INTRODUCTION TO COMPUTER GRAPHICS

Mr. Sumit Chauhan

Asst. Professor,
Management Education & Research Institute,
Guru Gobind Singh Indraprastha University,
New Delhi.

FIRST EDITION : 2011

Himalaya Publishing House

MUMBAI • NEW DELHI • NAGPUR • BENGALURU • HYDERABAD • CHENNAI • PUNE • LUCKNOW • AHMEDABAD • ERNAKULAM • BHUBANESWAR • INDORE • KOLKATA • GUWAHATI

First Edition : 2011

Published by : Mrs. Meena Pandey for **Himalaya Publishing House Pvt. Ltd.,**
"Ramdoot", Dr. Bhalerao Marg, Girgaon, **Mumbai - 400 004.**
Phone: 022-23860170/23863863, Fax: 022-23877178
E-mail: himpub@vsnl.com; Website: www.himpub.com

Branch Offices :

New Delhi : "Pooja Apartments", 4-B, Murari Lal Street, Ansari Road, Darya Ganj, New Delhi - 110 002. Phone: 011-23270392, 23278631; Fax: 011-23256286

Nagpur : Kundanlal Chandak Industrial Estate, Ghat Road, Nagpur - 440 018. Phone: 0712-2738731, 3296733; Telefax: 0712-2721215

Bengaluru : No. 16/1 (Old 12/1), 1st Floor, Next to Hotel Highlands, Madhava Nagar, Race Course Road, Bengaluru - 560 001. Phone: 080-32919385; Telefax: 080-22286611

Hyderabad : No. 3-4-184, Lingampally, Besides Raghavendra Swamy Matham, Kachiguda, Hyderabad - 500 027. Phone: 040-27560041, 27550139; Mobile: 09848130433

Chennai : No. 85/50, Bazullah Road, T. Nagar, Chennai - 600 017. Phone: 044-28144004/28144005

Pune : First Floor, "Laksha" Apartment, No. 527, Mehunpura, Shaniwarpeth (Near Prabhat Theatre), Pune - 411 030. Phone: 020-24496323/24496333

Lucknow : Jai Baba Bhavan, Church Road, Near Manas Complex and Dr. Awasthi Clinic, Aliganj, Lucknow - 226 024. Phone: 0522-2339329, 4068914; Mobile: 09305302158, 09415349385, 09389593752

Ahmedabad : 114, "SHAIL", 1st Floor, Opp. Madhu Sudan House, C.G. Road, Navrang Pura, Ahmedabad - 380 009. Phone: 079-26560126; Mobile: 09327324149, 09377088847

Ernakulam : 39/104 A, Lakshmi Apartment, Karikkamuri Cross Rd., Ernakulam, Cochin - 622011, Kerala. Phone: 0484-2378012, 2378016; Mobile: 09344199799

Bhubaneswar : 5 Station Square, Bhubaneswar - 751 001 (Odisha). Phone: 0674-2532129, Mobile: 09861046007

Indore : Kesardeep Avenue Extension, 73, Narayan Bagh, Flat No. 302, IIIrd Floor, Near Humpty Dumpty School, Indore - 452 007 (M.P.). Mobile: 09301386468

Kolkata : 108/4, Beliaghata Main Road, Near ID Hospital, Opp. SBI Bank, Kolkata - 700 010, Phone: 033-32449649, Mobile: 09910440956

Guwahati : House No. 15, Behind Pragjyotish College, Near Sharma Printing Press, P.O. Bharalumukh, Guwahati - 781009, (Assam). Mobile: 09883055590, 09883055536

DTP by : HPH, Editorial Office, Bhandup (Swapnali)

Printed at : Shri Krishna offset Press Delhi-93

Dedicated to
My Nanaji
(Late Shri. M.S. Raghav)
& My Parents
(Mr. B.S. Chauhan & Mrs. Santosh Chauhan)

Preface

It is indeed a matter of great pleasure to write the preface of the first edition of this book entitled as **"Introduction to Computer Graphics"**. Computer Graphics has always been one of the most visually spectacular branches of computer technology. It is also an extremely effective medium for communication between man and computer.

Over the years, those that I have met and worked with have continuously urged me to write a book, to put my knowledge down on paper, and to share my expertise of the subject. So at last, here it is.

Though many titles are available in the market today, still there was a need to capture some of the concepts under one cover from their scattered availability. This requirement infused with the idea of writing this text.

This book introduces the basic concepts of computer graphics, coupling the technical background and theory with practical examples and application programs throughout. Its user-friendly approach enables the reader to gain understanding through the practical examples and programs provided.

Features:

- presents computer graphics theory and practice in integrated combination
- uses numerous easy-to-understand examples, C programs and end-of-chapter exercises
- provides an ideal, self-contained introduction to computer graphics
- also includes solved short question answers and previous question papers of different universities as appendix.

This book provides an introduction to Computer Graphics for students who wish to learn the basic principles and techniques of the field. Readers of every kind will, I hope, find material in this book of their interest. Also, who want technical substance, can read as a general introduction to computer graphics. It can be used by instructors and students as a resource/text book to know the subject in a better way.

The contents of the book covers the maximum syllabus of BCA, B. Tech and MCA of GGSIP University (GGSIPU), Delhi University (DU), U.P. Technical University (UPTU), Punjab Technical University (PTU), Guru Jambeshwar University (GJU), Kurukshetra University, Maharishi Dayanand University (MDU), Indira Gandhi National Open University (IGNOU), West Bengal Technical University (WBUT) and many other technical universities.

Author

Acknowledgement

"One can pay back the loan of gold, but one dies forever in debt to those who are kind."

~Malayan Proverb

The hardest part of writing a book is attempting to acknowledge all those who helped, but knowing that you'll fail to mention everyone. Here is my first attempt to acknowledge everyone.

First of all, I'd like to thank my father Mr. B.S. Chauhan and my mother Mrs. Santosh Chauhan, who tempered each other's advice to give me the right mix of keeping my feet on the ground and reaching for the stars; my elder brother, Mr. Amit Chauhan, for his advice; and especially thank my wife Pallavi and daughter Iha, who continued to remain my source of inspiration.

I am heartily thankful to Prof. Lalit Aggarwal – Vice President, MERI Group of Institutions; Prof. Y.L. Grover – Director General; Mr. A.K. Aggarwal – Dean, MERI for their constant encouragement and support.

I'd also like to thank Dr. Manju Singh, Former Director, Sirifort College of Computer Technology & Management, for encouraging me to write book on topics that should cover the revised syllabus of professional courses of various technical universities.

My thanks to all my colleagues of Management Education & Research Institute, New Delhi for their extending support and making this whole experience enrichening in the successful completion of the book.

I am indeed debted to the team of Himalaya Publishing House for their suggestions and encouragement given in producing this book.

Many thanks to thousands of students to whom I've taught over the years for their tireless dedication to learn Computer Graphics. Their curiosity and persistence in getting the most out of my learning experience truly inspired me, and has contributed greatly to this book.

Suggestions for improvement of the book are indeed welcome.

Sumit Chauhan

Contents

Introduction to Computer Graphics

Detailed Contents

CHAPTER 1 Introduction to Graphics

1.1 INTRODUCTION

Computer graphics is generally regarded as a branch of computer science that deals with creation, storage and manipulation of models and images. In 1960, William Fetter coined term "Computer Graphics" to describe his new design methods that he was pursuing at Boeing. Computer graphics is the study of techniques to enhance and include communication between human and machine. It allows communication through pictures, charts and diagrams to people.

By graphics, we will refer to any sketch, drawing, or any other method that pictorially represent an object or data, or process to convey information, as a supplement to written descriptions. The sketch may be a picture stating nature's beauty, cartoon, building or human behaviour. It may be just few regular lines on the screen.

Computer graphics is all these — "a consciously managed and documented technology directed towards communicating information accurately and descriptively." Anything that can be described in the object space, as well as, in the image space is Computer Graphics such as:

- Digital representation and display of **spatial** and **non spatial data**.
- Visual Inspection of spatial and non-spatial data.
- Analysis and manipulation of spatial data.
- Digital representation of analog world.

1.2 GRAPHICS AREAS

It is very difficult to categorize any field like computer graphics, but most of graphics expert would agree on the following major areas:

- **Modeling** deals with geometrical/mathematical specifications of an object and its visual properties in a way so they can be stored. For example that a glass of water might be specified with a set of 3-D pixels along with some interpolation method to connect all the pixels.
- **Rendering is** the process of producing realistic images. It is a term inherited from art and deals with the creation of images.
- **Animation** is a method of creating an illusion of motion by flashing sequence of images at a specific rate. The speed should be more than 20 images per second.

There are also many other areas involved in computer graphics, but whether they are included in core graphics areas is just a matter of opinion.

- **Image processing** are techniques to modify or interpret existing pictures such as photographs.
- **Interactive graphics** provides a very utilitarian function by serving as one of the most natural means of communicating with a computer.

1.3 APPLICATION AREAS

Today, computer graphics is used in various areas ranging from everyday routines activities to specialized areas in different fields like education, training, advertising, business, industry, research, art, real estate, entertainment and animation.

Some of the major application areas are:

- Building Design and Construction, e.g., making prototypes.
- Entertainment, e.g., video games, film special effects.
- Animation, and e.g., cartoons and advertisement.
- Medical Technology, e.g., CAT (Computerized Axial Tomography).
- Engineering Field, e.g., CAD (Computer Aided Design).
- Simulated Environment, e.g., HMDs (Head Mounted Displays) used in flight simulators.

1.4 REPRESENTATIVE USES OF COMPUTER GRAPHICS

In today's world, usually in all the areas, computer graphics is helping in doing a number of things in an application area. For example:

(i) Computer Aided Design (CAD)	Design and drafting Mechanical parts Architecture Product design
(ii) Art	Paintings Interactive works
(iii) Education and Training	Process control (status displays in – refineries, power plant, computer network) Architecture Medicine Flight Simulation Virtual Reality training
(iv) Visualization	Geometrical representation Weather forecast (an accurate-schematic representation) Geography (Cartography, e.g., geographic maps.) Medicine (X-rays)
(v) Image Processing	MRI
(vi) Graphical User Interface	Interactive technique Icons Windowing
(vii) Entertainment	Virtual sets Animations Special effects in Films Video Games Commercials
(viii) Office Automation and Electronic Publishing	

1.5 COMPUTER GRAPHICS VERSUS IMAGE PROCESSING

Although methods used in computer graphics and image processing is moreover same, the two areas are concerned with fundamentally different operations. In *Computer Graphics*, a computer is used to create a picture. *Image processing,* on the other hand, applies techniques to modify or interpret existing pictures such as photographs.

Two principal applications of image processing are:

(a) Improving the quality of the picture.

(b) Machine perception of visual information as used in robotics.

Computer graphics concerns the pictorial synthesis of real or imaginary objects from their computer-based models; whereas the related field of image processing (also called picture processing) treats the converse process the analysis or the reconstruction of models of 2-D or 3-D objects from their pictures.

1.6 CLASSIFICATION OF COMPUTER GRAPHICS

There are different classifications in computer graphics given by various graphics practitioners. It is just a matter of opinion. Computer graphics can be categorized as follows:

- **Screen-based graphics:** By writing directly to screen, by manipulating screen elements, e.g., paint programs.
- **Model-based graphics:** By writing to internal data structure and the data structure is 'rendered' onto screen, e.g., drawing programs.

Computer graphics can also be classified as follows:

Passive/Non-interactive graphics – It involves the condition where the observer has no control over the image. Example: Titles shown on TV Logos and character generation etc.

Interactive Graphics – It provides a very utilitarian function by serving as one of the most natural means of communicating with a computer.

Interactive computer graphics involves 2-way communication between computer and user. The computer upon receiving signals from the input device can modify the displayed picture appropriately. To the user, it appears that the picture is changing instantaneously in response to his commands. He can give services of commands, each one generating a graphical response from the computer. In this way,; he maintains a conversation, or dialogue with the computer.

Interactive graphics is the most important means of producing pictures since the invention of photography and television, it has an added advantage that, we can make pictures not only of concrete, "real world" objects but also of abstract, synthetic objects (mathematical surfaces in 4-D), and of data that have no inherent geometry.

It is not confined to static images; even dynamically varying pictures can also be effectively shown.

Dynamics Input

Motion

Objects can be moved and tumbled with respect to a stationary observer.

The objects can remain stationery and the viewer can move around them, e.g., Flight simulator.

Update

It is the actual change of the shape, color, or other properties of the object being viewed.

Interactive computer graphics thus permits extensive, high-bandwidth user-computer interaction. This significantly enhances our ability to understand data, to perceive trends and to privatize real or imaginary objects.

1.7 COMPONENTS OF COMPUTER GRAPHICS

Computer Graphics consists of three components:

(1) Digital memory buffer (frame buffer)

(2) Monitor

(3) Video controller

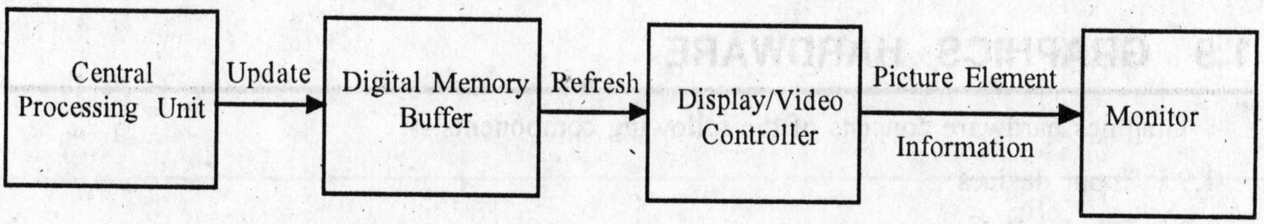

Fig. 1.1 Components Required to see the Output on Screen in the form of Pixels

(1) **Frame Buffer:** This is place where images or pictures are stored as an array in the form of 0's and 1's, 0 represents darkness and 1 represents image or picture.

Frame buffer is the video RAM (V-RAM) that is memory area that has the information about the image to be displayed on the screen. The amount of memory required to hold the image depends primarily on the resolution of the screen and also the color depth used per pixel. The formula to calculate how much video memory is required at a given resolution and bit depth is:-

$$\text{Memory in GB: } \frac{\text{X-resolution} \times \text{Y-resolution} \times \text{Bits per pixel}}{8 \times 1024 \times 1024 \times 1024}$$

(2) **Monitor:** The purpose of display devices is to convert electrical signals into visible images.

(3) **Video Controller:** It is an interface between digital memory buffer and TV monitor. The main function of this is to pass the contents of frame buffer to the monitor.

1.8 GRAPHICS PACKAGES

Graphics System: A graphics system may be defined as any collection of hardware and software designed to make it easier to use graphic input and output in computer programs.

Graphics Software: The software component of graphic system. There are two general classifications for graphics software:

(i) General programming packages

(ii) Special-purpose applications packages

(i) ***General programming packages:*** Provides an external set of graphics function that can be used in a high-level programming language such as C. Basic functions in a general package included those for generating picture components (straight lines, polygons, circles and other figures), setting color and intensity values, selecting views, and applying transformation.

(ii) ***Special-purpose applications packages*****:** These are designed for non-programmer so that users can generate displays without worrying about how graphic operations work. For example: various businesses, medical and CAD systems.

Thus, a graphic package is a set of function or subroutines used by an application program to generate pictures on a plotter or display and to handle graphical interaction.

1.9 GRAPHICS HARDWARE

Graphics hardware consists of the following components:-

1.9.1 Input devices

1.9.2 Display Devices

1.9.3 Display controllers

1.9.1 Input Devices

Various devices are available for data input on graphics workstations. These may be classified as:

1.9.1.1 Text Entry

➲ ***Buttons*****:** Buttons are very simple to use and easy to map with the functionality of any process. There are different types of buttons:

- fixed buttons with labels like ticket machines
- e.g., gaming machines and programmable keypads.

➲ ***Keyboard*****:** This device is meant for discrete entries. This is a primary device for entering text strings. It is very efficient device for inputting non-graphic data. It has various layouts.

1.9.1.2 Pointing Devices

1.9.1.2.1 Direct Pointing Devices:

➲ ***Light Pen:*** Detects burst of light from screen phosphor. It addresses individual pixels. It contains a light-sensitive cell, which detects the light from the screen enabling the computer to identify the location of the pen on the screen.

Disadvantages:

- It is a fragile device.
- It obscures part of screen.
- Users have to remove their hands from keyboard while accessing light pen.

➲ ***Pen-Pad:*** It is a pressure-sensitive pen and pad. It is very good for drawing. You can directly use Pen on screen. Common in PDAs to draw or write.

➲ ***Touch screen:*** You can directly control the screen using your fingers. Touch screens use sensors to detect the touch of finger.

Advantages:

- Intuitive to use.
- Good for public access systems like ATMs.
- Good durability in high-use environment.
- Enables users to choose from available options by simply touching the desired icon or menu item.

Disadvantages:

- Inaccurate.
- Greasiness on screen from fingers, e.g., ATM Machine, Touch screen phones etc.
- Obscures part of the screen.
- Users come too close to screen for comfort.

1.9.1.2.2 Indirect Pointing Devices:

➲ ***Mouse:*** A mouse functions as a pointing device used to position the screen cursor. You have to make selections with the help of the button placed on the top of the mouse.

Types of mouse based on mechanism:

(1) ***Mechanical Mouse:*** It uses a ball that makes contact with inside wheels when it is rolled on a plain surface.

(2) ***Optical Mouse:*** As the name suggests, a mouse that uses light to detect movement. It emits a ray of light and senses its reflection when it is moved. Initial optical mouse required a special mouse pad, but a new device doesn't require the same.

➲ ***Trackball:*** A trackball is a pointing device that works like an upside-down mouse. It is used in portable computers.

Advantages:

- It requires no space.
- Ball can be rotated with the fingers or palm of the hand, to produce screen cursor movement.
- It is very popular with notebooks and portable computers.

➲ *Joystick*: It is a small, vertical lever mounted on a base that is used to steer the screen cursor around. Most joysticks select screen positions with actual stick movement; other respond to the pressure on the stick. It is very robust and inexpensive. Often found in computer games.

➲ *Graphics Tablets*: Positional information with pen. A special pen is used against the pressure sensitive surface of the tablet to move the cursor. It provides substantial control for editing finely detailed graphic elements.

1.9.1.3 Scanners and Optical Character Recognition

➲ *Scanners:* Drawings, graphs, color, text can be stored for computer processing with an image scanner by passing an optical scanning mechanism over the information to be stored.

There are two types of scanners:

1. **Handheld scanner:** In this, user had to move the scanner over the document that has to be scanned.
2. **Flat bed scanner:** The document is placed on the glass plate and cover is closed. The document is scanned using a lamp.

Advantages:

- Enable direct data entry into a computer system.
- It reduces human effort.
- It increases data accuracy and data processing speed.
- Converts hard copy to soft copy.

➲ ***Optical character recognition***: We can convert paper documents into a word processing document without retyping or rekeying. It recognizes not only printed character but also handwriting, e.g.,: Bar code reader.

1.9.1.4 Other Input Devices

➲ ***Data Glove:***A *data glove* is an interactive device, resembling a glove worn on the hand. A glove equipped with sensors that sense the movements of the hand and interfaces those movements with a computer. It facilitates tactile sensing and fine-motion control in robotics and virtual reality environments. Data glove is one of electromechanical device.

Tactile sensing involves simulation of the sense of human touch and also includes the ability to perceive pressure, linear force, torque, temperature, and surface texture. Sensors used to detect the movement of the user's hand and fingers, and the translation of these motions into signals that can be used by a virtual hand, like in gaming or a robotic hand, like in remote-control surgery.

- *Foot Mouse:* A *footmouse* is a type of computer mouse that gives the users the ability to move the cursor and click the mouse buttons with their feet. It consists of two separate pedals. One pedal operates the pointer, while the other is used for button clicking. By default, a heel-click engages the right mouse button, while a toe-click engages the left mouse button.

  It is primarily used by users with disabilities or with high-back or neck problems. It is also promoted as a way to prevent such problems in the future and as a means to increase productivity by not having to move one's hand between the keyboard and mouse.

- *Speech Recognition*: Speech recognition is the ability of a machine or program to identify words and phrases in spoken language and convert them to a machine-readable format. Traditional speech recognition software has a limited vocabulary of words and phrases and may only identify these if they are spoken very clearly. More sophisticated software has the ability to accept natural speech. Speech recognition applications include call routing, speech-to-text, voice dialing and voice search.

1.9.2 Display Devices

The purpose of display devices is to convert electrical signals into visible images.

Display Types:

1.9.2.1 Cathode Ray Tubes (CRTs)

1.9.2.2 Raster Scan CRT

1.9.2.3 Random Scan CRT or Vector Display

1.9.2.4 Color CRT Monitors

1.9.2.5 Direct View Storage Tube (DVST)

Other Technologies:

1.9.2.6 Plasma Panel

1.9.2.7 Liquid-Crystal Display (LCD)

1.9.2.8 Light-emitting Diodes (LEDs)

1.9.2.1 Cathode Ray Tube (CRT)

Computer graphics may use many different output devices, such as monitors, printers, plotter etc. but most common display device is the CRT. Video monitor has always been the predominant display device for interactive computer graphics. The operations of most video monitors is based on the standard CRT design

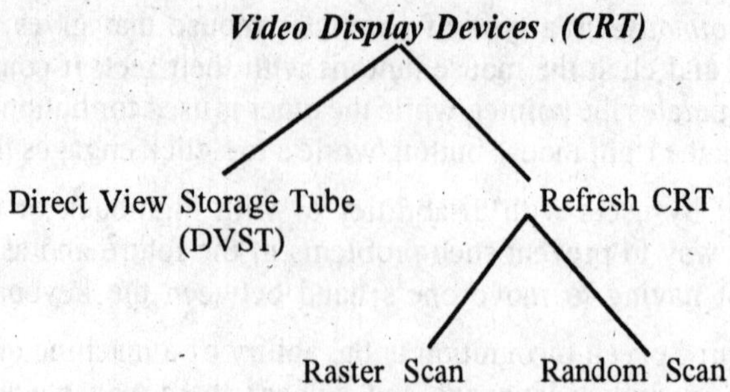

Fig. 1.2 Classification of Video Display Devices

The following figure illustrates the basic operation of CRT:

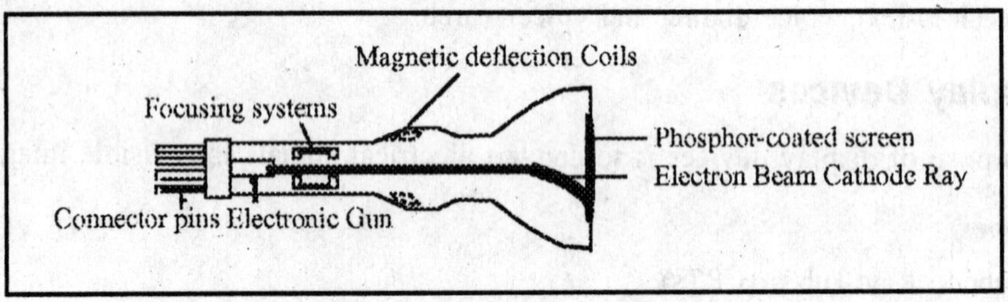

Fig. 1.3 Basic Design of Cathode Ray Tube (CRT)

A beam of e^- (cathode rays), emitted by and e^- gun passes through focusing and deflection systems that direct the beam toward specified positions on the phosphor-coated screen. The phosphor then units a small spot of light at each position contacted by the e^- beam. This is known as *phosphorescence* that decays slower but still rapidly (in about 15-20 milliseconds) so there is a need to refresh the screen by redrawing the image. One way to keep the phosphor glowing is to redraw the picture repeatedly by quickly directing the e^- beam back over the same points. This type of display is called a refresh CRT.

Fundamentals of CRT:

- ***Refresh Rate:*** The rate at which the pixels get refreshed in a unit time is called *Refresh Rate.* It is sufficiently high redisplay to avoid flickering.
- ***Pixel:*** It is the smallest addressable screen element also called *picture element.* Values of all pixels are stored in an array in computer's memory called *frame buffer.*
- ***Electron Gun:*** It makes use of electrostatic fields to focus and accelerate e^- beam.

Its primary components are:

➲ Heated metal cathode

➲ Control grid

- ***Deflection System:*** It can be controlled either with electric fields or with magnetic fields. Cathode ray tubes are commonly constructed with magnetic deflection coils mounted on the outside of the CRT envelope. There are two pairs of coils are used – horizontal deflection and vertical deflection. A primary requirement of the deflection system is that it deflects rapidly, since speed of deflection determines how much information can be displayed without flicker.

- ***Phosphors:*** The phosphors used in a graphic display are normally shown for their color characteristics and persistence. Three colors of phosphor (red, blue, green) RGB are used. Besides color, a major difference between phosphor is their *persistence,* i.e., how long the phosphor continue to emit light even after the CRT beam is removed.

- ***Persistence:*** The persistence is defined as the time it takes the emitted light from the screen to decay to 1/10th of its original intensity.

➲ Lower persistence phosphors require higher refresh rates to maintain picture without flicker. It is useful in animation.

➲ Higher persistence phosphors allow for a lower refresh rate to avoid flicker. It is useful for displaying highly complex, static pictures. This is poor for animation since a "trail" is left with moving objects.

Thus, depending on the persistence of the phosphor-coated inside the screen, the monitors require different refresh rates.

- ***Resolution:*** The maximum number of points/pixels that can be displayed without overlap is called the *resolution* of a screen and is usually given as the number of horizontal points versus the number of vertical points per unit area.

More the resolution => more the number of pixels

i.e., Number of pixels α resolution of the screen.

The maximum resolution may be determined by:

- Characteristics of the monitor for a random scan system.
- By combination of the monitor and graphics card memory for a raster scan system.

Resolution of CRT depends on:

(i) type of phosphor

(ii) intensity to be displayed

(iii) focusing system

(iv) deflecting system

High Resolution systems are often referred to as high-definition systems.

The figure 1.4 depicts the intensity distribution of a spot on the screen.

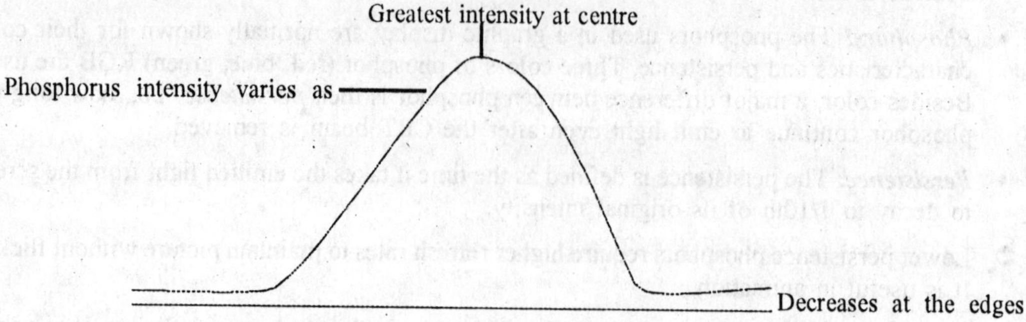

Fig. 1.4 Intensity Distribution of a Spot on the Screen

Spot size depends on intensity.

Aspect Ratio: The ratio of vertical pixels to horizontal pixels necessary to produce equal-length lines in both directions on the screen. It refers to the ratio of horizontal dimension/vertical dimension.

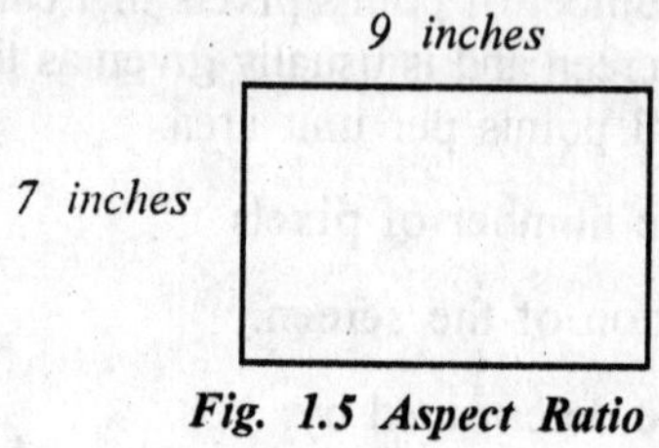

Fig. 1.5 Aspect Ratio

Aspect ratio = 9/7 =1.28

Features of CRT:-

(i) Rapid operation: display of an image in few milliseconds

(ii) High power consumption

(iii) Expensive

(iv) Good for graphics video and animation

(v) Reliable

(vi) Low cost

CRT is of two types:

1. Raster CRT
2. Random CRT

Rasterization is referred to as converting geometric primitives (lines, polygons) to pixels. It is also known as *scan conversion;* it is converting a continuous object such as a line or circle into discrete pixel. Rasterization is also known as discretizing/sampling. Raster displays store the display primitives (such as lines, characters and solidly shaded or patterned areas) in the refresh buffer in terms of their component pixels.

1.9.2.2 Raster Scan CRT

The device scans the screen from top to bottom in a regular pattern from left to right. Raster scan implies that the image is scanned onto the screen surface in a raster sequence, i.e., as a succession of equidistant scan lines, each scan line made up of pixels.

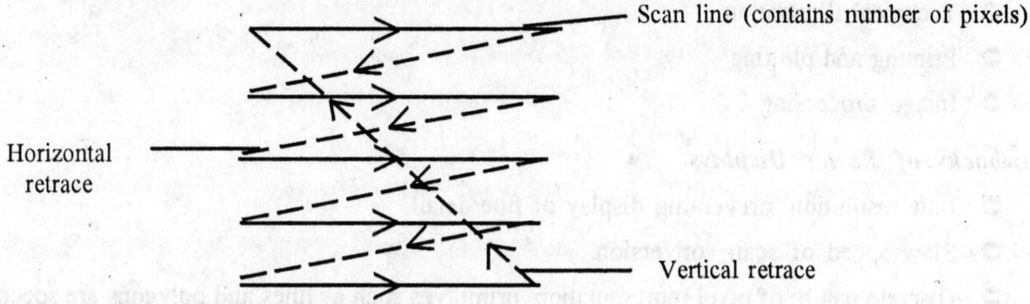

Fig. 1.6 Raster Scan

Picture definition is stored in a memory area called the *refresh buffer* or *frame buffer*. This memory area holds the set of intensity values for all the screen points. Stored intensity values are then retrieved from the refresh buffer and "painted" on the screen one row (scan line) at a time. Each screen point is referred to as a pixel.

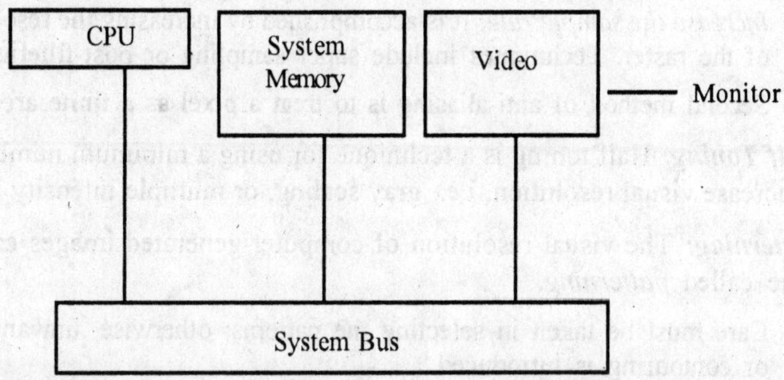

Fig. 1.7 Architecture of a Simple Raster Graphics System

In the raster scan display device, the screen is assumed to consist of a 2-D matrix. The term raster is used for 2-D matrix. Each point of the screen corresponding to a matrix element is called *pixel.*

Intensities of pixels are stored in an array in computer's memory called *frame buffer.* Refreshing on raster scan displays is carried out at the rate of 60 to 80 frames per second.

Raster scan displays owe their increase in popularity to two causes:-

- Need for greater realism in pictures.
- Cost of raster scan display equipments is decreasing.

Applications of Raster Scan Graphics

- Flight simulation
- Animation
- Design
- Technical Illustration
- Printing and plotting
- Image processing

Drawbacks of Raster Displays

- Low resolution, preventing display of fine detail.
- Slow speed of scan conversion.
- Discrete nature of pixel representation: primitives such as lines and polygons are specified in terms of their endpoints (vertices) and must be scan converted into their pixel components in their frame buffer. To provide effective anti-aliasing, it is necessary to understand the causes of aliasing itself. Fundamentally, the appearance of aliasing effects are due to the fact that lines, polygon edges, color boundaries, etc. is continuous, whereas, and raster device is discrete.

Fundamentally, there are two methods of *anti-aliasing*:

(i) *Increase the sample rate*: It is accomplished by increasing the resolution (number of pixels) of the raster. Techniques include super sampling or post-filtering.

(ii) Second method of anti-aliasing is to treat a pixel as a finite area rather than as a point.

Half Toning: Half toning is a technique for using a minimum number of intensity levels to obtain increase visual resolution, i.e., gray scaling, or multiple intensity levels.

Patterning: The visual resolution of computer-generated images can be increased using a technique called *patterning*.

- Care must be taken in selecting the patterns; otherwise, unwanted small-scale structure or contouring is introduced.
- To avoid introducing unwanted artifacts into the image, patterns should not be symmetrical.
- Patterns should present a growth sequence.
- Patterns result in loss of spatial resolution.
- Stair-step appearances referred to as *jaggies* are produced. This drawback arises from the nature of raster itself. Also known as *aliasing*.

Fig. 1.8 Jaggies

Thus, *jaggies* are the discontinuities which are particularly noticeable on systems with low resolution. To improve this, use anti-aliasing.

- Use high resolution screen and driver setting.
- Modified using virtual pixels.

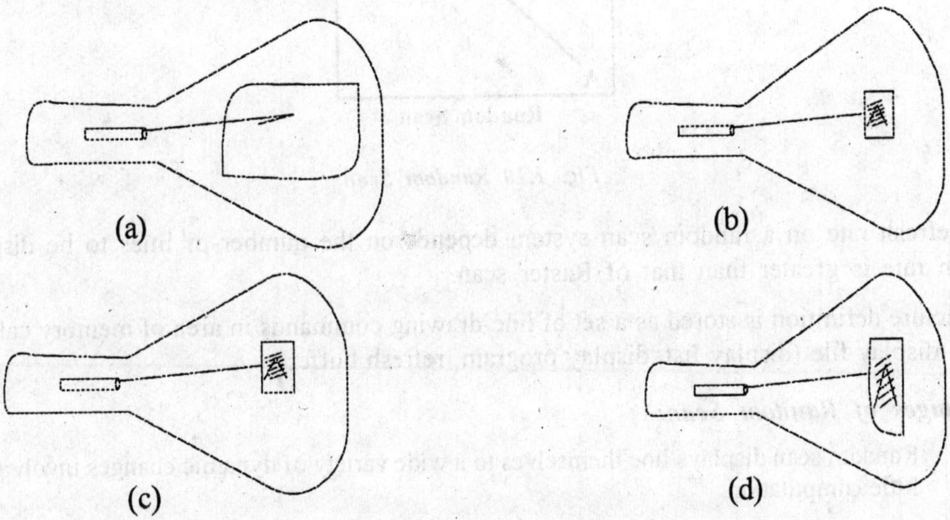

Fig. 1.9 A Raster Scan System from (a) to (d)

To reduce flicker rate:

- High scan rate (> 70 Hz).
- High persistence phosphor.
- *Interlacing*: Displays odd and even rows alternatively. In some raster display devices, a frame buffer is displayed in two passes. This kind of refreshing is called *interlacing*. In the 1st pass, the odd rows are refreshed and the even rows are refreshed in the 2nd pass. Interlacing is primarily used with monitors of slower refreshing rates.

1.9.2.3 Random Scan CRT:

Here, a beam is deflected from end point to end point, as dictated by the arbitrary order of display commands. It is also known as vector stroke, line drawing or calligraphic displays. The commands for plotting points, lines and characters are interpreted by the display processor. It sends digital and point coordinates to a vector generator that covert the digital coordinate values to analog voltages for beam-deflection circuits that displace the e⁻ beam writing on the CRT's phosphor coating.

Here, the e^- beam directly draws the picture.

- Turn e^- beam off. Move to A.
- Turn e^- beam on, and draw to B.
- Repeat move-drawn sequence.

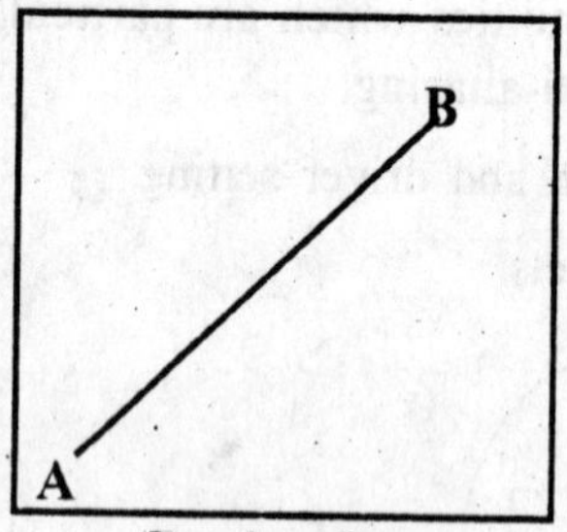

Fig. 1.10 Random Scan

Refresh rate on a random scan system depends on the number of lines to be displayed. Refresh rate is greater than that of Raster scan.

Picture definition is stored as a set of line-drawing commands in area of memory called the refresh display file (display list, display program, refresh buffer).

Advantages of Random Scan:

1. Random scan displays line themselves to a wide variety of dynamic changes involving very little computation.
2. Vector displays produce smooth lines drawings because the CRT beam directly follows the line path.
3. No *jaggies* are formed.
4. Very high resolution, limited only by monitor.
5. Easy animation, just draw at different positions.
6. Requires little memory.

Disadvantages of Random Scan:

- Requires "intelligent e^- beam", i.e., processor-controlled.
- Limited screen density before flickering, cannot draw a complex image.
- Limited color capability.
- Very expensive.

Typical applications: CAD and air traffic control display.

Raster Scan	Random Scan
(i) The device scans the screen from top to bottom in a regular pattern.	(i) The beam is deflected from end point to end point as dictated by an arbitrary order of display commands.
(ii) Picture definition is stored as intensity value of pixels in the memory area called frame buffer or refresh buffer.	(ii) Picture definition is stored as a set of line drawing commands in area of memory referred to as refresh display file.
(iii) Low resolution.	(iii) Very high resolution.
(iv) Jaggies are produced.	(iv) No jaggies.
(v) Refresh rate is low.	(v) Refresh rate is higher.
(vi) Cost is less.	(vi) Expensive.
(vii) It controls the intensity of each pixel (data) in the rectangular matrix (raster) of dots that covers the entire screen.	(vii) A display file for a line-drawing display contains only information about lines and characters to be drawn; the void areas of the screen are ignored.
(viii) Generate video images of extreme realism.	(viii) Flicker badly when displaying complex pictures.
(ix) Large capacity limited only by screen resolution.	(ix) Could not produce realistic image of solid objects.
(x) Changes generally involve large amounts of processing. It is therefore difficult to achieve the modification required for effective interaction.	(x) These displays end themselves to a wide variety of dynamic changes speed of involving very little computation.
(xi) Flexible as consists of number of intermediaries.	(xi) Inflexible.
(xii) Applications, Animation, Flight simulation etc.	(xii) High precision engineering drafting highly interactive solid-object design, and real line computer animation.

Fig. 1.11 Basic Differences between Raster Scan and Random Scan

1.9.2.4 Color CRT Monitors

A CRT monitor displays color pictures by using a combination of phosphors that emit different color light. By combining the emitted light from the different phosphors, a range of colors can be generated. The two basic techniques for producing color displays with a CRT are:

(a) Beam penetration method

(b) Shadow mask method

(a) Beam penetration method: It has been used with random scan monitors for displaying color pictures two layers of phosphor, usually red and, green, are coated onto the inside of the CRT screen, and the displayed color depends on how for the e⁻ beam penetrates into the phosphor layers.

- A beam of slow e⁻ excites only the outer RED layer.
- A beam of very fast e⁻ penetrates through the red layer and excites the inner green layer.
- An intermediate beam speeds, combinations of red and green lights are emitted to show two additional colors, orange and yellow.

Speed of e⁻ and screen color at any point, is controlled by the beam acceleration voltage.

Advantages and Disadvantages:

- Inexpensive way to produce color.
- Only 4 colors possible.
- Quality of picture is not so good.
- In order to change or switch colors, we need to change the beam-accelerating potential by significant amounts. When accelerating potential changes, the deflection system must react to compensate.

(b) Shadow mask CRT: The shadow mask color CRT can display a much wider range of colors than the beam penetration CRT, and is used in raster scan systems.

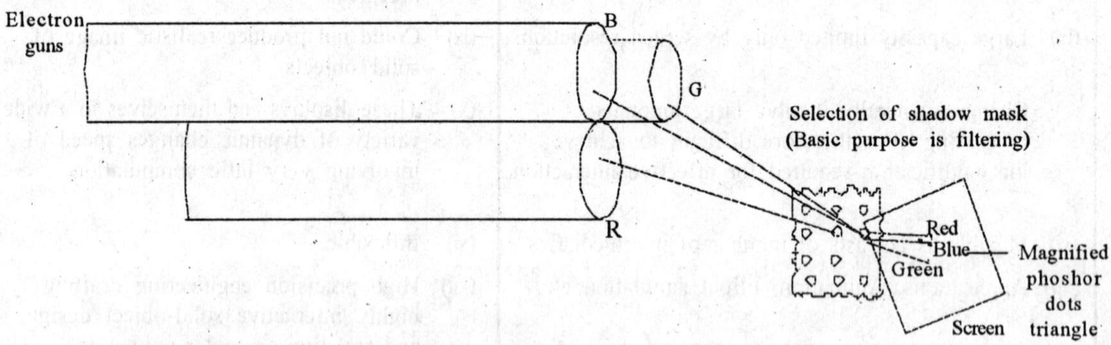

Fig. 1.12 Delta-delta Shadow Mask CRT

A shadow mask CRT has three phosphor colors at each pixel position:

- One phosphor dot emits: Red light
- Second phosphor dot emits: Green light
- Third phosphor dot emits: Blue light

This type of CRT has three e⁻ guns, one for each color dot and a shadow mask grid just behind the phosphor-coated screen. The three e⁻ beams are deflected and focused as a group onto the shadow mask, which contains a series of holes aligned with the phosphor dot patterns. When the three beams pass through a hole in the shadow mask, they activate a dot triangle, which appears as a small color spot on the screen. So, by combining different intensities from different guns we can get different colors.

Advantages

- It can provide a "reasonable" number of simultaneous colors without requiring large frame buffers.
- Helps expanding intensity range.
- To create a pseudo color displays of a monochromatic.

1.9.2.5 Direct View Storage Tubes (DVST)

Refresh line drawing displays based on the CRT have the disadvantage of high cost and tendency to flicker when the displayed picture is complex. These two problems have led to the development of display devices with inherent image storage capability.

The most widely used of these devices is the direct view storage tubes. It is a modified random scan system.

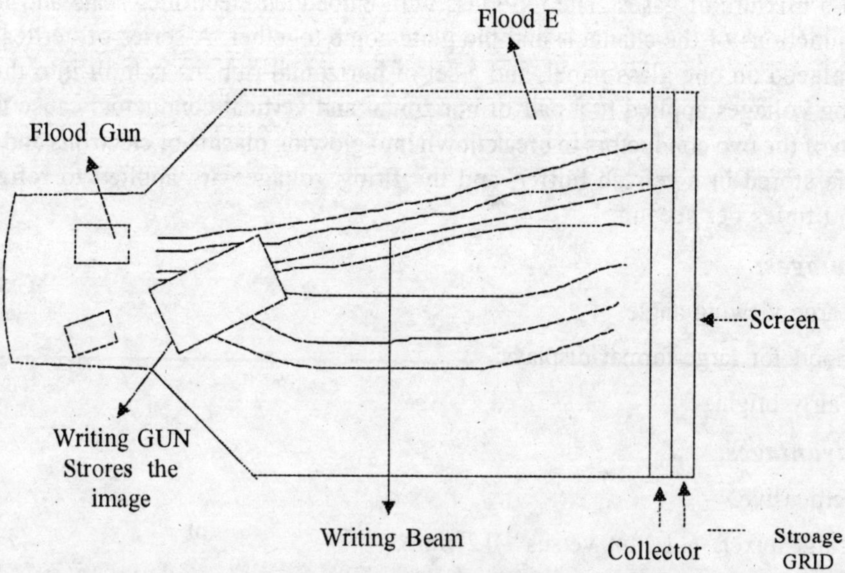

Fig. 1.13 The DVST

The DVST stores the picture information as a charge distribution behind the phosphor coated screen. Two guns are used:

- **Writing beam gun:** Used to store picture pattern.
- **Flood gun:** Maintains picture display.

Advantages:

- No flickering.
- No refreshing is needed.
- Very complex pictures can be displayed at very high resolution without flicker.

Disadvantages:

- Ordinarily do not display color.
- Selected parts of the picture cannot be erased, to eliminate a picture section, the entire screen must be erased and the modified picture redrawn.
- Inferior in terms of performance to refresh CRT.

Different Raster Output Devices: CRT monitors, LCDs, laser and dot matrix printers.

Different Non-Raster Output Devices: Vector display and plotters.

1.9.2.6 Plasma Panel

A form of display used in association with computer systems in which light output is produced from the interaction between an electric current and an ionized inert gas such as neon. Plasma panels also called gas-discharge displays are constructed by filling the region between two glass plates with a mixture of gases. The top glass with embedded electrodes seals and forms a pixel where the junctions of the channels and the plate come together. A series of vertical conducting ribbons is placed on one glass panel, and a set of horizontal ribbons is built into the other glass panel. Firing voltages applied to a pair of horizontal and vertical conductors cause the gas at the intersection of the two conductors to break down into glowing plasma of electrons and ions. Picture definition is stored in a refresh buffer, and the firing voltages are applied to refresh the pixel positions 60 times per second.

Advantages:

- Large viewing angle.
- Good for large-format displays.
- Fairly bright.

Disadvantages:

- Expensive.
- Large pixels (~1 mm versus ~0.2 mm).
- Phosphors gradually deplete.
- Less bright as compared to CRTs, using more power.

1.9.2.7 Liquid-crystal Display (LCD)

A screen display technology developed in 1963 at the David Sarnoff Research Center in Princeton, NJ. LCD displays utilize two sheets of polarizing material with a liquid crystal solution between them. An electric current passed through the liquid causes the crystals to align so that light cannot pass through them. Each crystal, therefore, is like a shutter, either allowing light to pass through or blocking the light. The contrast between the opaque and transparent areas forms visible characters.

Advantages:

- Very compact and light.
- Low power consumption.
- No geometric distortion.
- Little or no flicker depending on backlight technology.
- Not affected by screen burn-in.
- No high voltage or other hazards present during repair/service.
- Can be made in almost any size or shape.

Disadvantages:

- Limited viewing angle.
- Dead pixels may occur either during manufacturing or through use.
- Cannot be used with light guns/pens.

1.9.2.8 Light-emitting Diode (LED)

The light emitting diode, or LED monitor is a recent introduction in the field of display technology. As an upgraded version of LCD monitors, these monitors employ LED technology to deliver superior quality graphics. They are typically used outdoors in store signs and billboards. LED panels are sometimes used as form of lighting, for the purpose of general illumination, task lighting, or even stage lighting rather than display.

The LED was first invented in Russia in the 1920s, and introduced in America as a practical electronic component in 1962. Oleg Vladimirovich Losev was a radio technician who noticed that diodes used in radio receivers emitted light when current was passed through them. In 1927, he published details in a Russian journal of the first ever LED.

LEDs are based on the semiconductor diode. When the diode is forward biased (switched on), electrons are able to recombine with holes and energy is released in the form of light. This effect is called electroluminescence and the color of the light is determined by the energy gap of the semiconductor. The LED is usually small in area with integrated optical components to shape its radiation pattern and assist in reflection.

Advantages:

- Lower energy consumption.
- Longer lifetime.
- Improved robustness.
- Smaller size and faster switching.

Disadvantages:

- Relatively expensive.
- Require more precise current and heat management than traditional light sources.

1.9.3 Display Controllers

A **Video Display Controller** or **VDC** is an integrated circuit which is the main component in a video signal generator, a device responsible to pass the contents of the frame buffer to the monitor. It is an interface between digital memory buffer and TV monitor. Some Video Display Controllers also generate an Audio signal, but in that case it's not their main function.

Video Display Controllers were most often used in the old home-computers of the 80s, but also in some early video game systems.

1.10 SUMMARY

Graphical interfaces have replaced the character or textual interfaces. Nowadays, there are number of graphics areas like modeling, animation, rendering, image processing, etc. Computer graphics is classified as interactive and non-interactive graphics. There are three components of computer graphics: digital memory buffer, monitor, and video controller. Graphics hardware consists of input devices, display devices and display controllers. The display devices are also known as output devices. The most commonly used output devices in a graphics system is a video monitor. In this chapter, we have discussed all of the above topics.

1.11 GLOSSARY

- **Computer graphics:** Generally regarded as a branch of computer science that deals with creation, storage and manipulation of models and images.
- **Refresh Rate:** The rate at which the pixels get refreshed in a unit time is called Refresh Rate. It is sufficiently high redisplay to avoid flickering.
- **Pixel:** It is the smallest addressable screen element also called picture element. Values of all pixels are stored in an array in computer's memory called frame buffer.
- **Computer Graphics:** Consists of three components such as Digital memory buffer (frame buffer), Monitor, and Video controller.
- **Frame Buffer:** This is place where images or pictures are stored as an array in the form of 0's and 1's, 0 represents darkness and 1 represents image or picture.
- **Mouse:** A mouse functions as a pointing device used to position the screen cursor. You have to make selections with the help of the button placed on the top of the mouse. Mouse can be classified on the basis of Mechanism: mechanical mouse, and Optical mouse.
- **Persistence:** The persistence is defined as the time it takes the emitted light from the screen to decay to 1/10th of its original intensity.
- **Resolution:** The maximum number of points/pixels that can be displayed without overlap is called the resolution and is usually given as the number of horizontal points versus the number of vertical points per unit area.
- **Aspect Ratio:** The ratio of vertical pixels to horizontal pixels necessary to produce equal-length lines in both directions on the screen. It refers to the ratio of horizontal dimension/vertical dimension.

- **Patterning:** The visual resolution of computer generated images can be increased using a technique called patterning.
- **Jaggies:** Jaggies are the discontinuities which are particularly noticeable on systems with low resolution.
- **In Raster Scan:** The device scans the screen from top to bottom in a regular pattern.
- **In Random Scan:** The beam is deflected from endpoint to endpoint as dictated by an arbitrary order of display commands.

1.12 EXERCISE

Q1. What do you understand by computer graphics?

Q2. What is the difference between computer graphics and image processing?

Q3. What are the major application areas of computer graphics?

Q4. How many mega bytes does a frame buffer need in 600 × 400 pixel?

Q5. What do you understand by input and output devices?

Q6. What is the difference between Raster scan and Random scan?

Q7. Write short notes on:

(i) Resolution

(ii) Pixel

(iii) Aspect ratio

(iv) Persistence

(v) Trackball

(vi) Graphics system

E N D

CHAPTER 2 Scan Conversion

2.1 INTRODUCTION

Scan conversion is a technique for changing the vertical/horizontal scan frequency of video signal for different purposes and applications. The device which performs this conversion is called *scan converter.*

The application of scan conversion is wide and covers video projectors, cinema equipment, TV and video capture cards, standard and HDTV televisions, LCD monitors and many different aspects of picture and video processing.

2.2 RASTER VERSUS VECTOR GRAPHICS

Before an object can be shown on a computer monitor or a printer, a model describing the geometry of the object is required, unless the object is an image in itself. Usually, modeling of elementary objects is done in the framework of vector graphics. If a complex object has to be modeled, the combination of elementary objects are used like lines, rectangles, circles, ellipses or arcs.

Computer Monitors, printers and also different formats of storing images like JPEG, bitmaps are all based on raster graphics, also called pixel-oriented graphics.

In order to display vector-oriented graphics in the form of raster graphics, all geometrical models or shapes must be converted into pixels. This process and method is also known as *Scan Conversion.*

2.3 POINT DRAWING

The basic building blocks for pictures are referred to as output primitives. theThey include character strings and geometric entries, such as points, straight lines, curved lines, filled areas (polygons, circles, etc.) and shapes defined with arrays of color points. Attributes are the properties of output primitives are to be displayed. They include intensity and color specifications, line styles, text styles, and area filling patterns.

Point-plotting techniques are based on the use of a Cartesian coordinate system points are addressed by their x and y coordinates; the value of x increases from left to right and y increases from bottom to top.

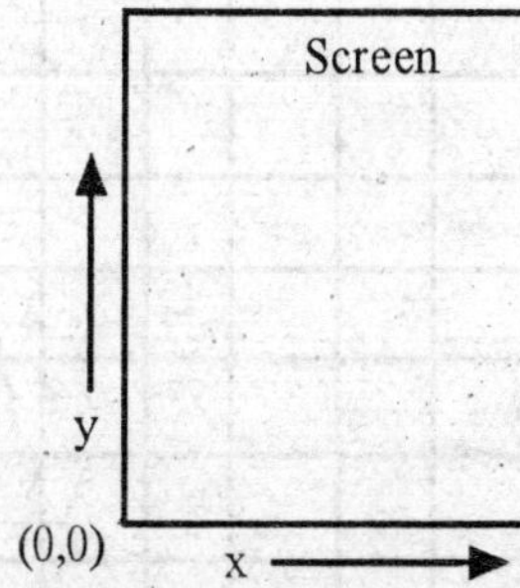

Fig. 2.1 The Cartesian Screen Coordinate System

2.4 LINE DRAWING ALGORITHMS

Following are the factors considered while drawing lines by line drawing algorithms:

- Lines should appear straight, i.e., they start and end accurately.
- Lines should terminate accurately.
- Lines should have constant density and constant brightness.
- Lines density should be independent of line length and angle.
- Lines should be drawn rapidly.

2.4.1 Nature of Line Segment

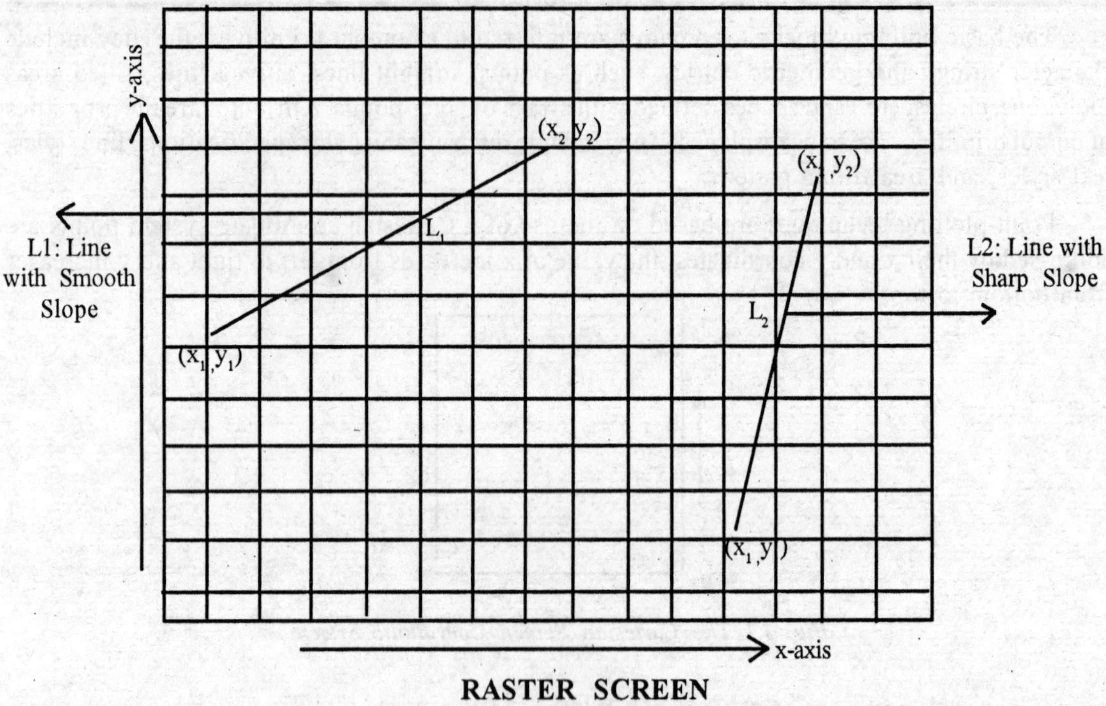

Fig. 2.2 Nature of Line Segment

x-axis represents columns, y-axis represents rows

L1: Here, change in number of columns is more than change in number of rows, i.e., $\Delta x > \Delta y$ where $\Delta x = x_2 - x_1$ and $\Delta y = y_2 - y_1$ ...(2.1)

L2: Here, change in number of rows is more than change in number of columns, i.e., $\Delta y > \Delta x$ where $\Delta x = x_2 - x_1$ and $\Delta y = y_2 - y_1$ ...(2.2)

2.4.2 Digital Differential Analyzer (DDA) Method

The basis of the DDA method is to take unit steps along one coordinate and computer the corresponding values along the other coordinate. The unit steps are always along the coordinate of greatest change, e.g., if $\Delta x = 8$ and $\Delta y = 5$, then we would take unit steps along x and compute the steps along y.

Let us assume a line of positive slope and draw from x_1, y_1 to x_2, y_2.

{slope = m = $\Delta y/\Delta x$, i.e., change in y coordinates/change in x coordinates}

If m <= 1.0 then

let x_step = 1 {$\Delta x = 1$, $\Delta y = 0$ or 1}

Else m > 1.0

let y_step = 1 {$\Delta y = 1$, x_step = 0 or 1}

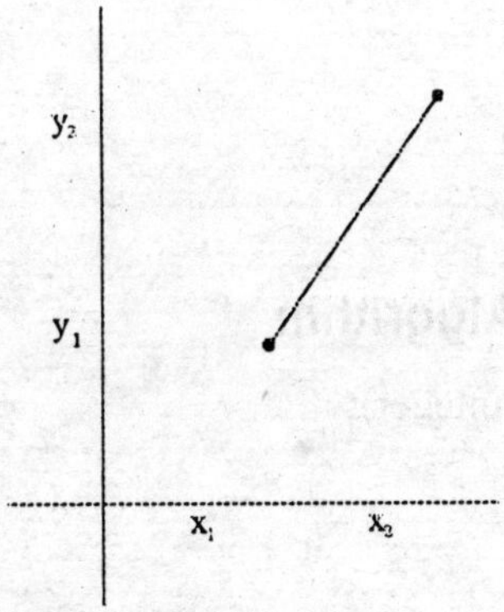

Fig. 2.3 Line Segment between (x_1,y_1) and (x_2,y_2)

Always remember that steps are along the longest change. It means if change in x coordinates is greater than change in y coordinates then x_step = 1 and y_step = 0 or 1, and *vice versa.*

{m <= 1.0} for x_step = 1, $\Delta y/\Delta x = m$

by putting the value of change in x, i.e., $\Delta x = 1$.

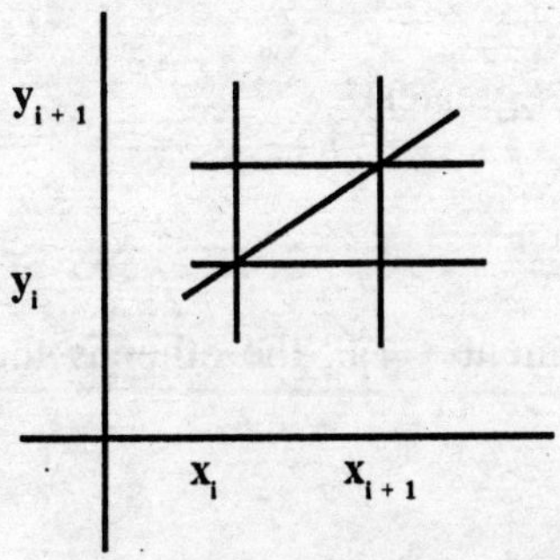

Fig. 2.4 Showing Step i and i+1

=>$\Delta y/1 = m$, $\Delta y = m$

Change in y coordinates can be written as $\Delta y = y_2 - y_1$

=> $\Delta y = m = y_{i+1} - y_i$

=> $y_{i+1} = y_i + m$ ...(2.3)

{m > 1} for y_step = 1,

by putting the value of change in y, i.e., $\Delta y = 1$

$m = 1/\Delta x$ => $\Delta x = 1/m$

Change in x coordinates can be written as $\Delta x = x_2 - x_1$

=> $x_{i+1} - x_i = 1/m$

=> $x_{i+1} = x_i + 1/m$ ...(2.4)

If, instead, we draw from x_2,y_2 to x_1,y_1 then:

(a) $\Delta x = -1; \qquad y_{i+1} = y_i - m$ ...(2.5)

(b) $\Delta y = -1; \qquad x_{i+1} = x_i - \dfrac{1}{m}$ ...(2.6)

2.4.3 Pseudocode of DDA Algorithm

```
Procedure DDA (x1, y1, x2, y2: integer);
var
dx, dy, steps: integer;
x_increment, y_increment, x, y: real;
begin
dx: = x2 – x1; dy: = y2 – y1;
if abs(dx) > abs(dy) then
steps: = abs(dx); {Change in x is greater}
else
steps: = abs(dy); {Change in y is greater}
x_ increment: = dx/steps;
y_ increment: = dy/steps;
{either x_ increment or y_ increment = 1.0, the other is the slope;}
x: = x1;
y: = y1;
set_pixel (round(x), round(y));
for I: = 1 to steps do
begin
x: = x + x_increment;
y: = y + y_increment;
set_pixel (round(x), round(y));
end; {DDA}
```

2.4.4 C Program

```
/*PROGRAM TO DRAW A LINE USING DDA ALGORITHM*/
#include<stdio.h>
#include<graphics.h>
#include<conio.h>
```

```
#include <stdlib.h>
#include <ctype.h>
void line_DDA(int ,int ,int ,int);
void main()
{
int gdriver = DETECT,gmode; /* request auto detection */
int x1,x2,y1,y2;
char c,ch;            /* take coordinates of line */
do
{
clrscr();
printf("\n\t\t Program to draw a line using DDA algorithm");
printf("\n Enter the value of x1 coordinate: ");
scanf("%d",&x1);
printf("\n Enter the value of y1 coordinate: ");
scanf("%d",&y1);
printf("\n Enter the value of x2 coordinate: ");
scanf("%d",&x2);
printf("\n Enter the value of y2 coordinate: ");
scanf("%d",&y2);            /* draw a line */
initgraph(&gdriver,&gmode, "d:\\tc\\"); /* initialize graphics mode */
line_DDA(x1,y1,x2,y2);
printf("\n\n Do you want to continue? y/n/n");
ch = getche();
c = tolower(ch);
while((c != 'n')&&(c != 'y'))
{
printf("\b");
c = getche();
}
}
while(c == 'y');
```

```
}
void line_DDA (int x1,int y1,int x2,int y2)
{
int dx,dy,steps,k;
float x,y,x_increment,y_increment;
dx = x2 - x1;
dy = y2 - y1;
if(abs(dx) > abs(dy))
steps = abs(dx);
else
steps = abs(dy);
x_increment = dx/steps;
y_increment = dy/steps;
x = x1;
y = y2;
putpixel(x,y,1);
for(k=0;k < steps;k++)
{
x =x+ x_increment;
y =y+ y_increment;
putpixel(x,y,1);
}
}
```

Advantages of DDA Algorithm

In the real world of limited precision displays, we must generate only addressable points. This can be done by rounding to the nearest integer after each incremental step.

- One advantage of this arrangement is that it allows us to detect changes in x and y hence it avoids plotting the same point again.
- Each line is computed with just two additions, eliminating multiplication.
- Faster method.

Example 2.1: Consider a line from (4, 6) to (8, 9). Use the simple DDA algorithm to rasterize this line.

Solution: Line (4, 6) to (8, 9)

$$x_2 - x_1 = 8 - 4 = 4$$

$$y_2 - y_1 = 9 - 6 = 3$$

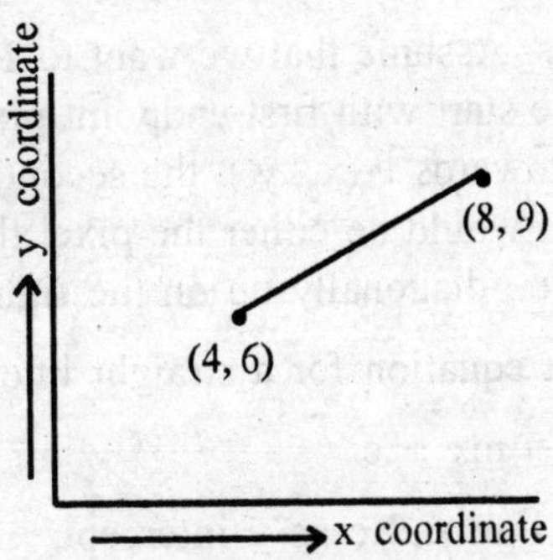

Fig. 2.5 Line Segment

As abs$|x_2 - x_1|$ > abs$|y_2 - y_1|$ i.e., abs(dx) > abs(dy)

=> Length: = abs$|x_2 - x_1|$ = 4

x increment = 4/4 = 1

y increment = 3/4 = 0.75

x = 4 + 1 = 5 y = 6 + 0.75 = 6.75

x = 5 + 1 = 6 y = 6.75 + 0.75 = 7.50

x = 6 + 1 = 7 y = 7.50 + 0.75 = 8.25

x = 7 + 1 = 8 y = 8.25 + 0.75 = 9

2.4.5 What's wrong with DDA?

- It requires floating point operations.
- These operations are expensive to implement in hardware.
- They are not really necessary if the endpoints are integers.
- Rounding off can cause the calculated pixel positions to drift away from the true line path for long line segments.
- Rounding operations and floating point arithmetic are still time-consuming.

2.4.6 Derivation of Bresenham's Line Algorithm for $|m| < 1$

The main drawback of DDA algorithm is that it is very time-onsuming as it includes floating point arithmetic and rounding off operations. The drawback was overcome by Bresenham's line drawing algorithm, since it highly efficient incremental method for scan converting lines and produces accurate results using only integer addition, subtraction and multiplication by powers of 2.

The basic principle followed by Bresenham's line algorithm is to find the best pixel to represent the straight line. To accomplish this, algorithm always increases by unit steps either in x direction or y direction depending upon the slope (i.e., m) of the line. The increment in other variable is decided on the basis of the distance between the true path of the line and the nearest pixel. This distance is called the *decision parameter.*

The method works as follows. Assume that we want to scan convert the line L1 as shown in figure 2.2 where $0 < m < 1$. We start with first endpoint pixel $P_1(x_1, y_1)$, then the subsequent pixels would be on the right and towards $P_2(x_2, y_2)$, the second endpoint. Once a pixel has been selected at any step, the next pixel would be either the pixel that is to the right to it, or the one that is to the right and up to it (i.e., diagonally up on the right).

The Cartesian slope-intercept equation for a straight line

$$y = mx + c \qquad \text{...(2.7)}$$

where m is the slope of the line and c as y intercept.

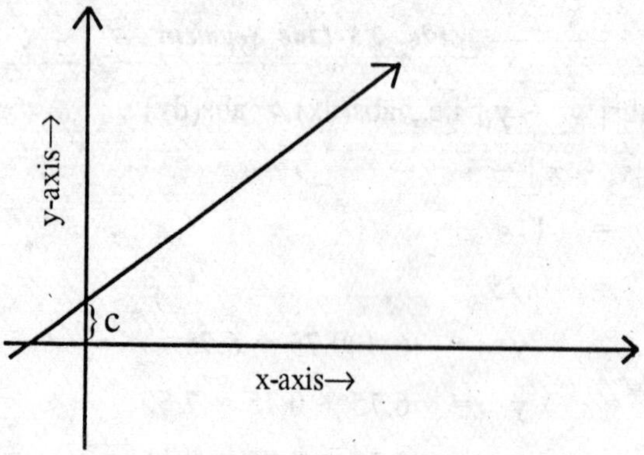

Fig. 2.6 Slope Intercept form

If (x_1, y_1) and (x_2, y_2) are the two endpoints of the line, then the slope of the line is

$$m = (y_2 - y_1)/(x_2 - x_1) = \Delta y/\Delta x \qquad \text{...(2.8)}$$

To elaborate Bresenham's approach, we first consider the scan conversion process for lines with positive slope less than 1. Pixel positions along the line path are then determined by sampling at unit x intervals. Starting from the first, i.e., left endpoint (x_1,y_1) of a given line of positive slope less than 1, we step to each successive column (i.e., x position) and plot the pixel whose scan line y value is closest to the true line. Figure 2.7 demonstrates the kth step in the process. We assume that, we have determined the pixel at (x_k,y_k) to be displayed, we next need to decide which pixel to plot at $k+1^{th}$ step, either (x_k+1, y_k) or $(x_k +1, y_k + 1)$.

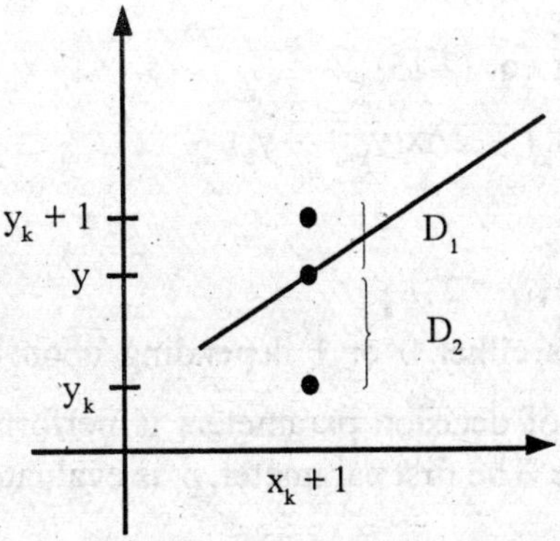

Fig. 2.7 k^{th} Step and Secision Parameter

At $k+1^{th}$ step, we label vertical pixel separations from the mathematical line path as D_1 and D_2. The *y* coordinate on the mathematical line at pixel column position x_k+1 is calculated as:

$$y = m(x_k+1) + c \qquad ...(2.9)$$

Then

$$D_1 = y - y_k$$
$$= m(x_k+1) + c - y_k \qquad ...(2.10)$$

and

$$D_2 = (y_k+1) - y$$
$$= y_k+1 - m(x_k+1) - c$$

The difference between these 2 separations is:

$$D_1 - D_2 = 2m(x_k +1) - 2y_k + 2c - 1 \qquad ...(2.11)$$

A decision parameter p_k for the kth step in the line algorithm can be obtained by rearranging the above equation so that it involves only integer calculations. We accomplish this by substituting $m = \Delta y / \Delta x$, where Δy and Δx are the vertical and horizontal separations of the endpoint positions respectively, and defining:

$$p_k = \Delta x(D_1 - D_2)$$
$$= 2\Delta y.x_k - 2\Delta x.y_k + D \qquad ...(2.12)$$

The sign of p_k is same as the sign of $D_1 - D_2$, since $\Delta x > 0$ for our example. Parameter D is constant and has the value $D = 2\Delta y + \Delta x(2c - 1)$, which is independent of pixel position and will be eliminated in the recursive calculation for p_k, if the pixel at y_k is closer to the line path than the pixel at y_k+1 (that is $D_1 < D_2$), then decision parameter p_k is positive. In that case, we plot the lower pixel $(x_k +1, y_k)$, otherwise we plot the upper pixel$(x_k +1, y_k + 1)$.

Increment occurs in unit steps in either the x or y directions; therefore we obtain the values of successive decision parameters using integer calculations. At step k+1, the decision parameter is evaluated from Eq. 2.12 as:

$$p_{k+1} = 2\Delta y.x_{k+1} - 2\Delta x.y_{k+1} + D \qquad ...(2.13)$$

Subtracting Eq. (2.12) from eq. (2.13)

$$p_{k+1} - p_k = 2\Delta y(x_{k+1} - x_k) - 2\Delta x(y_{k+1} - y_k)$$

But $x_k+1 = x_k+1$, so that

$$p_{k+1} = p_k + 2\Delta y - 2\Delta x(y_{k+1} - y_k) \qquad ...(2.14)$$

where the term $y_{k+1} - y_k$ is either 0 or 1 depending upon the sign of parameter p_k.

This recursive calculation of decision parameters is performed at each integer x starting from the left coordinate of the line. The first parameter, p_0 is evaluated at the starting pixel position (x_1, y_1) and with $m = \Delta y/\Delta x$ as:

$$p_0 = 2\Delta y - \Delta x$$

i.e., from Eq. 2.11 $p_0 = \Delta x(2m(x_1+1) - 2y_1 + 2c - 1)$, i.e., $\Delta x(D_1 - D_2)$

$$p_0 = \Delta x(2(mx_1 + c - y_1) + 2m - 1)$$

Since, $mx_1 + c - y_1 = 0$ and $m = \Delta y/\Delta x$, we have

$$= \Delta x\ (2\Delta y/\Delta x - 1)$$

$$= 2\Delta y - \Delta x \qquad ...(2.15)$$

An accurate and efficient raster line-generating algorithm, developed by Bresenham, scans convert lines using only incremental integer calculations. It is a recursive algorithm.

2.4.7 Bresenham's Line Drawing Algorithm for |m|< 1

(i) Start.

(ii) Input the two line endpoints and store the left endpoint in (x_1, y_1).

(iii) Plot the first point, i.e., (x_1, y_1).

(iv) Calculate constants Δx, Δy, $2\Delta y$, and $2\Delta y - \Delta x$.

(v) Calculate the value for the decision parameter at initial point

$p_0 = 2\Delta y - \Delta x$.

(vi) At each x_k along the line, starting from k = 0, check whether:

If $p_k < 0$, the next point to plot is (x_{k+1}, y_k) and decision parameter would be

$p_{k+1} = p_k + 2\Delta y$

Otherwise (i.e., if $p_k\ \alpha \geq 0$), the next point to plot is (x_{k+1}, y_{k+1}) and decision parameter would be

$p_{k+1} = p_k + 2\Delta y - 2\Delta x$

(vii) Repeat step (iv) Δx times.

(viii) Stop.

2.4.8 C Program

```
/*PROGRAM TO DRAW A LINE USING BRESENHAM'S ALOGRITHM*/
#include <stdio.h>
#include <graphics.h>
#include <stdlib.h>
#include <stdio.h>
#include <conio.h>
void bln(float x1,float y1,float x2,float y2,int color)
{
float dx,dy,m,p,inc1,inc2;
dx=x2-x1;
dy=y2-y1;
m=dy/dx;
if(m>1)
outtextxy(100,100, "SLOPE GREATER THAN 1");
else
{
p=2*dy-dx;
inc1=2*dy;
inc2=2*(dy-dx);
putpixel(x1,y1,color);
while(x1<=x2)
{
if(p<0)
p+=inc1;
else
{
y1++;
p+=inc2;
}
x1++;
putpixel(x1,y1,color);
```

```
}
}
}
int main(void)
{
int gdriver = DETECT, gmode, errorcode;
initgraph(&gdriver, &gmode, "d:\\tc\\");
errorcode = graphresult();
printf("\n\t\t Program to draw a line using Bresenhams algorithm");
if (errorcode != grOk)
{
printf("Graphics error: %s\n", grapherrormsg(errorcode));
printf("Press any key to halt:");
getch();
exit(1);
}
bln(10,10,60,60,14);
getch();
closegraph();
return 0;
}
```

Example 2.2: Draw the line with endpoints (20, 12) and (30, 18) using Bresenham's algorithm.

Solution:

Here, slope, $m = \dfrac{y_2 - y_1}{x_2 - x_1} = \dfrac{18-12}{30-20} = \dfrac{6}{10} = 0.6$

$\Delta x = 10$ and $\Delta y = 6$

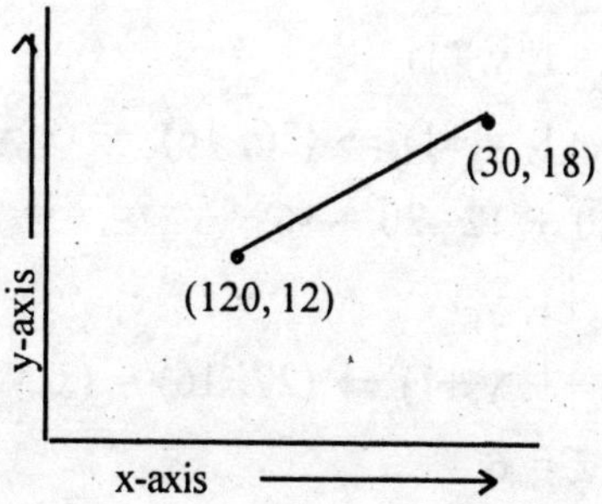

Fig. 2.8 Line Segment

The initial decision parameter has the value

(1) $p_0 = 2\Delta y - \Delta x$

$\Rightarrow$ $p_0 = 2(6) - 10 = 12 - 10 = 2$

And the increments for calculating successive decision parameters.

$2\Delta y = 12$, and $2\Delta y - 2\Delta x = -8$

As $p_0 > 1$

$\Rightarrow$ Next point (x_k+1, y_k)

$(x_0 + 1, y_0) \approx (x_1, y_1)$

(21, 13)

And $p_{0+1} = p_0 + 2\Delta y - 2\Delta x$

$p_1 = 2 - 8 = -6$

(2) $-6 < 0 \Rightarrow$ Next point (x_k+1, y_k)

$(x_1+1, y_1) \Rightarrow (22,13) \approx (x_2,y_2)$

$p_{1+1} = p_1 + 2\Delta y = -6 + 12 = 6 \Rightarrow 6$

(3) $6 > 0 \Rightarrow$ Next point (x_k+1, y_k+1)

$(x_2+1, y_2+1) \Rightarrow (23, 14) \approx (x_3,y_3)$

$p_{2+1} = p_2 + 12 - 20 = 18 - 20 = -2$

(4) $-2 < 0 \Rightarrow$ Next point (x_k+1, y_k)

$(x_3+1, y_3+1) \Rightarrow (24, 14) \approx (x_4,y_4)$

$p_{3+1} = p_3 + 12 = -2 + 12 = 10$

(5) $10 > 0 \Rightarrow$ Next point (x_k+1, y_k+1)

$(x_4+1, y_4+1) \Rightarrow (25, 15) \approx (x_5,y_5)$

$p_{4+1} = p_4 + 12 - 20 = 10 + 12 - 20 = 2$

(6) $2 > 0 \Rightarrow$ Next point (x_k+1, y_k+1)

$$(x_5+1, y_5+1) \Rightarrow (26, 16) \approx (x_6, y_6)$$

$p_{5+1} = p_5 + 12 - 20 + 20 + 12 - 20 = -6$

(7) $-6 < 0 \Rightarrow$ Next point (x_k+1, y_k)

$$(x_6+1, y_6+1) \Rightarrow (27, 16) \approx (x_7, y_7)$$

$p_{6+1} = p_6 + 12 = -6 + 12 = 6$

(8) $6 > 0 \Rightarrow$ Next point (x_k+1, y_k+1)

$$(x_7+1, y_7+1) \Rightarrow (28, 17) \approx (x_8, y_8)$$

$p_{7+1} = p_7 + 12 - 20 = 6 + 12 - 20 = -2$

(9) $-2 < 0 \Rightarrow$ Next point (x_k+1, y_k)

$$(x_8+1, y_8+1) \Rightarrow (29, 17) \approx (x_9, y_9)$$

$p_{8+1} = p_8 + 12 = -2 + 12 = 10$

(10) $10 > 0 \Rightarrow$ Next point (x_k+1, y_k+1)

$$(x_9+1, y_9+1) \Rightarrow (30, 18) \approx (x_{10}, y_{10})$$

And hence we proceed further in the similar manner.

k	p_k	(x_k+1, y_k+1)	k	p_k	(x_k+1, y_k+1)
0	2	(21, 13)	5	2	(26, 16)
1	-6	(22, 13)	6	-6	(27, 16)
2	6	(23, 14)	7	6	(28, 17)
3	-2	(24, 14)	8	-2	(29, 17)
4	10	(25, 15)	9	10	(30, 18)

2.4.9 Advantages of Using Bresenham's Line Algorithm

- Bresenham's Algorithm avoids generating duplicate points.
- As it avoids multiplications and divisions, it is well suited for implementation in hardware or on simple microprocessors.
- It uses only integer arithmetic thus avoiding the Round function, thus allowing calculations to be performed accurately.
- It works only on integers.
- Line intensity varies with its angle.

2.5 CIRCLE SCAN CONVERSION

2.5.1 8-way Symmetry

A Circle is a Symmetrical figure. Any algorithm of Scan converting a circle can take advantage of the circle's symmetry to plot different points corresponding to the each value that the algorithm calculates. For example, if point P_1 in figure. 2.9 were calculated with a circle algorithm, and if you are using eight-way symmetry then seven more points could be found by reflection. The reflection is accomplished by reversing the x, y coordinates as in point P_2, exchanging the x, y coordinates and reflecting about the y-axis, i.e., x =0 as in point P_3, reflecting about the y-axis as in point in P_5, reversing the x, y, coordinates, reflecting about the y-axis in point P_4 and reflecting about the x-axis as in point $-P_6$, reversing the x, y coordinates and reflecting about the y-axis as in point P_7, and reflecting about the x-axis as in point P_8.

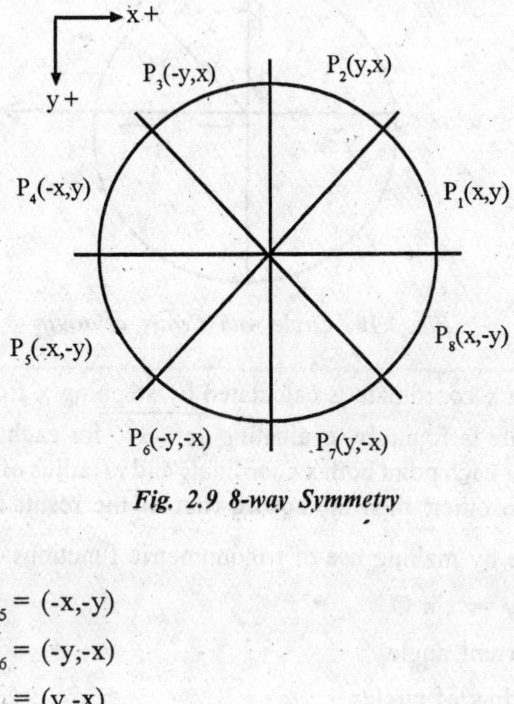

Fig. 2.9 8-way Symmetry

To Summarize:

$P_1 = (x,y)$ $P_5 = (-x,-y)$

$P_2 = (y,x)$ $P_6 = (-y,-x)$

$P_3 = (-y,x)$ $P_7 = (y,-x)$

$P_4 = (-x,y)$ $P_8 = (x,-y)$

2.5.2 Definition of a Circle

There are two standard methods of mathematically defining a circle:

2.5.2.1 Center at Origin

1. Defines a circle with the second-order polynomial equation:

$$y^2 = r^2 - x^2 \qquad (2.16)$$

where x = x coordinate

y = y coordinate

r = radius of the circle

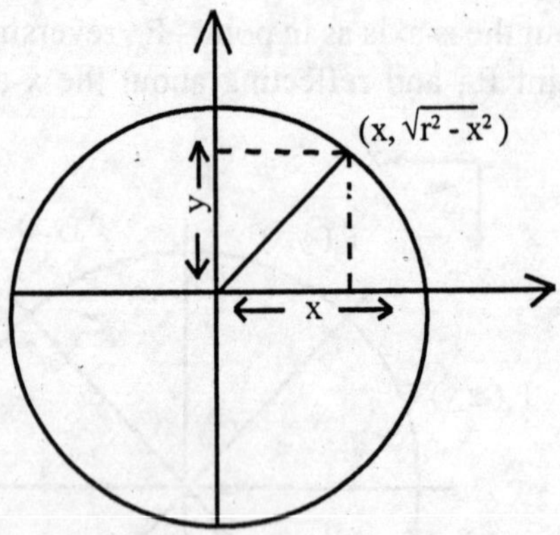

Fig. 2.10 Circle with Centre at origin

In this method, each x coordinate is calculated by stepping x from 0 to $r/\sqrt{2}$, from 90° to 45°, and each y coordinate is found by evaluating $\sqrt{r^2 - x^2}$ for each step of x. This method is highly inefficient since for each point both x coordinate and r (radius of the circle) must be squared and subtracted from each other; then the square root of the result must be found.

2. Defines a circle by making use of trigonometric functions:

$$x = r \cos Ø, \quad y = r \sin Ø \qquad ...(2.17)$$

where Ø = current angle

r = radius of circle

x = x coordinate

y = y coordinate

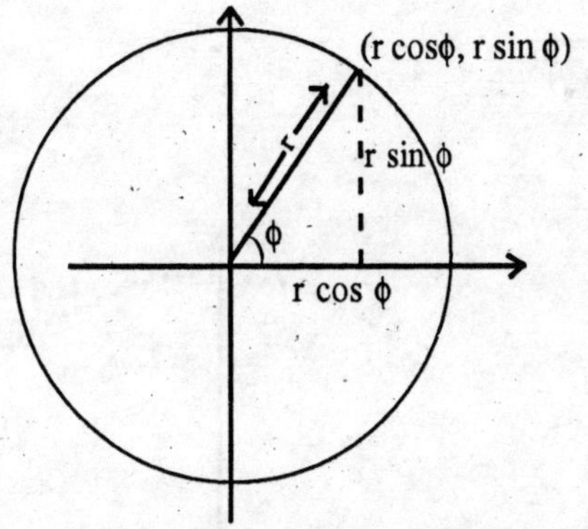

Fig. 2.11 Trignometric Equation of a Circle

By this method, Ø is stepped from 0° to 45°, and each value of x and y is calculated. However, computation of trigonometric functions are even more time-consuming than the calculations required by the first method.

2.5.2.2 Center at an Arbitrary Point

1. A circle is defined as the set of points that are all at a given distance 'r' from a center position (x_c, y_c).

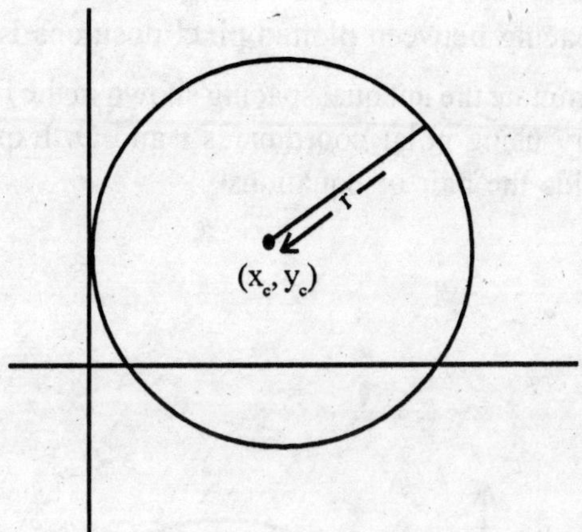

Fig. 2.12 Circle with Centre (x_c, y_c)

This distance relationship is expressed by a Pythagorean Theorem in Cartesian coordinates

$$(x - x_c)^2 + (y - y_c)^2 = r^2 \qquad ...(2.18)$$

We could use this equation to calculate the position of points on a circle circumference by stepping along the x-axis in unit steps from $x_c - r$ to $x_c + r$ and calculating the corresponding y values at each position as:

Explicit definition

$$y = y_c \pm \sqrt{r^2 - (x - x_c)^2} \qquad ...(2.19)$$

Where,

$-r \le (x - x_c) \le 1$

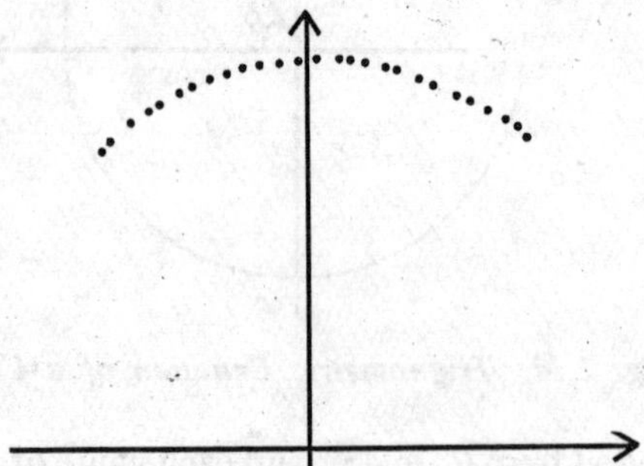

Fig. 2.13 Unequal Spacing

Disadvantages:

- This is not the best method for generating a circle.
- It involves considerable computation at each step.
- Moreover, the spacing between plotted pixel positions is not uniform.

2. Another way to eliminate the unequal spacing shown in the figure 2.13 is to calculate points along the circular boundary using polar coordinates r and Ø. Expressing the circle equation in parametric polar form yields the pair of equations

$$x = x_c + r\cos Ø \qquad ...(2.20)$$

$$y = y_c + r\sin Ø \qquad ...(2.21)$$

Where Ø ε [0, 2π]

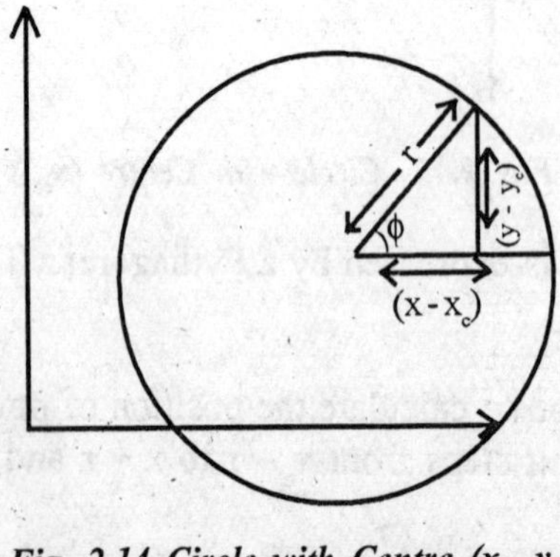

Fig. 2.14 Circle with Centre (x_c, y_c)

When a display is generated with these equations using a fixed angular step size, a circle is plotted with equally spaced points along the circumference.

Computation can be reduced by considering the symmetry of circles. The shape of the circle is similar in each quadrant.

Determining pixel positions along a circle circumference involves good deal of computation time. The Cartesian equation involves multiplications and square root calculations while the parametric equations contain multiplications and trigonometric calculations.

2.5.3 Derivation of Bresenham's Circle Algorithm

As discussed earlier, if a circle is to be plotted efficiently, you should avoid the use of trigonometric and power functions. Bresenham's method of drawing the circle is an efficient method since it avoids trigonometric and power functions, involves only simple integer operations.

More efficient circle algorithms are based on incremental calculation of decision parameters, which involves only simple integer operations, as in case of *Bresenham's Algorithm.*

- *Bresenham's circle algorithm* avoids the square root calculation.
- Here, the decision parameter for finding the closest pixel to the circumference at each sampling step is set up.
- Here, thus the successive decision parameters are attained using incremental calculations.

The **Bresenham's circle algorithm** is a midpoint method that calculates pixel positions along the circumference of a circle using integer additions and subtraction, assuming that the circle parameters are specified in integer screen coordinates.

If we follow the eight way symmetry to generate or scan convert a circle then only one octant of the circle needs to be generated. The other points can be calculated by successive reflections.

Scan converting a circle using Bresenham's algorithm works as follows. If the eight-way symmetry of a circle is used to generate a circle, algorithm will plot 1/8th part of the circle from 90° to 45°. As circle is drawn from 90° to 45°, the x moves in positive direction and y moves in negative direction.

To achieve best approximation to the true circle, we have to select those pixels in the raster that falls the least distance from the true circle. If points are generated from 90° to 45°, each new point closest to the true circle can be found by applying either of two options:

(a) Increment in positive x direction by one unit

or

(b) Increment in positive x direction by one unit and decrement in negative y direction by one unit.

Therefore, a method of selecting between these two options is all that is necessary to find the points closest to the true circle.

Let us assume that, we have determined the pixel (x_k, y_k) to be displayed, we next need to decide which pixel to plot at k+1th step, either S (x_k+1, y_k) or P (x_k +1, y_k-1). We have to select S or P, depending on which is close to the circle, and for that we have to perform some test.

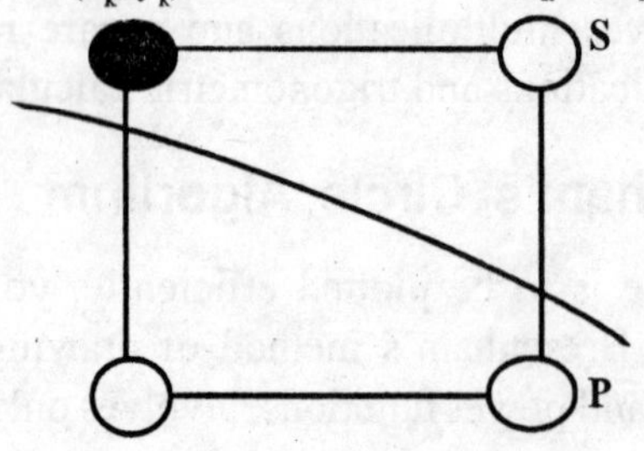

Fig. 2.15 Section of the Display Screen where a Circle is to be Plotted

Let the distance from the origin to pixel S squared minus the distance to the true circle squared = D(S)

since S(x_k + 1, y_k)S $\quad D(S) = (x_k + 1)^2 + y_k^{\ 2} - r^2$ ...(2.22)

Then let the distance from the origin to pixel P Squared minus the distance to the true circle squared = D(P)

Since P(x_k + 1, y_k - 1), $\quad D(P) = (x_k + 1)^2 + (y_k - 1)^2 - r^2$ ...(2.23)

Function D gives relative measurement of the distance from the center of pixel to the true circle. Since D(S) will always be positive (S lies outside the true circle) and D(P) will always be negative (P is inside the true circle), a decision variable

$p_k = D(S) + D(P)$ ...(2.24)

Therefore, $p_k = 2(x_k + 1)^2 + y_k^{\ 2} (y_k - 1) - 2r^2$ ...(2.25)

If $p_k < 0$, i.e., |D(S)|< |D(P)|, then pixel S is selected i.e., only x is incremented by one unit. If $p_k \geq 0$, i.e., |D(S)| > |D(P)| then pixel P is selected, i.e., x is incremented by one unit and y is decremented by one unit.

If $p_k < 0$

$x_{k+1} = x_k + 1$

$y_{k+1} = y_k$

Else

$x_{k+1} = x_k + 1$

$y_{k+1} = y_k - 1$

Decision variable for k+1th step:

$p_{k+1} = (2x_{k+1} + 1)^2 + y^2_{k+1} + (y_{k+1} - 1)^2 - 2r^2$ ...(2.26)

Subtracting Eq.2.25 from Eq.2.26

$p_{k+1} - p_k = 2(x_{k+1} + 1)^2 + y^2 + (y_{k+1} - 1)^2 - 2(x_k+1)^2 - y_k^2 - (y_k - 1)^2$ ...(2.27)

Since $x_{k+1} = x_{k+1}$, we have

$p_{k+1} = p_k + 4x_k + 2(y^2_{k+1} - y^2_k) - 2(y_{k+1} - y_k) + 6$ ...(2.28)

If S is selected then $y_{k+1} = y_k$

$p_{k+1} = p_k + 4x_k + 6$ ...(2.29)

Otherwise, if P is selected then $y_{k+1} = y_k - 1$

$p_{k+1} = p_k + 4(x_k - y_k) + 10$ ...(2.30)

The equation of p_k at starting point, i.e., x = 0 and y = r is as follows:

$p_k = D(S) + D(P)$

$= 2(x_k + 1)^2 + y_k^2 + (y_k - 1)^2 - 2r^2$

$= 2(0 + 1)^2 + r^2 + (r - 1)^2 - 2r^2$

$= 2 + r^2 + r^2 + 1 - 2r - 2r^2$

$= 3 - 2r$ ...(2.31)

2.5.4 Bresenham's Circle Drawing Algorithm

1. Input radius 'r' of the circle.
2. Calculate the initial value of the decision parameter/variable

   $p_k = 3 - 2r$
3. Load the initial point of the circle in the frame buffer (0,r).
4. If we are using eight-way symmetry to plot the pixels, then until (x < = y) we have to perform following steps:

   if (p_0<0) then

   p = p + 4x + 6

   x= x + 1

   else

   p = p + 4(x-y) + 10

   x = x − 1

   y = y − 1
5. Plot (x,y).
6. Determine and plot the corresponding symmetry points in other octants also.
7. Stop.

2.5.5 C Program

```
/*PROGRAM TO DRAW A CIRCLE USING BRESENHAM's CIRCLE DRAWING
ALGORITHM*/
#include <graphics.h>
#include <stdlib.h>
#include <stdio.h>
#include <conio.h>
void bcircle(int h,int k,int r,int color)
{
int x=0,y=r;
float d=3-2*r;
while(x<=y)
{
putpixel(x+h,y+k,color);
putpixel(x+h,-y+k,color);
putpixel(-x+h,y+k,color);
putpixel(-x+h,-y+k,color);
putpixel(-y+h,-x+k,color);
putpixel(-y+h,x+k,color);
putpixel(y+h,x+k,color);
putpixel(y+h,-x+k,color);
if(d<0)
d+=4*x+6;
else
{
d+=4*(x-y)+10;
y--;
}
x++;
}
}
int main(void)
```

```
{
int gdriver = DETECT, gmode, errorcode;
initgraph(&gdriver, &gmode, "d:\\tc\\");
errorcode = graphresult();
printf("\n\t\t Program to draw a Circle using Bresenham's algorithm");
if(errorcode != grOk) /* an error occurred */
{
printf("Graphics error: %s\n", grapherrormsg(errorcode));
printf("Press any key to halt:");
getch();
exit(1); /* return with error code */
}
bcircle(300,300,50,10);
getch();
closegraph();
}
```

Example 2.3: Plot a circle by Bresenham's algorithm with whose radius is 3 and center is (0,0).

Solution: Initial point $= (0, r) = (0,3)$

Now, decision parameter at initial point $p = 3 - 2r$

$= 3 - 2 * 3 = 3 - 6$

$= -3$

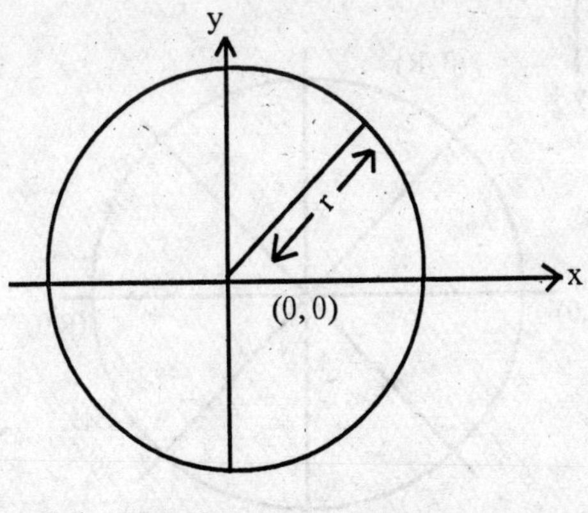

Fig. 2.16 Circle with r = 3 and Centre at Origin

Now $p < 0$ then S is chosen and x is incremented by one unit.

$x = x + 1 = 1$

$y = y = 3$

Next point to plot (1,3)

$$
\begin{aligned}
\text{Now} \quad p &= p + 4x + 6 \\
&= -3 + 4(1) + 6 = -3 + 4 + 6 \\
&= 7
\end{aligned}
$$

Now $p > 0$ then p is chosen and x is incremented by one unit and y is decremented by one unit.

$$x = x + 1 = 1 + 1 = 2$$

$$y = 3 - 1 = 2$$

Next point to plot (2, 2).

Since the value of x is equal to value of y, so no more further calculations are required in the octant from 90° to 45°.

2.5.6 Derivation of Midpoint Circle Algorithm

Midpoint circle is another incremental algorithm that is very similar to Bresenham's approach. As in the faster line algorithm, we sample at unit intervals and find out the closest pixel position to the specified circle path at each step. We can set up our algorithm to calculate pixel positions around a circle path centered at the coordinate origin (0,0).

If we follow the eight-way symmetry to generate or scan convert a circle, then only one octant of the circle needs to be generated. The other points can be calculated by successive reflections.

To apply the midpoint method, we first define the equation of a circle with (0,0) as its centre as:

$$F_{Cir}(x,y) = x^2 + y^2 - r^2 \qquad \text{...(2.32)}$$

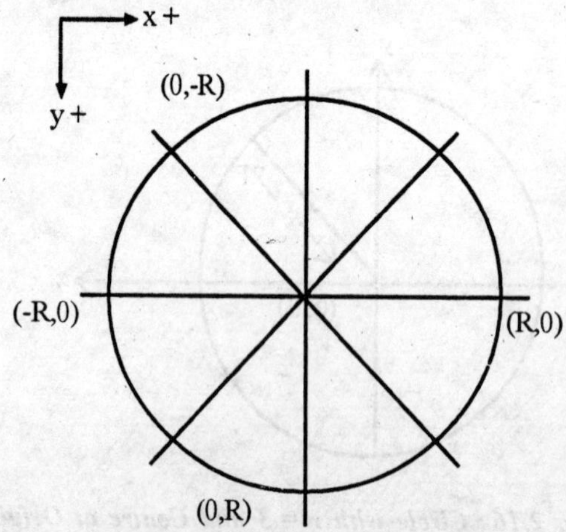

Fig. 2.17 Circle with Radius R and Centre at Origin.

Any point (x,y) on the boundary of the circle with radius r satisfies the equation $F_{Cir}(x,y) = 0$. If the point (x,y) is inside the circle, the circle function, $F_{Cir}(x,y)$ is negative. and if the point is outside the circle, the circle function $F_{Cir}(x,y)$ is positive. To summarize, the relative position of any point (x,y) can be determined by checking the sign of the circle function:

$$F_{Cir}(x,y)\begin{cases} < 0, \text{if } (x,y) \text{ lies inside the circle} \\ = 0, \text{if } (x,y) \text{ lies on the circle} \\ > 0, \text{if } (x,y) \text{ lies outside the circle} \end{cases} \quad ...(2.33)$$

In fig. 2.18, we have plotted the pixel at (x_k, y_k), now we next need to determine $E(x_k+1, y_k)$ or SE (x_k+1, y_k-1) is closer to the true circle.

Now consider the coordinates of the point M $(x_k+1, y_k-½)$, halfway between E and SE. M is called the midpoint and we use it to define a decision parameter:

$$p_k = F_{cir}(x_k+1, y_k-½) = F_{cir}(M) = (x_k+1)^2 + (y_k-½)^2 - r^2 \quad ...(2.34)$$

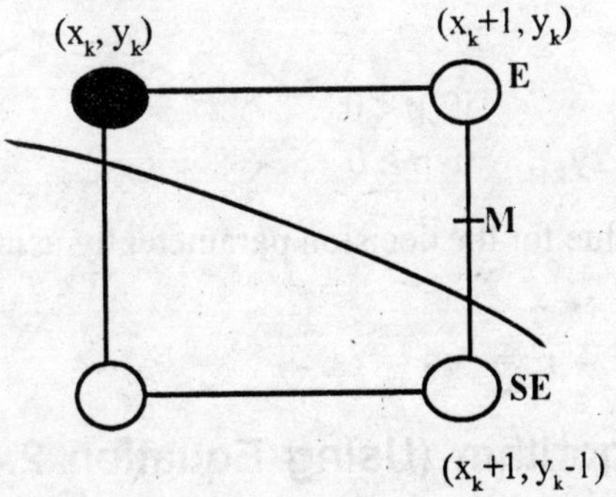

Fig. 2.18 kth Step in Midpoint Circle Scan Conversion

If $p_k < 0$, i.e., negative, the midpoint M is inside the circle, and we choose pixel E, else if $p_k > 0$, i.e., positive, the midpoint M is outside the circle, and we choose pixel SE and if $p_k = 0$, then the midpoint M is on the circle, and we choose pixel SE. Similarly, the decision parameter for next step is:

$$p_{k+1} = (x_{k+1}+1)^2 + (y_{k+1} - ½)^2 - r^2 \quad ...(2.35)$$

Subtracting eq. 2.34 from eq. 2.35

$$p_{k+1} - p_k = [(x_k+1)+1]^2 + (x_k+1)^2 + (y_{k+1} - ½)^2 - (y_k - \frac{1}{2})^2 \quad ...(2.36)$$

Since $x_{k+1} = x_k+1$, we have

$$p_{k+1} = p_k + 2(x_k+1) + 1 + (y^2_{k+1} - y^2_k) - (y_{k+1} - y_k) \quad ...(2.37)$$

If pixel E is chosen (i.e. $p_k < 0$), we have $y_{k+1} = y_k$

$$p_{k+1} = p_k + 2(x_k + 1) + 1 + (y_k^2 - y_k^2) - (y_k - y_k)$$

$$= p_k + 2x_k + 2 + 1 = p_k + 2x_k + 3 \quad ...(2.38)$$

If pixel SE is chosen (i.e., $p_k \geq 0$), we have $y_{k+1} = y_k - 1$

Thus,

$$p_{k+1} = (p_k + 2(x_k+1) + 1 + (y_k - 1)^2 - y_k) - (y_k - 1 - y_k)$$

$$= p_k + 2x_k + 2 + 1 + (y_k^2 + 1 - 2y_k - y_k) + 1$$

$$= p_k + 2x_k - 2y_k + 5$$

Summarize:

$$p_{k+1} = \begin{cases} p_k + 2x_k + 3 & \text{if } p > 0 \\ p_k + 2(x_k - y_k) + 5 & \text{if } p_k \geq 0 \end{cases} \quad \text{...(2.39)}$$

By putting $x_k+1 = x_{k+1}$ in equation 2.36

we get equation 2.39 as

$$p_{k+1} = \begin{cases} p_k + 2x_{k+1} + 1 & \text{if } p < 0 \\ p_k + 2(x_k + 1) + 1 - 2y_{k+1} & \text{if } p \geq 0 \end{cases} \quad \text{...(2.40)}$$

Finally, we calculate the initial value for the decision parameter by using eq. 2.34 and initial point as (0,r)

$$p_k = (0 + 1)^2 + (r - ½)^2 - r^2 = 5/4 - r \quad \text{...(2.41)}$$

2.5.7 Midpoint Circle Algorithm (Using Equation 2.40)

(1) Input radius r and circle center (x_c, y_c), and obtain the first point on the circumference of a circle entered on the origin as

$$(x_0, y_0) = (0, r)$$

(2) Calculate the initial value of the decision parameter as

$$p_0 = \frac{5}{4} - r \text{ where r is non-integer}$$

{for r an integer we take $p_0 = 1 - r$}

(3) At each x_k position, starting at k = 0, perform the following test:

If, $p_k < 0$ the next point along the circle centered on (0, 0) is (x_{k+1}, y_k) and

$$p_{k+1} = p_k + 2x_{k+1} + 1$$

Otherwise, the next point along the circle is $(x_k+1, y_k - 1)$ (i.e., $p_k \geq 0$)

$$p_{k+1} = p_k + 2(x_k+1) + 1 - 2y_{k+1}$$

where $2x_{k+1} = 2x_k + 2$ and $2y_{k+1} = 2y_k - 2$

(4) Determine symmetry points in the other seven octants.

(5) Move each calculated pixel position (x, y) onto the circular path centered on (x_c, y_c) and plot the coordinate values.

$x = x + x_c; y = y + y_c$

(6) Repeat steps 3 through 5 until $x \geq y$

2.5.8 C Program

```
/*PROGRAM TO DRAW A CIRCLE USING MID POINT CIRCLE DRAWING
ALGORITHM*/
#include <graphics.h>
#include <stdlib.h>
#include <stdio.h>
#include <conio.h>
void midptcircle(int h,int k,int r,int color)
{
int x=0,y=r;
float d=5/4-r;
while(x<=y)
{
putpixel(x+h,y+k,color);
putpixel(x+h,-y+k,color);
putpixel(-x+h,y+k,color);
putpixel(-x+h,-y+k,color);
putpixel(-y+h,-x+k,color);
putpixel(-y+h,x+k,color);
putpixel(y+h,x+k,color);
putpixel(y+h,-x+k,color);
if(d<0)
d+=2*x+3;
else
{
d+=2*(x-y)+5;
y--;
}
x++;
```

```
}
}
int main(void)
{
int gdriver = DETECT, gmode, errorcode;
initgraph(&gdriver, &gmode, "d:\\tc\\");
errorcode = graphresult();
printf("\n\t\t Program to draw a Circle line using Mid point algorithm");
if (errorcode != grOk) /* an error occurred */
{
printf("Graphics error: %s\n", grapherrormsg(errorcode));
printf("Press any key to halt:");
getch();
exit(1); /* return with error code */
}
midptcircle(300,300,50,10);
getch();
closegraph();
return 0;
}
```

Example 2.4: Given a circle radius x = 10, we demonstrate the midpoint circle algorithm by determining positions along the circle octant in the first quadrant from x = 0 to x = y.

Solution:

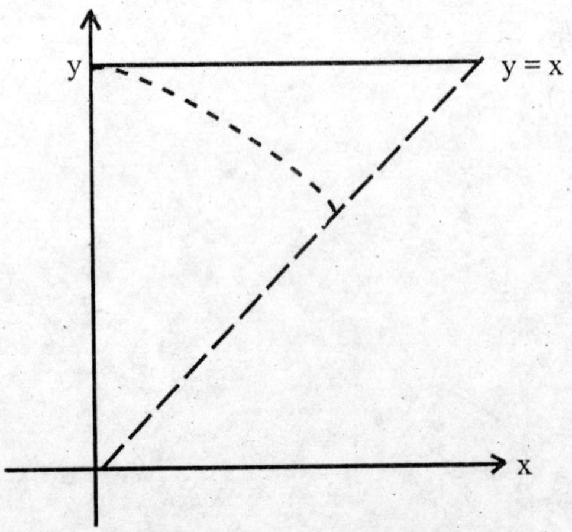

Fig. 2.19 Circle in First Quadrant

The initial value of the decision parameter is

$p_0 = 1 - r = -9$

Initial point is $(x_0, y_0) = (0, 10)$

(i) $p_k < 0$ i.e., $-9 < 0$

$\Rightarrow$ x is increasing but y is constant

$\Rightarrow (1, 10)$

Also $p_{k+1} = p_k + 2x_{k+1} + 1$

$\Rightarrow p_{k+1} = 9 + 2 + 1$ $\{2x_{k+1} = 2x_{k+2} = 0 + 2 = 2\}$

$= -9 + 3 = -6$

(ii) Again $-6 < 0$

$\Rightarrow$ x is increasing whereas y is constant

$\Rightarrow (2, 10)$

Then

$\Rightarrow p_{k+1} = p_k + 2x_{k+1} + 1$

$= -6 + 4 + 1$ $\{2x_{k+}1 = 2x_{k+2} = 2 \times 1 + 2 = 4\}$

$= -6 + 5 = -1$

(iii) Again $-1 < 0$

$\Rightarrow$ x is increasing but y is constant

$\Rightarrow (3, 10)$

Also $p_{k+1} = p_k + 2x_{k+1} + 1$

$\Rightarrow p_{k+1} = -1 + 6 + 1 = 6$ $\{2x_{k+1} = 2x_{k+2} = 2 \times 2 + 2 = 6\}$

(iv) Again $6 > 0$

$\Rightarrow$ x is increasing and y is decreasing

$\Rightarrow (4, 9)$

Also $p_{k+1} = p_k + 2x_{k+1} + 1 - 2y_{k+1}$

$\Rightarrow p_{k+1} = 6 + 8 + 1 - 18$ $2x_{k+1} = 2x_{k+2} = 2 \times 3 + 2 = 8$

$= 15 - 18 = -3$

(v) Again $-3 < 0$

$\Rightarrow$ x is increasing but y is constant

$\Rightarrow (5, 9)$

Also $p_{x+1} = p_k + 2x_{x+1} + 1$

$\Rightarrow p_{k+1} = -3 + 10 + 1 = 8$ $2x_{k+1} = 2x_{k+2} = 2 \times s\ 2 + 2 = 6$

(vi) Again $p_k = 8 > 0$

$\Rightarrow$ x is increasing and y is decreasing

$\Rightarrow$ (6,8)

Also $p_{k+1} = p_k + 2x_{k+1} + 1 - 2y_{k+1}$

$= 8 + 12 + 1 - 16 = 5$

(vii) Again $p_k = 5 < 0$

$\Rightarrow$ x is increasing and y is decreasing

$\Rightarrow$ (7,7)

k	p_k	(x_{k+1}, y_{k+1})	$2x_{k+1}$	$2y_{k+1}$
0	-9	(1, 10)	2	20
1	-6	(2, 10)	4	20
2	-1	(3, 10)	6	20
3	6	(4, 9)	8	18
4	-3	(5, 9)	10	18
5	8	(6, 8)	12	16
6	5	(7, 7)	14	14

Example 2.5: An arc is to be drawn from (2, 10) to (8, 8) in a circle of radius 10 using Mid-point circle algorithm.

Solution: $(x_0, y_0) = (2, 10)$ $r = 10$

$p_0 = 1 - r = 1 - 10 = -9$

(i) $p_0 = -9 < 0$

$\Rightarrow$ x increases and y remains constant

(3, 10)

then $p_{k+1} = p_k + 2x_{k+1} + 1$

$= -9 + 2 \times 2 + 2 + 1 = -9 + 7 = -2$

(ii) $p_0 = -2 < 0$

$\Rightarrow$ x increases and y remains constant

(4, 10)

then $p_{k+1} = p_k + 2x_{k+1} + 1$

$= -2 + 8 + 1 = -7$

(iii) $p_0 = -7 < 0$

$\Rightarrow$ x increases and y decreases

(5, 10)

then $p_{k+1} = p_k + 2x_{k+1} + 1 - 2y_{k+1}$

$= -7+11= 4$

(iv) $p_0 = 4 > 0$

$\Rightarrow$ x increases and y decreases

(6, 9)

then $p_{k+1} = p_k + 2x_{k+1} + 1$

$= 4+2 \times 6+2+1- (2 \times 10-2) = 4 + 13 - 18 = -1$

(v) $p_0 = -1 < 0$

$\Rightarrow$ x increases and y decreases

(7, 9)

then $p_{k+1} = p_k + 2x_{k+1} + 1$

$= -1+2 \times 6+2+1= -1 + 12+3 = 14$

(vi) $p_0 = 14 > 0$

$\Rightarrow$ x increases and y decreases

(8, 8)

2.6 ELLIPSE GENERATION

2.6.1 Ellipse Equation

Ellipse is an elongated circle.

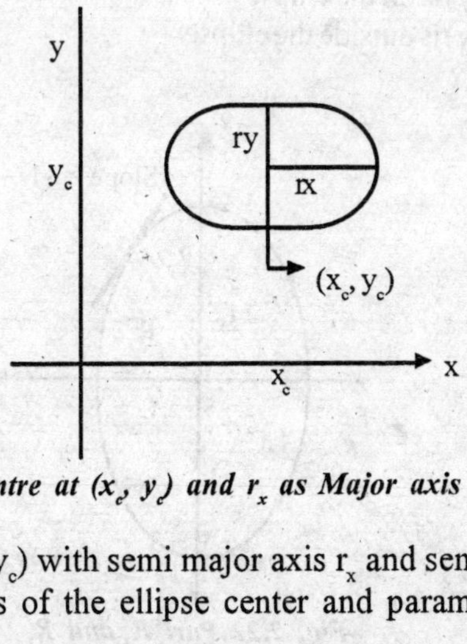

Fig. 2.20 Ellipse with Centre at (x_c, y_c) and r_x as Major axis and r_y as Minor axis

Here ellipse centered at (x_c, y_c) with semi major axis r_x and semi minor axis r_y. The equation of ellipse can be written in terms of the ellipse center and parameters r_x and r_y.

$$\left(\frac{x-x_c}{r_x}\right)^2+\left(\frac{y-y_c}{r_y}\right)=1 \quad \text{...(2.42)}$$

Symmetry of an ellipse calculation of a point x is one quadrant yield the ellipse points shown in other 3 quadrants.

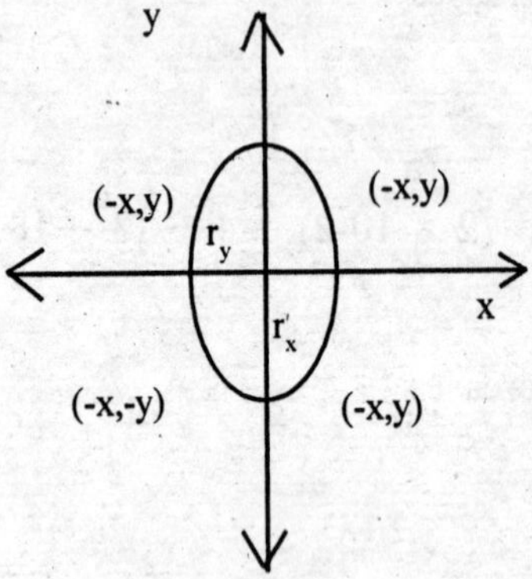

Fig. 2.21 Four-way Symmetry in Ellipse

For $(x_c, y_c) = (0, 0)$,

$$\left(\frac{x}{r_x}\right)^2+\left(\frac{y}{r_y}\right)^2=1 \quad \text{...(2.43)}$$

$$\text{Ellipse } (x, y) = r_y^2x^2 + r_x^2y^2 - r_x^2r_y^2 \quad \text{...(2.44)}$$

2.6.2 Derivation of Mid Point Ellipse Algorithm

$$f_{elp}(x, y) \text{ is } \begin{cases} < 0, \text{If } (x, y) \text{ is inside the ellipse} \\ = 0, \text{If } (x, y) \text{ is on the ellipse} \\ > 0, \text{If } (x, y) \text{ is outside the ellipse} \end{cases} \quad \text{...(2.45)}$$

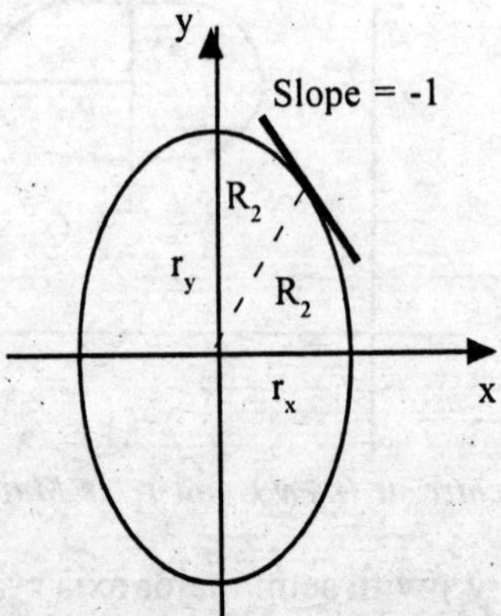

Fig. 2.22 Part R_1 and R_2

First quadrant is divided into two parts i.e., R_1 and R_2. We have divided these regions by considering the slope of the curve. If slope of the curve is less than -1, its R_1 and when slope of the curve is greater than -1, then its R_2.

The slope of the curve defined by f(x,y) = 0 is dy/dx = -fx/fy, where fx and fy are partial derivatives of f(x,y) w.r.t x and y, respectively, so $fx = 2r_y^2x$, $fy = 2r_x^2y$, and $dy/dx = -2r_y2x/2r_x^2y$

At the boundary of R_1 and R_2: dy/dx = -1 and $2r_y^2x = 2r_x^2y$ and, as soon as $2r_y^2x > 2r_x^2y$, we move out the R_1.

Starting at $(0, r_y)$, we take unit steps in the x direction until the slope of the curve is less than -1 and have to take unit steps in the y direction over the remainder of the curve in the first quadrant.

For R_1:-

Assume that the midpoint between the two pixels at k^{th} position in R_1

$$p_k = f_{elp}(x_k+1, y_k - ½)$$

$$= r_y^2(x_k+1)^2 + r_x^2(y_k - ½)^2 - r_x^2r_y^2 \qquad ...(2.46)$$

if $p_k < 0$, the midpoint $M(x_k+1, y_k - ½)$ is inside the ellipse and pixel E is selected. Else if $p_k \geq 0$, the midpoint is outside (or on) the ellipse and pixel SE is selected.

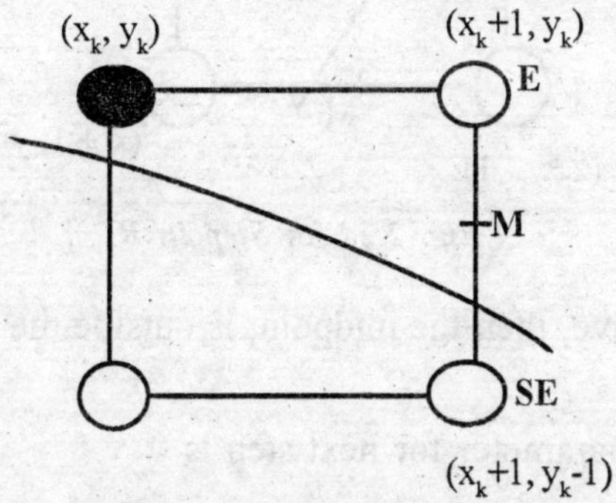

Fig. 2.23 kth Step R_1

Similarly, the decision parameter for next step is

$$p_{k+1} = f_{elp}(x_{k+1} +1, y_{k+1} - ½)$$

$$= r_y^2 [(x_{k+1}+1)]^2 + r_x^2 (y_{k+1} - ½)^2 - r_x^2r_y^2 \qquad ...(2.47)$$

Subtracting eq. 2.46 from eq. 2.47

$$p_{k+1} - p_k = r_y^2 [(x_{k+1} +1)]^2 + r_x^2 (y_{k+1} - ½)^2 - r_x^2r_y^2 - r_y^2 (x_k+1)^2 - r_x^2 (y_k - ½)_1^2 + r_x^2r_y^2$$

Since $x_{k+1} = x_k+1$

$$p_{k+1} = p_k + 2r_y^2 (x_k+1) + r_y^2 + r_x^2 [(y_{k+1} - ½)^2 - (y_k - ½)^2]$$

If $p_k < 0$, $y_{k+1} = y_k$ (E is selected)

$$p_{k+1} = p_k + 2r_y^2 (x_k+1) + r_y^2 \qquad ...(2.48)$$

If $p_k \geq 0$, $y_{k+1} = y_k - 1$ (SE is selected)

$$p_{k+1} = p_k + 2r_y^2 x_{k+1} + r_y^2 - 2r_x^2 y_{k+1}$$

(2.49)

The initial value of decision parameter for R_1 at $(0, r_y)$

$$p_0 = r_y^2 (0+1)^2 + r_x^2 (r_y - ½)^2 - r_x^2 r_y^2 \quad ...(2.50)$$

For R_2:-

Assume that the midpoint between the two pixels at jth position in R_2.

$$q_j = f_{elp}(x_j + ½, y_j - 1)$$

$$= r_y^2(x_j + ½)^2 + r_x^2(y_j - 1)^2 - r_x^2 r_y^2 \quad ...(2.51)$$

If $q_j \leq 0$, i.e., q_j is negative or zero, then the midpoint is inside the ellipse, and we select the pixel $(x_j + 1, y_j - 1)$

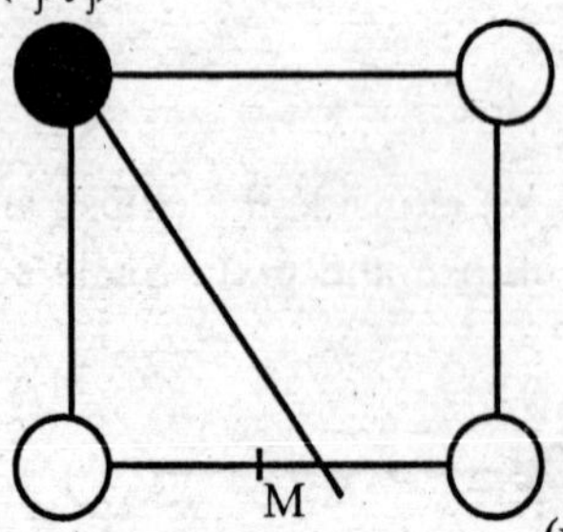

Fig. 2.24 jth Step in R_2

If $q_j > 0$, i.e., q_j is positive, then the midpoint is outside the ellipse, and we select the pixel $(x_j, y_j - 1)$.

Similarly, the decision parameter for next step is

$$q_{j+1} = r_y^2(x_{j+1} + ½)^2 + r_x^2(y_{j+1} - 1)^2 - r_x^2 r_y^2 \quad ...(2.52)$$

Subtracting Eq. 2.51 from 2.52

$$q_{j+1} - q_j = r_y^2 (x_{j+1} + ½)^2 + r_x^2 (y_{j+1} - 1)^2 - r_x^2 r_y^2 - r_y^2 (x_j + ½)^2 - r_x^2 (y_j - 1)^2 + r_x^2 r_y^2$$

Since $y_{j+1} = y_j - 1$

$$q_{j+1} = q_j + r_x^2 [(y_j - 2)^2 - (y_j - 1)^2] + r_y^2 [x_{j+1} + ½)^2 - (x_j + ½)^2]$$

$$q_{j+1} = q_j - 2r_x^2 (y_j - 1) + r_x^2 + r_y^2 [(x_{j+1} + ½)^2 - (x_j + ½)^2] \quad ...(2.53)$$

If $q_j \leq 0$, $x_{j+1} = x_j + 1$

$$q_{j+1} = q_j + 2r_x^2 x_{j+1} - 2r_x^2 y_{j+1} + r_x^2 \quad ...(2.54)$$

If $q_j > 0$, $x_{j+1} = x_j$

$$q_{j+1} = q_j - 2r_x^2 y_{j+1} + r_x^2 \quad ...(2.55)$$

Decision parameter at first point of R_2 can be obtained by evaluating the eqnation 2.51 at the last position in R_1.

$$q_0 = f_{elp}(x_0 + ½, y_0\text{-}1)$$

$$= r_y^2(x_0 + ½)^2 + r_x^2(y_0\text{-}1)^2 - r_x^2 r_y^2 \quad ...(2.56)$$

Thus, the ellipse function $f_{elp}(x, y)$ serves as the decision parameter in the mid point algorithm

2.6.3 Midpoint Algorithm for Ellipse Generation

(i) Input r_x, r_y and ellipse center (x_c, y_c) and obtain the first point.

$(x_0, y_0) = (0, r_y)$,

(ii) Initial value of the decision parameter in region R_1

$p_0 = r_y^2\text{-}r_x^2 r_y + 1/4 r_x^2$

(iii) If $p_k < 0$ then (x_k+1, y_k)

and $p_{k+1} = p_k + 2r^2_y x_{k+1} + r^2_y$

(iv) If $p_k > 0$ then $(x_{k+1}, y_k\text{-}1)$

and $p_{k+1} = p_k + 2r^2_y x_{k+1} \text{-} 2\ r_x^2 y_{k+1} + r^2_y$

with $2r^2_y x_{k+1} = 2r^2_y x_{k+1} \text{-} 2r^2_y$ and $2\ r_x^2 y_{k+1} = 2\ r_x^2 y_k \text{-} 2r_x^2$

(v) Calculate initial value of decision parameter in region R_2 using the last points (x_0, y_0) calculated in region R_1 as

$q_j = r_y^2\ (x_0 + ½)^2 + r_x^2\ (y_0\text{-}1)^2 - r_x^2 r_y^2$

(vi) If $q_j > 0$ then $(x_j\ , y_j - 1)$

and $q_{j+1} = q_j - 2r^2_x y_{j+1} + r_x^2$

(vii) If $q_j <= 0$ then $(x_j+1, yj - 1)$

and $q_j+1 = q_j - 2r_x^2 y_{j+1} + 2r_y^2 x_{j+1} + r_x^2$

(viii) Determine symmetry points for other 3 quadrants.

2.6.4 C Program

/*PROGAM TO DRAW AN ELLIPSE USING MIDPOINT ELLIPSE DRAWING ALGORITHM*/

```
#include <graphics.h>
#include <stdlib.h>
#include <stdio.h>
#include <conio.h>
void main()
{
```

```
float x,y,rx2,ry2,p1,p2;
int xc,yc,gm,gd=DETECT,rx,ry;
printf("ENTER RX AND RY:");
scanf("%d %d",&rx,&ry);
printf("ENTER THE COORDINATES OF THE CENTER:");
scanf("%d %d",&xc,&yc);
initgraph(&gd,&gm,"D:\\tc\\");
putpixel(xc,yc,15);
x=0;
y=ry;
rx2=pow(rx,2);
ry2=pow(ry,2);
p1=ry2-(rx2*ry)+(0.25*rx2);
while((ry2*x)<(rx2*y))
{
if(p1<0)
{ x++;
p1=p1+(2*ry2*x)+ry2;
}
else
{
x++;
y;
p1=p1+(2*ry2*x)-(2*rx2*y)+ry2;
}
putpixel(xc+x,yc+y,15);
putpixel(xc-x,yc+y,15);
putpixel(xc+x,yc-y,15);
putpixel(xc-x,yc-y,15);
}
p2=(ry2)*pow((x+0.5),2)+(rx2)*pow((y-1),2)-(rx2*ry2);
```

```
while(y>0)
{
if (p2>0)
{
y--;
p2=p2-(2*rx2*y) +rx2;
}
else
{
x++; y--;
p2=p2+ (2*ry2*x)-(2*rx2*y)+rx2;
}
putpixel(xc+x,yc+y,15);
putpixel(xc-x,yc+y,15);
putpixel(xc+x,yc-y,15);
putpixel(xc-x,yc-y,15);
}
getch();
closegraph();
}
```

Example 2.6: Determine raster position along the ellipse path when ellipse parameters are r_x = p8 and $r_y = 6$.

Solution: $(x_0, y_0) = (0, r_y) = (0, 6)$

$$p_0 = r_y^2 - r_x^2 r_y + \frac{1}{4} r_x^2 = (6)^2 - (8)^2 \times 6 + \frac{1}{4} \times (8)^2$$

$$= 36 - 64 \times 6 \times \frac{1}{4} + 64$$

$$= 36 - 64 \times 6 + 16 = 36 - 384 + 16$$

$$= -332$$

(i) $p_0 < 0 \Rightarrow (x_k+1, y_k)$

$\Rightarrow (1, 6) = (x_1, y_1)$

$p_{k+1} = p_k + 2r_y^2(x_k+1) + r_y^2$

$\Rightarrow p_1 = p_0 + 72 + 36$

$= -332 + 72 - 36 = -224$

(ii) $\Rightarrow p_1 < 0 \Rightarrow (x_k+1, y_k) \Rightarrow (2, 6) = (x_2, y_2)$

$p_2 = p_1 + 2r^2_y(x_k+1) + r^2_y$

$= -224 + 2 \times 36 \times 2 + 36$

$= -224 + 144 + 36 = -224 + 180 = -44$

(iii) Again $p_2 < 0 \Rightarrow (x_k+1, y_k) = (3, 6)$

$p_3 = p_2 + 2 \times 36 \times 3 + 36$

$= -44 + 216 + 36 = 208$

(iv) Here $p_3 > 0 \Rightarrow (x_k+1, y_k-1) = (4, 5)$

and $p_{k+1} = p_k + 2r^2_y(x_k+1) - 2r^2_x(y_k-1) + r^2_y$

$= 208 + 2(36).4 - 2(64).5 + 36$

$208 + 208 - 640 + 36 = -108$

(v) Again $-108 < 0$

Again $p_4 < 0 \Rightarrow (x_k+1, y_k) = (5, 5)$

$p_4 = p_3 + 2 \times 36 \times 5 + 36$

$= -108 + 360 + 36 = 288$

288

(vi) Here $p_5 > 0 \Rightarrow (x_k+1, y_k-1) = (6, 4)$

and $p_{k+1} = p_k + 2r^2_y(x_k+1) - 2r^2_x(y_k-1) + r^2_y$

$= 288 + 432 - 512 + 36$

$= 244$

(vii) Here $p_6 > 0 \Rightarrow (x_k+1, y_k-1) = (7, 3)$

and $p_{k+1} = p_k + 2r^2_y(x_k+1) - 2r^2_x(y_k-1) + r^2_y$

$= 244 + 504 - 384 + 36$

$= 400 > 0$

But here we see that, value of $2r^2_y(x_k+1) = 504$

And $2r^2_x(y_{k+1}) = 384$

$2r^2_y(x_{k+1}) > 2r^2_x(y_{k+1})$

Hence, we move out of R_1 and enters R_2.

k	P_k	(x_{k+1}, y_{k+1})	$2r_y^2x_{k+1}$		$2r_x^2y_{k+1}$
0	-332	(1, 6)	72	<	768
1	-224	(2, 6)	144	<	768
2	-44	(3, 6)	216	<	768
3	208	(4, 5)	288	<	640
4	-108	(5, 5)	360	<	640
5	288	(6, 4)	432	<	512
6	244	(7, 3)	504	>	384

We can move out of region R_1, since $2r_y^2x > 2r_x^2y$

For region R_2, initial point is $(x_0, y_0) = (7, 3)$

$$q_0 = \left(x_0 + \frac{1}{2}\right)^2 + r_x^2(y_0-1)^2 - r_x^2r_y^2$$

By substituting;

$$q_0 = 36\left(7+\frac{1}{2}\right)^2 + 64(3-1)^2 - 64 \times 36$$

$$= 36\left(\frac{14+1}{2}\right)^2 + 64(2)^2 - 64 \times 36 = 36\left(\frac{15}{2}\right)^2 + 64 \times 4 - 64 \times 36$$

$$= 36\left(\frac{15}{2}\right)^2 + 256 - 2304 = 36 \times \frac{225}{4} + 256 - 2304$$

$= 2025 + 256 - 2304 = 2281 - 2304 = -23$

Here $q_0 < 0 \Rightarrow (x_1, y_1) = (x_j+1, y_j-1) = (8, 2)$

& $q_0 = q_0+2r^2_yx_j+1-2r^2_xy_j-1+r_x^2$

$= -23 + 2 \times 36 \times 8 - 2 \times 64 \times 2 + 64 = 640 - 279 = 361$

Here $q > 0 \Rightarrow (x_2, y_2) = (x_j, y_j-1) = (8, 1)$

& $q = q_1-2r_x^2y_j-1+r_x^2$

$= 361 - 2 \times 641 + 64 = 361 - 128 + 64 = 361 - 64 = 297 > 0$

Here $q_2 > 0 \Rightarrow (x_3, y_3) = (x_j, y_j-1) = (8, 0)$

We will continue the iterations until $r_y = 0$.

2.7 SUMMARY

A point P is specified on screen with an ordered pair of numbers (x, y), where *x* is the horizontal distance from the origin and *y* is the vertical distance from the origin. To represent a line, we require two end points and then by using any line drawing algorithm we can calculate which pixels on screen has to be "turn ON" and which has to be " turn OFF". Similarly by using circle and ellipse drawing algorithms, we can draw circle and an ellipse. In this chapter, we have discussed different scan converting algorithms of line, circle and ellipse.

2.8 GLOSSARY

- Scan conversion is a technique for changing the vertical/horizontal scan frequency of video signal for different purposes and applications.
- In order to display vector-oriented graphics in the form of raster graphics, all geometrical models or shapes must be converted into pixels.
- On Raster screen, x-axis represents columns and y-axis represents rows.
- DDA line allows us to detect changes in x and y hence it avoids plotting the same point again.
- In DDA, each line is computed with just two additions, eliminating multiplication.
- DDA requires floating point operations.
- In DDA, Rounding off can cause the calculated pixel positions to drift away from the true line path for long line segments.
- The distance between the true path of the line and the nearest pixel is called the *decision parameter* in Bresenham's line.
- The value for the decision parameter at initial point in Bresenham's line:

  $p_0 = 2\Delta y - \Delta x$.
- If $p_k < 0$, the next point to plot is (x_{k+1}, y_k) and decision parameter in Bresenham's line would be $p_{k+1} = p_k + 2\Delta y$. Otherwise (i.e., if $p_k \geq 0$), the next point to plot is (x_{k+1}, y_{k+1}) and decision parameter would be $p_{k+1} = p_k + 2\Delta y - 2\Delta x$.
- Initial value of the decision parameter/variable in Bresenham's Circle

  $p_k = 3 - 2r$
- If (p_0<0) then and decision parameter in Bresenham's Circle would be:

  $p = p + 4x + 6$

  else

  $p = p + 4(x-y) + 10$
- Midpoint circle algorithm

- Initial value of the decision parameter in Midpoint Circle as

  $p0 = \frac{5}{4} - r$ where r is noninteger

- In Midpoint circle, if ($p_k < 0$), the next point along the circle centered on (0, 0) is (x_{k+1}, y_k) and $p_{k+1} = p_k + 2x_{k+1} + 1$

  Otherwise, the next point along the circle is (x_k+1, y_k -1) (i.e., $p_k \geq 0$)

  $p_{k+1} = p_k + 2x_{k+1} + 1 - 2y_{k+1}$

  where $2x_k+1 = 2x_k+1$ and $2y_{k+1} = 2y_k+2$

- If (x, y) is inside the ellipse

$$\text{If } f_{elp}(x,y) \text{ is} \begin{cases} < 0, \text{If } (x,y) \text{ is inside the ellipse} \\ = 0, \text{If } (x,y) \text{ is on the ellipse} \\ > 0, \text{If } (x,y) \text{ is outside the ellipse} \end{cases}$$

2.9 EXERCISE

Q1. Consider a line from (0, 0) to (6, 7). Use the simple DDA algorithm to rasterize this line.

Q2. Write the steps required to scan convert a circle using Bresenham's algorithm.

Q3. Consider a line from (5, 7) to (12, 11). Use the Bresenham's line algorithm to rasterize this line.

Q4. Using midpoint circle algorithm plot a circle whose radius = 8 units.

Q5. Write an algorithm for the midpoint circle algorithm in which decision parameter p is updated using x_{k+1} and y_{k+1} instead of x_k and y_k.

Q6. Plot a circle by Bresenham's algorithm whose radius is 5 and center is (0, 0).

Q7. How DDA differs from Bresenham's line drawing algorithm.

Q8. What do you mean by anti-aliasing?

Q9. Discuss ellipse generating algorithm.

Q10. Using Bresenham's algorithm, draw a circle whose center is (0, 0) and radius is 9 units.

E N D

CHAPTER 3

2-D Transformations

3.1 INTRODUCTION

Sometimes, it is essential to change the way objects appear. The need for transformation arises when various objects, each defined independently in its own coordinate system, need to be positioned in a master coordinate or real world coordinate system. The effects of transformations on object include changing the size of the object, its position on the screen, or its orientation. Implementation of such a change on object is called *transformation.*

There are two points of view for describing such a change on an object. The first point of view is that the object itself moves relative to a fix coordinate system or background. Mathematically, this viewpoint is described by applying *geometric transformation* to each point of an object. The second point of view states that the object is held fixed at a point, while the coordinate system is moved relative to the object. This effect is attained through the use of *coordinate transformations*.

Uses of transformation:

- **MODELING** – Position and resize parts of a complex model.
- **VIEWING** – Define and positions the virtual camera.
- **ANIMATION** – Define how objects move or change with time.

The basic geometric transformations are translation, rotation and scaling. Two more geometric transformations are shear and reflection.

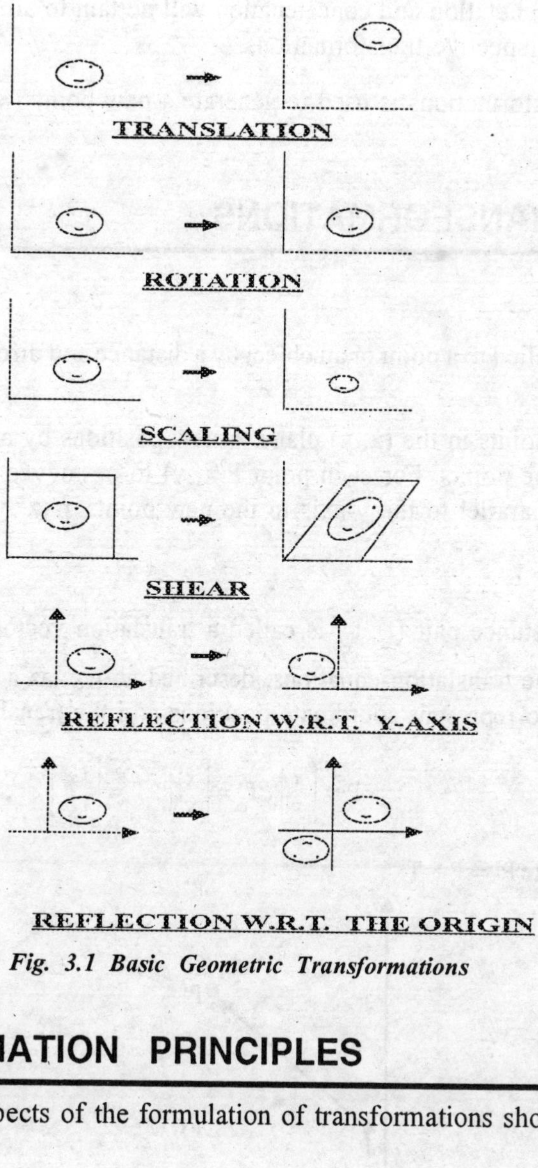

Fig. 3.1 Basic Geometric Transformations

3.2 TRANSFORMATION PRINCIPLES

The following two aspects of the formulation of transformations should be emphasized:

3.2.1 Denotation

A transformation is a single mathematical entity and as such can be denoted by a single name or symbol.

3.2.2 Concatenation

Two transformations can be combined, or concatenated, to yield a single transformation. Thus, transformation A might be a translation and transformation B a scaling. The concatenation property allows us to determine a transformation C = AB whose effect is to translate and then scale.

The principles of denotation and concatenation will pertain to all transformations: clipping, windowing, 3-D and perspective transformations.

Each of these transformations is used to generate a new point (x', y') from the coordinates of a point (x, y).

3.3 BASIC TRANSFORMATIONS

3.3.1 Translation

A translation is applied to a point or an object by a distance and direction, from one coordinate location to another.

We can translate points in the (x, y) plane to new positions by adding translation amounts to the coordinates of the points. For each point P(x, y) to be moved by t_x units parallel to the x-axis and by t_y units parallel to the y-axis to the new points $p'(x', y')$.

$$x' = x + t_x \quad y' = y + t_y \qquad ...(3.1)$$

The translation distance pair (t_x, t_y) is called a translation vector or shift vector.

We can express the translation equations, described above, as a single matrix equation by using column vectors to represent coordinate positions and the translation vector:

$$P = \begin{bmatrix} x \\ y \end{bmatrix}, P' = \begin{bmatrix} x' \\ y' \end{bmatrix}, T = \begin{bmatrix} t_x \\ t_y \end{bmatrix}$$

Thus, we can state $P' = P + T$ ...(3.2)

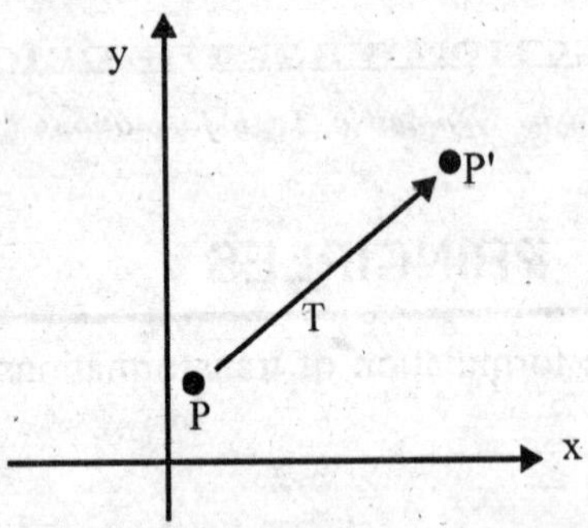

Fig. 3.2 Translating a Point from Position P to Position with Translating Vector T

Translation is a rigid-body transformation that moves objects without deformation, i.e., every point on the object is translated by the same amount. Hence, it preserves lengths and angles.

We could translate an object by applying the equations to every point of the object. Because each line in an object is made up of an infinite number of points, however, this process would take an infinitely long time. Fortunately, we can translate all the points on a line by translating only the line's endpoints and by drawing a new line between the translated endpoints.

3.3.2 Rotation

A two dimensional rotation is applied to object by repositioning it along a circular path in the xy plane. The convention is that the direction of rotation is anticlockwise if θ positive angle, and are clockwise, i.e., from y-axis towards x-axis if θ is negative angle. To generate, rotation we specify a rotation angle θ and the position (x_r, y_r) of the rotation point (or pivot point) about which the object is to be rotated.

3.3.3 Derivation of the Rotation Equation

Rotation of an object through angle θ about the origin.

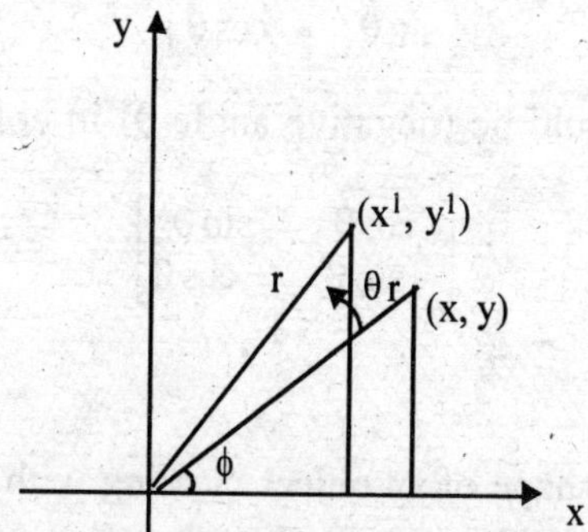

Fig. 3.3 Rotation of an Object

Here, r is the constant distance of the point from the origin; angle θ is the original angular position of the point from the x-axis and θ is the rotation angle.

Using standard trigonometric identifies, we can express the transformed coordinates in terms of angles θ and ϕ as

$$\left\{\begin{array}{l} x = r\cos(\phi+\theta) = r\cos\phi\cos\theta - r\sin\phi\sin\theta \\ y = r\sin(\phi+\theta) = r\sin\theta\cos\phi + r\sin\phi\sin\theta \end{array}\right\} \quad ...(3.3)$$

The original coordinates of the point in polar coordinates are

$x = r\cos\phi$ and $y = r\sin\phi$ ...(3.4)

Substituting expression 3.4 in 3.3, we obtain the transformation equal for rotating a point at position (x, y) through an angle θ about the origin:

$x' = x\cos\theta - y\sin\theta$ ...(3.5)

$y' = x\sin\theta + y\cos\theta$ ...(3.6)

In matrix form (Column Major order):

$$\begin{bmatrix} x' \\ y' \end{bmatrix} = \begin{bmatrix} \cos\theta & -\sin\theta \\ \sin\theta & \cos\theta \end{bmatrix} \cdot \begin{bmatrix} x \\ y \end{bmatrix}$$

$$P' = R(\theta).P$$

$$[R(\theta)] = \begin{bmatrix} \cos\theta & -\sin\theta \\ \sin\theta & \cos\theta \end{bmatrix}$$

$$[R(\theta)] = \cos^2\theta + \sin^2\theta = 1 \qquad ...(3.7)$$

Determinant of a pure rotation matrix is always +1. Rotation is a rigid body transformation it preserves lengths in object and angles between parts of objects.

Finally, the transformation matrix for 2-D rotation by angle θ in

➲ Counterclockwise direction would be (positive angle θ) in column major order:

$$\begin{bmatrix} \cos\theta & -\sin\theta \\ \sin\theta & \cos\theta \end{bmatrix} \qquad ...(3.8)$$

➲ Clockwise direction would be (negative angle θ) in column major order:

$$\begin{bmatrix} \cos\theta & \sin\theta \\ -\sin\theta & \cos\theta \end{bmatrix} \qquad ...(3.9)$$

3.3.4 Scaling

Scaling changes the size or shape of an object. Scaling with respect to origin can be carried out by multiplying the co-ordinate values (x, y) of each vertex of an object by scaling factors S_x and S_y respectively to produce the coordinates (x′, y′).

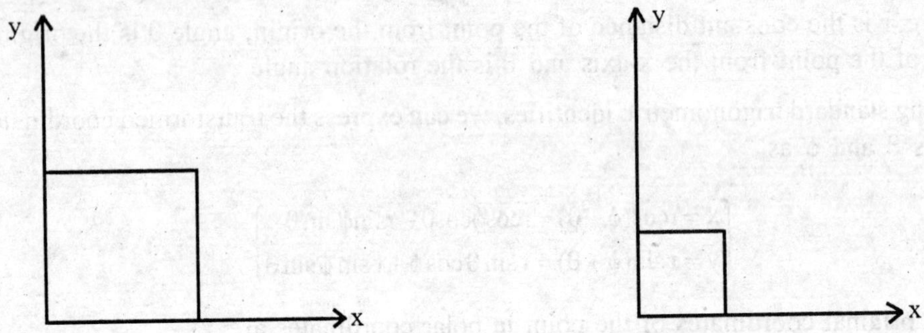

(a) Object before Scaling *(b) Object after Scaling*

Fig. 3.4

In matrix form

$$\begin{bmatrix} x' \\ y' \end{bmatrix} = \begin{pmatrix} S_x & 0 \\ 0 & S_Y \end{pmatrix} \cdot \begin{bmatrix} x \\ y \end{bmatrix}$$

$P' = S \, . \, P$ ...(3.10)

$x' = S_x * x$ ...(3.11)

$y' = S_y * y$ ...(3.12)

Scaling factors with value less than one move objects closer to the coordinate origin and reduces size of object, while scaling factors with value greater than one, move objects farther to the origin and produces an enlargement. The relative object proportions are maintained, when $S_x = S_y$, also known as *Uniform Scaling*. The relative object proportions are changed when $S_x \neq S_y$, results in *Differential Scaling*. It does not preserve lengths, even does not preserve angle (except when scaling is uniform).

3.3.5 C Program

```
/*PROGRAM TO TRANSLATE, ROTATE AND SCALE IN 2-D*/
#include <stdio.h>
#include <conio.h>
#include <graphics.h>
#include <math.h>
void translate();
void scale();
void rotate();
void main()
{
int ch;
int gd=DETECT,gm;
init graph(&gd,&gm,"d:\\tc\\");
setcolor(6);
outtextxy(100,88, "Object.");
rectangle(100,150,150,100);
printf("MENU");
printf("\n 1)Translate\n 2)Scale\n 3)Rotate");
printf("\nEnter your choice:");
scanf("%d",&ch);
cleardevice();
switch(ch)
{
case 1: translate();
break;
case 2: scale();
```

```
break;
case 3: rotate();
break;
default: printf("You have entered wrong choice");
break;
}
getch();
closegraph();
}
void translate()
{
int tx,ty;
setcolor(2);
outtextxy(240,10,"TRANSLATION");
outtextxy(238,20,"------");
printf("\n Enter tx: ");
scanf("%d",&tx);
printf("\n Enter ty: ");
scanf("%d",&ty);
cleardevice();
rectangle(100,150,150,100);
printf("\n After Translation");
rectangle(100+tx,150+ty,150+tx,100+ty);
}
void scale()
{
int sx,sy;
setcolor(2);
outtextxy(240,10,"SCALING");
outtextxy(238,20,"-------");
printf("\n Enter sx: ");
scanf("%d",&sx);
```

```
printf("\n Enter sy: ");
scanf("%d",&sy);
cleardevice();
rectangle(100,150,150,100);
printf("\n After Scaling");
rectangle(100*sx,150*sy,150*sx,100*sy);
}
void rotate()
{
float theta;
int x1,x2,x3,x4;
int y1,y2,y3,y4;
int ax1,ax2,ax3,ax4,ay1,ay2,ay3,ay4;
int refx,refy;
printf("\n Enter the angle for rotation:");
scanf("%f",&theta);
theta=theta*(3.14/180);
cleardevice();
setcolor(2);
outtextxy(240,10, "ROTATE");
outtextxy(238,20,"--------");
refx=100;
refy=100;
x1=100;
y1=100;
x2=150;
y2=100;
x3=150;
y3=150;
x4=100;
y4=150;
```

```
ax1=refy+(x1-refx)*cos(theta)-(y1-refy)*sin(theta);
ay1=refy+(x1-refx)*sin(theta)+(y1-refy)*cos(theta);
ax2=refy+(x2-refx)*cos(theta)-(y2-refy)*sin(theta);
ay2=refy+(x2-refx)*sin(theta)+(y2-refy)*cos(theta);
ax3=refy+(x3-refx)*cos(theta)-(y3-refy)*sin(theta);
ay3=refy+(x3-refx)*sin(theta)+(y3-refy)*cos(theta);
ax4=refy+(x4-refx)*cos(theta)-(y4-refy)*sin(theta);
ay4=refy+(x4-refx)*sin(theta)+(y4-refy)*cos(theta);
rectangle(100,150,150,100);
line(ax1,ay1,ax2,ay2);
line(ax2,ay2,ax3,ay3);
line(ax3,ay3,ax4,ay4);
line(ax4,ay4,ax1,ay1);
}
```

3.4 HOMOGENEOUS COORDINATES AND MATRIX REPRESENTATION OF 2-D TRANSFORMATIONS

The matrix representations of all basic transformations (translation, scaling and rotation) are:

$$P' = T + P$$

$$P' = S.P$$

$$P' = R.P \qquad ...(3.13)$$

As we see, translation is treated differently (as an addition) from scaling and rotation (as multiplications). We would like to treat all three transformations in a consistent way, so that they can be combined easily to eliminate the calculation of intermediate coordinate's value.

If points are expressed in homogeneous coordinates, all three transformations can be treated as multiplications, i.e., we devise a representation in which translation can be implemented by matrix multiplication.

- In homogeneous coordinates, we add a third coordinate to a point. Instead of being represented by a pair of numbers (x, y), each point is represented by a triple (x, y, h).
- Provides with a symmetric and aligned matrix.
- It is useful for describing and manipulating graphical objects.
- We can represent finite and infinite coordinates.
- At the same time, we can say that two sets of homogeneous coordinates (x, y, h) and (x′, y′, h′) represent the same point if and only if one is a multiple of the other. Thus,

(2, 4, 5) and (4, 8, 10) are the same points representation by different coordinate triples. At least one among all the homogeneous coordinates must be non zero: (0, 0, 0) is not allowed. If 'h' coordinate is non zero, we can divide through by it: (x, y, h) represents the same point as (x/h, y/h, 1). When $h \neq 0$, we normally do this division, and the numbers x/h and y/h are called the Cartesian coordinates of the homogeneous point. The points with h = 0 are called points of infinity.

All three transformations when treated as multiplications, increases the efficiency and performance of the system.

Triples of coordinates typically represent points in 3-space, but here we are using them to represent points in 2-space. Thus, now we represent the translation equations in the form of a 3 × 3 matrix as:

$$\begin{bmatrix} x' \\ y' \\ 1 \end{bmatrix} = \begin{bmatrix} 1 & 0 & t_x \\ 0 & 1 & t_y \\ 0 & 0 & 1 \end{bmatrix} . \begin{bmatrix} x \\ y \\ 1 \end{bmatrix} \quad \text{...(3.14)}$$

Similarly, the scaling equations are represented in matrix form as:

$$\begin{bmatrix} x' \\ y' \\ 1 \end{bmatrix} = \begin{bmatrix} S_x & 0 & 0 \\ 0 & S_y & 0 \\ 0 & 0 & 1 \end{bmatrix} . \begin{bmatrix} x \\ y \\ 1 \end{bmatrix}$$

$$P' = S \cdot P \quad \text{...(3.15)}$$

Finally, the rotation equations can be represented as:

$$\begin{bmatrix} x' \\ y' \\ 1 \end{bmatrix} = \begin{bmatrix} \cos\theta & -\sin\theta & 0 \\ \sin\theta & \cos\theta & 0 \\ 0 & 0 & 1 \end{bmatrix} . \begin{bmatrix} x \\ y \\ 1 \end{bmatrix}$$

$$P' = R(\theta) \cdot P \quad \text{...(3.16)}$$

Thus, to express any two-dimensional transformation as a matrix multiplication, we represent each Cartesian coordinate position (x, y) with the homogeneous coordinate triple (x_h, y_h, h)

Where,

$$x = \frac{x_h}{h} \text{ and } y = \frac{y_h}{h} \quad \text{...(3.17)}$$

Thus, a general homogeneous coordinate representation can be written as (x/h, y/h, 1). This is an efficient formulation, since it allows us to reduce computations by applying the composite matrix.

3.5 CONCATENATED TRANSFORMATIONS

It is the sequence of transformations into one transformation by the concatenation process.

Example 3.1: Prove that Successive Translations are additive.

$$\begin{bmatrix} x' \\ y' \\ 1 \end{bmatrix} = \begin{bmatrix} 1 & 0 & t_x \\ 0 & 1 & t_y \\ 0 & 0 & 1 \end{bmatrix} \begin{bmatrix} x \\ y \\ 1 \end{bmatrix}$$

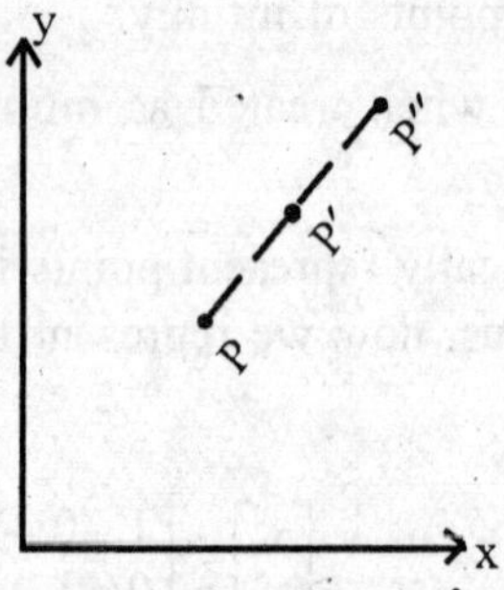

Fig. 3.5 Successive Translation from P to P′ and P′ to P″

$P' = T(t_x, t_y).P$

If a point P is translated by $T(t_{x_1}, t_{y_1})$ to P′ and then translated by $T(t_{x2}, t_{y2})$ to P″, then

$$P' = T(t_{x_1}, t_{y_1}) P \quad ...(3.18)$$

$$P'' = T(t_{x_2}, t_{y_2}) .P' \quad ...(3.19)$$

Substituting (3.18) in (3.19), we get

$$P''=T(t_{x_2}, t_{y_2}) \cdot T(t_{x_1}, t_{y_1}).P \quad ...(3.20)$$

The matrix product $T(t_{x_2}, t_{y_2}) \cdot T(t_{x_1}, t_{y_1})$ is

$$= \begin{bmatrix} 1 & 0 & t_{x_1} \\ 0 & 1 & t_{y_1} \\ 0 & 0 & 1 \end{bmatrix} \begin{bmatrix} 1 & 0 & t_{x_2} \\ 0 & 1 & t_{y_2} \\ 0 & 0 & 1 \end{bmatrix} \cdot \begin{bmatrix} x \\ y \\ 1 \end{bmatrix}$$

$$= \begin{bmatrix} 1+0+0 & 0+0+0 & t_{x_1} + 0 + t_{x_2} \\ 0+0+0 & 0+1+0 & 0 + t_{y_1} + t_{y_2} \\ 0+0+0 & 0+0+0 & 0+0+1 \end{bmatrix}$$

Thus, the net translation is $T(t_{x_1} + t_{x_2}, t_{y_1} + t_{y_2})$ (3.21)

Example 3.2: Prove that Successive Scalings are multiplicative.

$$\begin{bmatrix} x' \\ y' \\ 1 \end{bmatrix} = \begin{bmatrix} S_x & 0 & 0 \\ 0 & S_y & 0 \\ 0 & 0 & 1 \end{bmatrix} \begin{bmatrix} x \\ y \\ 1 \end{bmatrix}$$

$P' = S(S_x, S_y).P$

It a point P is scaled by $S(S_{x1}, S_{y1})$ to P′ and then scaled by (S_{x2}, S_{y2}) to P″, then
$P' = S(S_{x1}, S_{y1}).P$ ...(3.22)

$P'' = S(S_{x_2}, S_{y_2}).P$ ...(3.23)

Substituting (3.16) in (3.17) we get;

$P'' = S(S_{x_2}, S_{y_2}).\ S(S_{x_1}, S_{y_1}).P$ ...(3.24)

The matrix product of $S(S_{x_2}, S_{y_2}).S(S_{x_1}, S_{y_1})$ is:

$$= \begin{bmatrix} S_{x_2} & 0 & 0 \\ 0 & S_{y_2} & 0 \\ 0 & 0 & 1 \end{bmatrix} \begin{bmatrix} S_{x_1} & 0 & 0 \\ 0 & S_{y_1} & 0 \\ 0 & 0 & 1 \end{bmatrix}$$

$$= \begin{bmatrix} S_{x_2}.S_{x_1} + 0 + 0 & 0 + 0 + 0 & 0 + 0 + 0 \\ 0 + 0 + 0 & 0 + S_{y_2}.S_{y_1} + 0 & 0 + 0 + 0 \\ 0 + 0 + 0 & 0 + 0 + 0 & 0 + 0 + 1 \end{bmatrix} \quad ...(3.25)$$

$$= \begin{bmatrix} S_{x_2}.S_{x_1} & 0 & 0 \\ 0 & S_{y_2}.S_{y_1} & 0 \\ 0 & 0 & 1 \end{bmatrix}$$

Thus, the net scaling is $S(S_{x_1}.S_{x_2}, S_{y_1}.S_{y_2})$ ...(3.26)

Hence, Successive Scalings are multiplicative.

Example 3.3: Prove that Successive Rotation's are additive:

$$\begin{bmatrix} x' \\ y' \\ 1 \end{bmatrix} = \begin{bmatrix} \cos\theta & -\sin\theta & 0 \\ \sin\theta & \cos\theta & 0 \\ 0 & 0 & 1 \end{bmatrix} = \begin{bmatrix} x' \\ y' \\ 1 \end{bmatrix}$$

$$P' = R(\theta).P$$

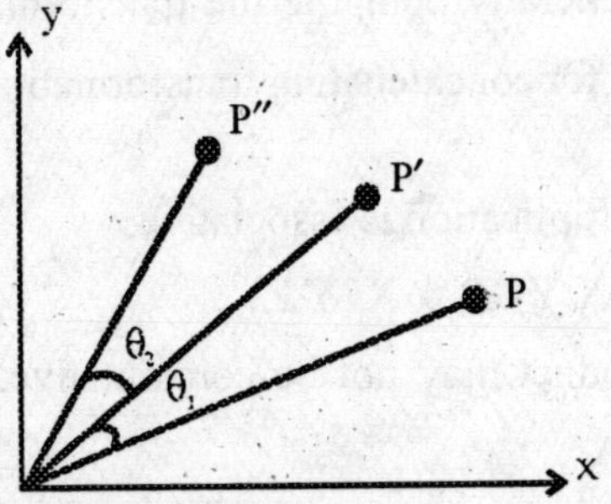

Fig. 3.6 Successive rotation by θ_1 and θ_2

If a point P is rotated by $R(\theta_1)$ to P′ and then rotated by $R(\theta_2)$ to P″, then

$P'=R(\theta_1).P$ ...(3.27)

$P''=R(\theta_2).P'$ ...(3.28)

Substituting (3.27) in (3.28) we get;

$P''=R(\theta_2).R(\theta_1).P$ ...(3.29)

The matrix product of $R(\theta_2).R(\theta_1)$ is

$$= \begin{bmatrix} \cos\theta_1 & -\sin\theta_1 & 0 \\ \sin\theta_1 & \cos\theta_1 & 0 \\ 0 & 0 & 1 \end{bmatrix} . \begin{bmatrix} \cos\theta_2 & -\sin\theta_2 & 0 \\ \sin\theta_2 & \cos\theta_2 & 0 \\ 0 & 0 & 1 \end{bmatrix}$$

$$= \begin{bmatrix} \cos\theta_1 \cos\theta_2 - \sin\theta_1 \sin\theta_2 + 0 & -\cos\theta_1 \sin\theta_2 - \sin\theta_1 \cos n\theta_2 + 0 & 0+0+0 \\ \sin\theta_1 \cos\theta_2 + \cos\theta_1 \sin\theta_2 + 0 & -\sin\theta_1 \sin\theta_2 + \cos\theta_1 \cos\theta_2 + 0 & 0+0+0 \\ 0+0+0 & 0+0+0 & 0+0+1 \end{bmatrix}$$

$$= \begin{bmatrix} \cos\theta_1 \cos\theta_2 - \sin\theta_1 \sin\theta_2 & -(\cos\theta_1 \sin\theta_2 + \sin\theta_1 \cos\theta_2) & 0 \\ \sin\theta_1 \cos\theta_2 + \sin\theta_1 \cos\theta_2 & (\cos\theta_1 \cos\theta_2 - \sin\theta_1 \sin\theta_2) & 0 \\ 0 & 0 & 1 \end{bmatrix}$$

$$= \begin{bmatrix} \cos(\theta_1+\theta_2) & -\sin(\theta_1+\theta_2) & 0 \\ \sin(\theta_1+\theta_2) & \cos(\theta_1+\theta_2) & 0 \\ 0 & 0 & 1 \end{bmatrix} \quad (3.30)$$

Thus, the net rotation is $R(\theta_1 + \theta_2) = R(\theta_1) + R(\theta_2)$ (3.31)

⇒ Hence, Successive rotations are additive

⇒ $P' = R(\theta_1 + \theta_2).P$

3.5.1 Advantages of Concatenated Transformations

Use of concatenated transformations has several advantages:

- We can represent it more compactly than a sequence.
- We can generally compute the transformation with fewer arithmetic operations.

However, rules for concatenating transformation equations are quite complex. Concatenation properties:-

- Matrix multiplication is associative.

  $X.Y.Z = (X.Y).Z = X.(Y.Z)$ ...(3.32)

- Matrix Product may not be commutative.

  $A.B = B.A$ ...(3.33)

It means if we have to translate and scale an object, we must be careful about the order in which the composite matrix is evaluated. In some cases, we have transformations all of same type, then the order in which matrix is evaluated doesn't matter for, e.g., the multiplication of transformation matrices is commutative.

The general, 2-D transformation matrix, representing a combination all basic transformations are expressed as

$$\begin{bmatrix} x' \\ y' \\ 1 \end{bmatrix} = \begin{bmatrix} rs_{xx} & rs_{xy} & trs_x \\ re_{yx} & rs_{yy} & trs_y \\ 0 & 0 & 1 \end{bmatrix} = \begin{bmatrix} x \\ y \\ 1 \end{bmatrix} \quad ...(3.34)$$

Where the element rs_{xy} are the multiplicative rotation-scaling terms in the transformation that contains rotation angles and scaling factors only, whereas, trs_x contains translation distances, rotational angles and scaling factors.

3.6 OTHER TRANSFORMATIONS

3.6.1 Reflection

A reflection is a transformation that produces a mirror image of an object. In 2-D, the reflection is also described as the rotation transformation by $\theta = 180^0$.

➲ **Reflection about the line y = 0, the x-axis,** is accomplished with the transformation matrix

$$\begin{bmatrix} 1 & 0 & 0 \\ 0 & -1 & 0 \\ 0 & 0 & 1 \end{bmatrix}$$

In this transformation, x values remains the same, but "flips" the y values of object coordinate.

$$x' = x$$

$$y' = -y \quad ...(3.35)$$

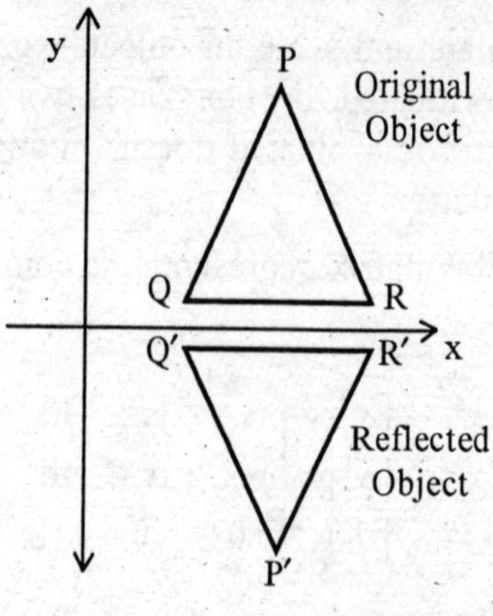

Fig. 3.7 Reflection of an Object about the x-axis

Reflection about x-axis (i.e., y = 0) is represented in matrix form as:

$$\begin{bmatrix} x' \\ y' \\ 1 \end{bmatrix} = \begin{bmatrix} 1 & 0 & 0 \\ 0 & -1 & 0 \\ 0 & 0 & 1 \end{bmatrix} * \begin{bmatrix} x \\ y \\ 1 \end{bmatrix}$$

$$P' = R_{ref(x)} * P \qquad ...(3.36)$$

➲ **The reflection about the x = 0 (y axis)** change x coordinates while keeping y coordinates remains the same. The matrix for this transformation is:

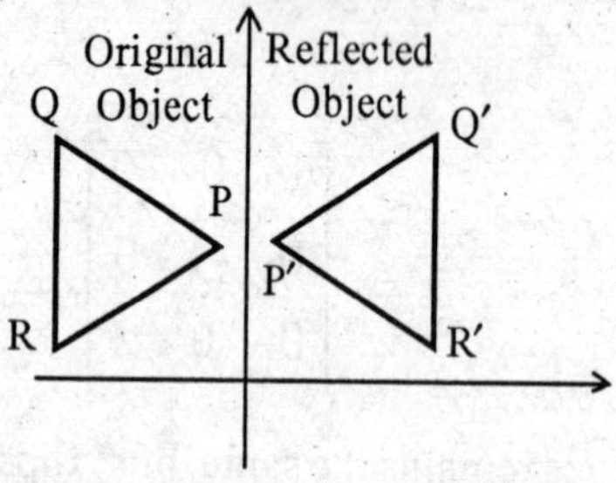

Fig. 3.8 Reflection of an Object about the y–axis

In this transformation y values remain the same, but flips the x values of object coordinate.

$x' = -x$

$y' = y \qquad ...(3.37)$

Reflection about y-axis (i.e., x = 0) is represented in matrix form as:

$$\begin{bmatrix} x' \\ y' \\ 1 \end{bmatrix} = \begin{bmatrix} -1 & 0 & 0 \\ 0 & 1 & 0 \\ 0 & 0 & 1 \end{bmatrix} * \begin{bmatrix} x \\ y \\ 1 \end{bmatrix}$$

$$P' = R_{ref(y)} * P \qquad ...(3.38)$$

- **Reflection about the origin (x = 0, y = 0)** :In this reflection, we actually assuming the object is first quadrant and choose the mirror line as axis perpendicular to the xy plane and crossing through the origin as in fig. 3.9. In this case, after reflection both x and y coordinate of the object are flipped.

$x' = -x$

$y' = -y$ ...(3.39)

The matrix for this transformation

$$\begin{bmatrix} -1 & 0 & 0 \\ 0 & -1 & 0 \\ 0 & 0 & 1 \end{bmatrix}$$

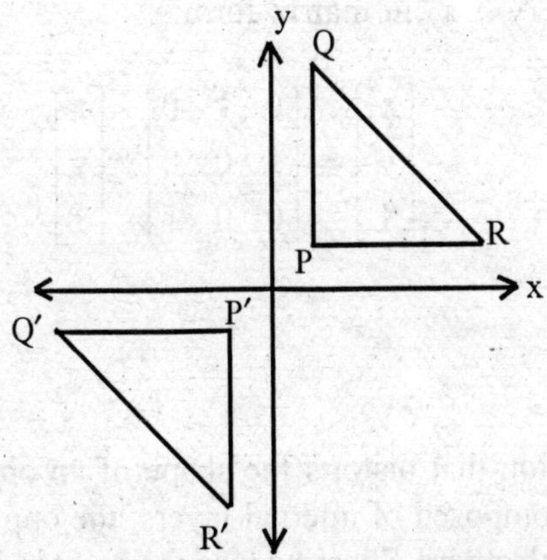

Fig. 3.9 Reflection about the Origin

Reflection about the origin (x = 0, y = 0), in matrix form,

$$\begin{bmatrix} x' \\ y' \\ 1 \end{bmatrix} = \begin{bmatrix} -1 & 0 & 0 \\ 0 & -1 & 0 \\ 0 & 0 & 1 \end{bmatrix} * \begin{bmatrix} x \\ y \\ 1 \end{bmatrix}$$

$$P' = R_{ref(x\,=\,0,\;y\,=\,0)} . P \qquad ...(3.40)$$

- **Reflection about the line y = x:** In this case, both the coordinates of an object x, y exchanges themselves, i.e., point (x,y) when reflected about the line y = x, becomes (y,x)

$x' = y$

$y' = x$ ...(3.41)

The matrix for this transformation is:

$$\begin{bmatrix} 0 & 1 & 0 \\ 1 & 0 & 0 \\ 0 & 0 & 1 \end{bmatrix}$$

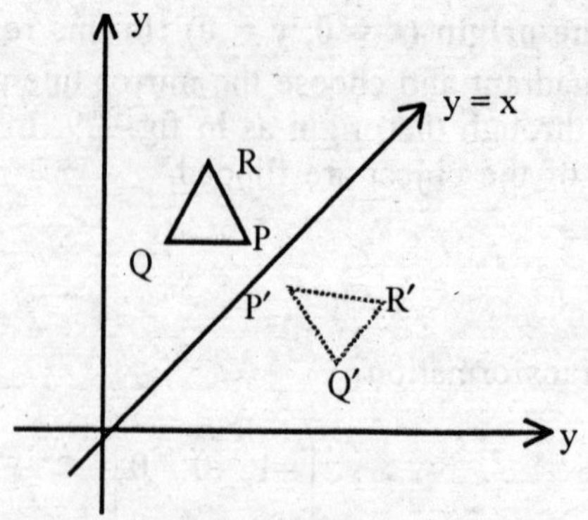

Fig. 3.10 Reflection about the Line y = x

Reflection about the line (y = x) in matrix form:

$$\begin{bmatrix} x' \\ y' \\ 1 \end{bmatrix} = \begin{bmatrix} 0 & 1 & 0 \\ 1 & 0 & 0 \\ 0 & 0 & 1 \end{bmatrix} * \begin{bmatrix} x \\ y \\ 1 \end{bmatrix}$$

$$P' = R_{refl(y=x)}\ P \qquad \text{...(3.42)}$$

3.6.2 Shear

Shearing is a transformation that distorts the shape of an object, such that in output shape appears as if the object were composed of internal layers; the opposite and parallel layers of any object are simply slides over each otherd. Shearing means a point is dragged in a particular direction. This means some coordinate will be affected while other are not. Shearing occurs along a line.

Shearing is of two kinds:

- A shear along x-axis. (X-Shear)
- A shear along y-axis. (Y-Shear)

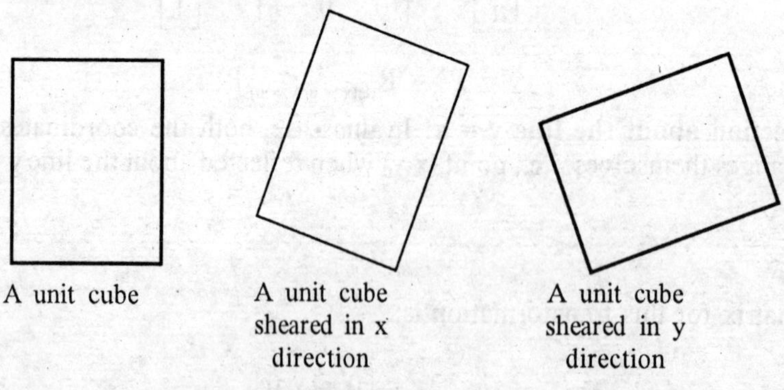

Fig. 3.11 Shearing

$$SH_x = \begin{bmatrix} 1 & a & 0 \\ 0 & 1 & 0 \\ 0 & 0 & 1 \end{bmatrix} \text{ SHEARS ALONG THE X-AXIS}$$

which transforms coordinate x and y as:

$$x' = x + a.y,\ y' = y \qquad \text{...(3.43)}$$

$$SH_y = \begin{bmatrix} 1 & 0 & 0 \\ b & 1 & 0 \\ 0 & 0 & 1 \end{bmatrix} \text{ SHEARS ALONG THE Y-AXIS}$$

which transforms coordinate x and y as:

$$x' = x,\ y' = b.x + y \qquad \text{...(3.44)}$$

3.6.3 C Program

```
/*PROGRAM TO PERFORM 2-D REFLECTION AND SHEARING*/
#include <stdio.h>
#include <process.h>
#include <conio.h>
#include <graphics.h>
#include <math.h>
void disp(int n,float c[][3])
{
float maxx,maxy;
int i;
maxx=getmaxx();
maxy=getmaxy();
maxx=maxx/2;
maxy=maxy/2;
i=0;
while(i<n-1)
{
line(maxx+c[i][0],maxy-c[i][1],maxx+c[i+1][0],maxy-c[i+1][1]);
i++;
```

```
}
i=n-1;
line(maxx+c[i][0],maxy-c[i][1],maxx+c[0][0],maxy-c[0][1]);
setcolor(GREEN);
line(0,maxy,maxx*2,maxy);
line(maxx,0,maxx,maxy*2);
setcolor(WHITE);
}
void mul(int n,float b[][3],float c[][3],float a[][3])
{
int i,j,k;
for(i=0;i<n;i++)
for(j=0;j<3;j++)
a[i][j]=0;
for(i=0;i<n;i++)
for(j=0;j<3;j++)
for(k=0;k<3;k++)
{
a[i][j] = a[i][j] + (c[i][k] * b[k][j]);
}
}
void reflection(int n,float c[][3])
{
float b[10][3],a[10][3];
int i=0,ch,j;
cleardevice();
printf("\n\t* * MENU * *");
printf("\n\t 1) ABOUT X-AXIS");
printf("\n\t 2) ABOUT Y-AXIS");
printf("\n\t 3) ABOUT ORIGIN");
printf("\n\t 4) ABOUT X=Y");
printf("\n\t 5) ABOUT -X=Y");
```

```
printf("\n\t 6) EXIT");
printf("\n\t ENTER YOUR CHOICE:");
scanf("%d",&ch);
clrscr();
cleardevice();
disp(n,c);
for(i=0;i<3;i++)
for(j=0;j<3;j++)
{
b[i][j]=0;
if(i==j)
b[i][j]=1;
}
switch(ch)
{
case 1:
b[1][1]=-1;
break;
case 2:
b[0][0]=-1;
break;
case 3:
b[0][0]=-1;
b[1][1]=-1;
break;
case 4:
b[0][0]=0;
b[1][1]=0;
b[0][1]=1;
b[1][0]=1;
break;
case 5:
```

```
b[0][0]=0;
b[1][1]=0;
b[0][1]=-1;
b[1][0]=-1;
break;
case 6:
break;
default:
printf("\n\tINVALID CHOICE !");
break;
}
mul(n,b,c,a);
setcolor(RED);
disp(n,a);
}
void shearing(int n,float c[][3])
{
float b[10][3],sh,a[10][3];
int i=0,ch,j;
cleardevice();
printf("\n\t* * * MENU * * *");
printf("\n\t1) X SHEARING");
printf("\n\t2) Y SHEARING");
printf("\n\t3) EXIT ");
printf("\n\tENTER YOUR CHOICE :" );
scanf("%d",&ch);
if(ch==3)
return;
printf("\n\tENTER THE VALUE for SHEARING:" );
scanf("%f",&sh);
clrscr();
cleardevice();
```

```
for(i=0;i<3;i++)
for(j=0;j<3;j++)
b[i][j]=0;
for(i=0;i<3;i++)
b[i][i]=1;
switch(ch)
{
case 1:
b[1][0]=sh;
break;
case 2:
b[0][1]=sh;
break;
case 3:
break;
default:
printf("\n\tINVALID CHOICE !" );
break;
}
mul(n,b,c,a);
setcolor(RED);
disp(n,a);
}
void main()
{
int i,j,k,cho,n,gd=DETECT,gm;
float c[10][3],tx,ty,sx,sy,ra;
initgraph(&gd,&gm,"d:\\tc\\");
printf("\n Enter the number of vertices :" );
scanf("%d",&n);
for(i=0;i<n;i++)
{
```

```
printf("\nEnter the co-ordinates of the %d vertex :",i+1);
scanf("%f %f",&c[i][0],&c[i][1]);
c[i][2]=1;
}
do
{
clrscr();
cleardevice();
printf("\n\t\t\t * * * MENU * * *");
printf("\n\t 1) REFLECTION" );
printf("\n\t 2) SHEARING");
printf("\n\t 3) EXIT");
printf("\n\t ENTER YOUR CHOICE:" );
scanf("%d",&cho);
switch(cho)
{
case 1:
clrscr();
cleardevice();
setcolor(BLUE);
disp(n,c);
reflection(n,c);
getch();
break;
case 2:
clrscr();
cleardevice();
setcolor(BLUE);
disp(n,c);
shearing(n,c);
getch();
break;
```

```
case 3 :
exit(0);
break;
default:
printf("\n\tInvalid choice !!");
break;
}
}while(cho!=3)
getch();
closegraph();
}
```

3.7 COMPOSITE TRANSFORMATIONS

3.7.1 Reflection with Respect to an Arbitrary Line

Consider the reflection of an object PQRS with respect to an arbitrary line y = mx + b as shown in fig. 3.12.

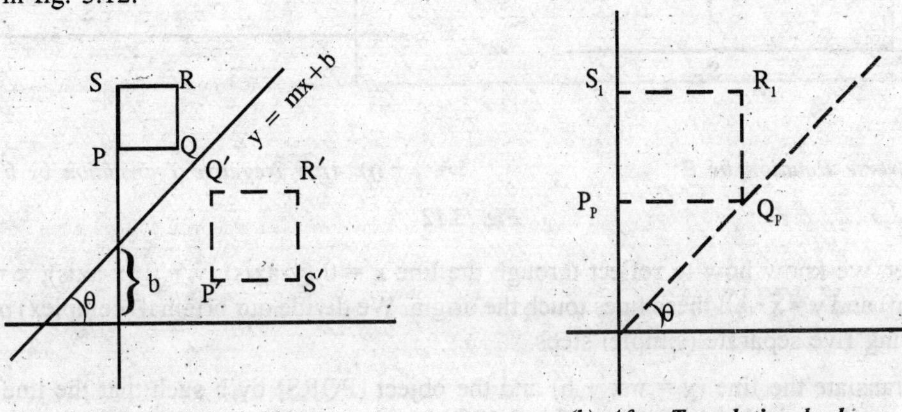

(a) PQRS – Original Object
P′Q′R′S′ – reflected object w.r.t. y = mx + b

(b) After Translation by b

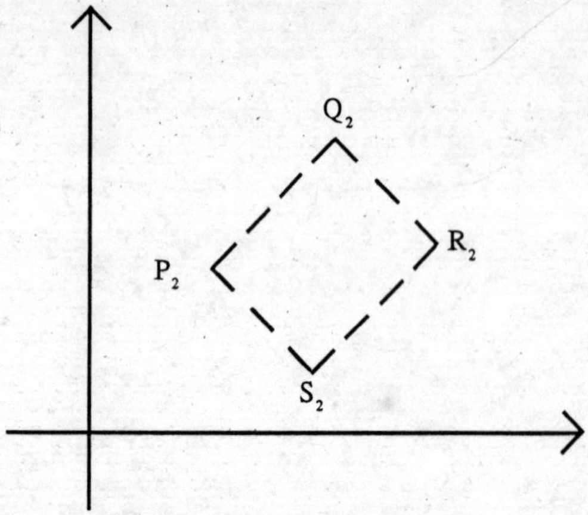

(c) After Rotation by an Angle $-\theta$

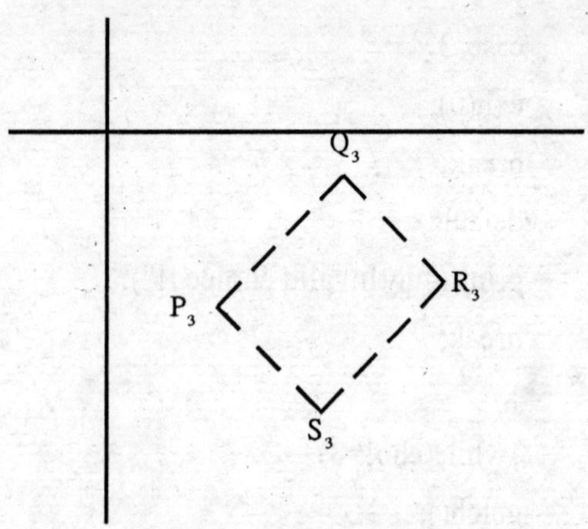

(d) After Reflection about y-axis

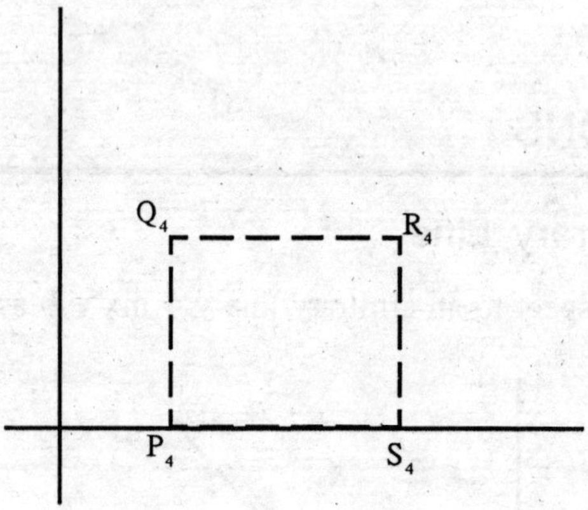

(e) After Reverse Rotation by θ

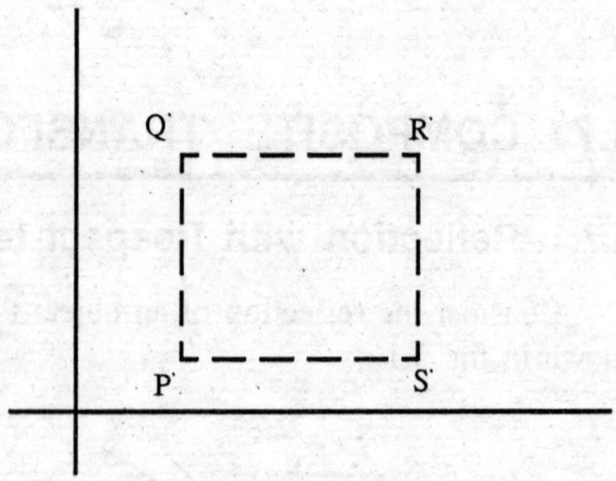

(f) After Negative Translation by b

Fig. 3.12

Till yet, we know how to reflect through the line x = 0 (y-axis), y = 0 (x-axis), x = 0 and y = 0 (origin) and y = x. All these lines touch the origin. We divide our original (complex) problem into following five separate (simple) steps.

Step 1: Translate the line (y = mx + b) and the object (PQRS) by b such that the line should pass through the origin as in fig. 3.12(b).

Step 2: Rotate the line and the object with respect to the origin by an angle such that the line coincides with one of the coordinate axis i.e. either x-axis or y-axis. as in fig.3. 12(c).

Step 3: Reflect the object with respect to the coincided axis. as in fig. 3.12(d).

Step 4: Rotate the line and object w.r.t. the origin by an angle -θ such that the line and object will get shifted to translate position.

Step 5: Translate inverse by 'b' to shift the object and the line back to its original position.

The net Transformation matrix is:

$$[M_{ref}] = [T]\ [R(\theta)]\ [R_{ref}]\ [R\ (\theta)]^{-1}\ [T]^{-1} \qquad ...(3.45)$$

where:

T – Translation matrix

$R(\theta)$ – Rotation matrix by angle θ

R_{ref} – Reflection about an axis

$[R(\theta)]^{-1}$ – Inverse rotation matrix

$[T]^{-1}$ – Inverse translation by b

A similar approach is used to shear an object about an arbitrary point or reference lines.

3.7.2 2-D Rotation of an Object by an Angle θ with Respect to an Arbitrary Point

Consider the rotation of an object with respect to an arbitrary point A_1 as shown in fig. 3.13(a). Till yet, we only know to rotate with respect to origin. We divide our actual (complex) problem into following three separate (simple) problems:

1. Translate the object such that A_1 is at the origin, as in fig. 3.13(b).
2. Rotate the object w.r.t origin by angle θ as in fig. 1.13(c).
3. Translate the object such that the point at the origin returns back to the original position of A_1.

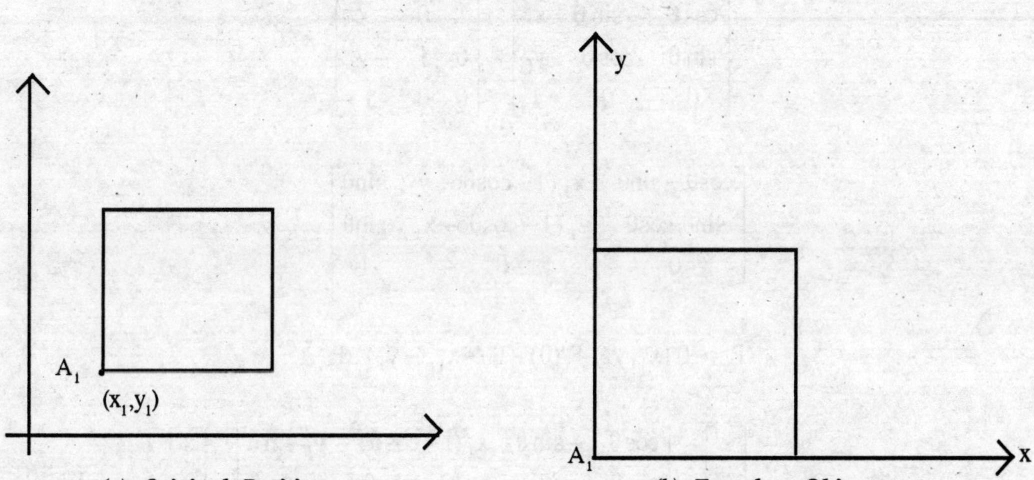

(a) Original Position *(b) Translate Object*

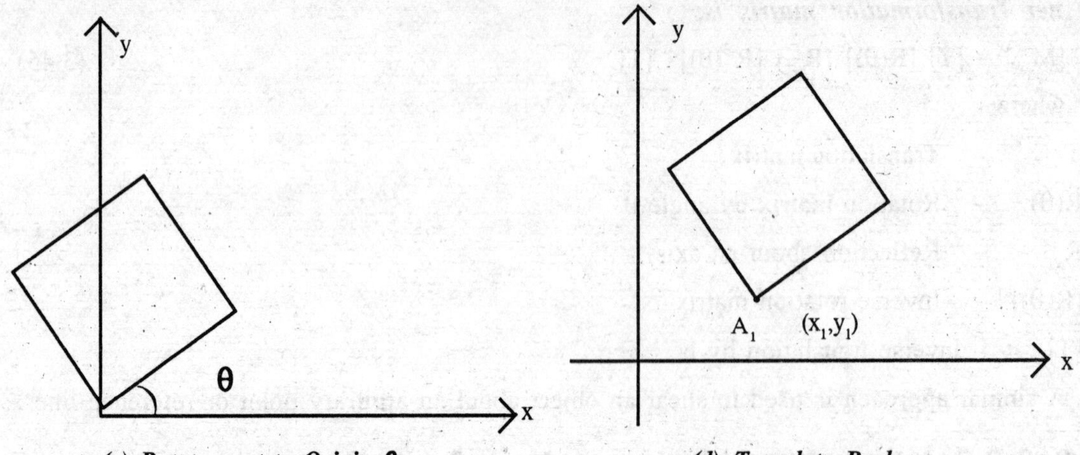

(c) Rotate w.r.t to Origin θ *(d) Translate Back*

Fig. 3.13

Three steps representation in matrix form:

$$T\,(x_1,\ y_1)\ .\ R(\theta)\ .\ T(-x_1,\ -y_1)$$

$$= \begin{bmatrix} 1 & 0 & x_1 \\ 0 & 1 & y_1 \\ 0 & 0 & 1 \end{bmatrix} * \begin{bmatrix} \cos\theta & -\sin\theta & 0 \\ \sin\theta & \cos\theta & 0 \\ 1 & 1 & 1 \end{bmatrix} * \begin{bmatrix} 1 & 0 & -x_1 \\ 0 & 1 & -y_1 \\ 0 & 0 & 1 \end{bmatrix}$$

$$= \begin{bmatrix} \cos\theta & -\sin\theta & x_1 \\ \sin\theta & \cos\theta & y_1 \\ 0 & 0 & 1 \end{bmatrix} * \begin{bmatrix} 1 & 0 & -x_1 \\ 0 & 1 & -y_1 \\ 0 & 0 & 1 \end{bmatrix}$$

$$\begin{bmatrix} \cos\theta - \sin\theta & x_1\,(1-\cos\theta o + y \quad \sin\theta \\ \sin\theta\ \cos\theta & y_1\,(1-\cos\theta o - x_1 \quad \sin\theta \\ 0 & 0 \quad\quad 1 \end{bmatrix}$$

$$P' = T\,(x_1, y_1).R\,(\theta)\,.\,T\,(-x_1, -y_1)\,.\,P$$

$$\begin{bmatrix} x' \\ y' \\ 1 \end{bmatrix} = \begin{bmatrix} \cos\theta & -\sin\theta & x_1\,(1-\cos\theta) + y_1\,\sin\theta \\ \sin\theta & \cos\theta & y_1\,(1-\cos\theta) - x_1\,\sin\theta \\ 0 & 0 & 1 \end{bmatrix} . \begin{bmatrix} x \\ y \\ 1 \end{bmatrix} \qquad ...(3.46)$$

3.7.3 Scale an Object with Respect to an Arbitrary Point

This method or technique is also known as composition of 2-D transformations. Similarly, we can scale an object with respect to an arbitrary point A_1 (x_1, y_1). Firstly, translate the object such that A_1 is at origin, then scale the object and then translate the object such that the point at the origin returns back to the original position of A_1. Matrix representation of the next transformation is:

$$M_s = T(x_1, y_1) \cdot S(S_x, S_y) \cdot T(-x_1, -y_1) = \quad ...(3.47)$$

$$\begin{bmatrix} 1 & 0 & x_1 \\ 0 & 1 & y_1 \\ 0 & 0 & 1 \end{bmatrix} * \begin{bmatrix} S_x & 0 & 0 \\ 0 & S_y & 0 \\ 0 & 0 & 1 \end{bmatrix} * \begin{bmatrix} 1 & 0 & -x_1 \\ 0 & 1 & -y_1 \\ 0 & 0 & 1 \end{bmatrix}$$

$$\begin{bmatrix} S_x & 0 & x_1(1-S_x) \\ 0 & S_y & y_1(1-S_y) \\ 0 & 0 & 1 \end{bmatrix}$$

$$\Rightarrow P' = M_s \cdot P$$

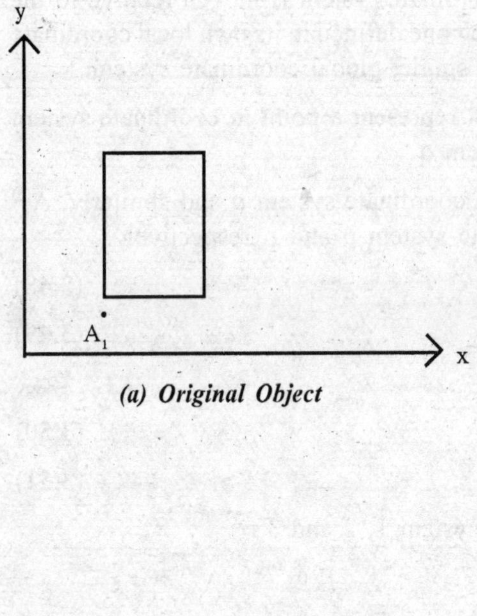

(a) Original Object

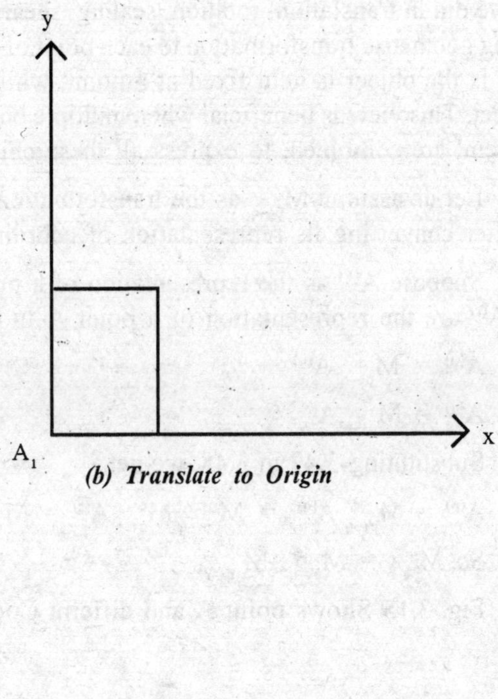

(b) Translate to Origin

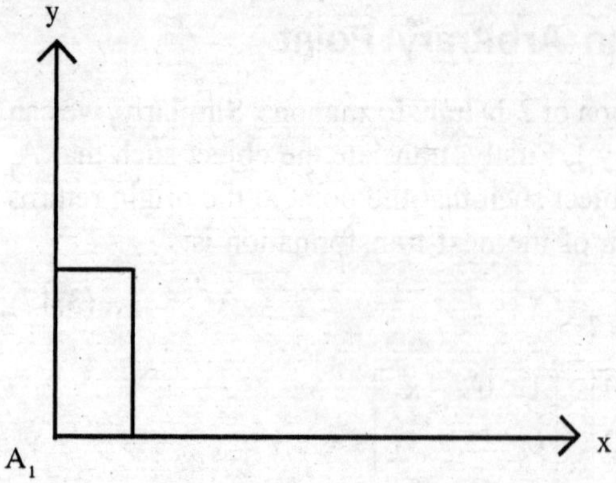

(c) Scaling w.r.t to Origin

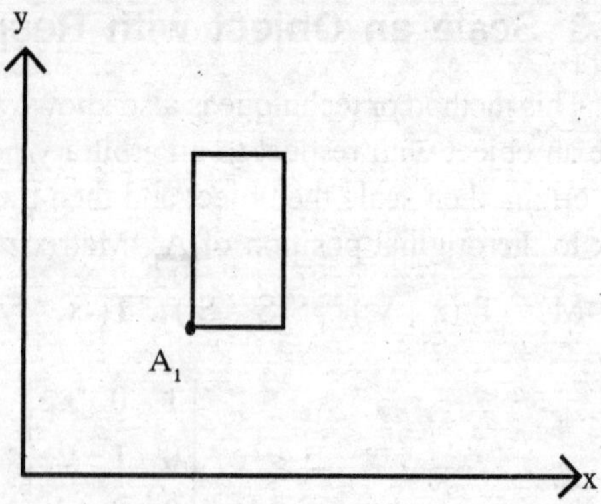

(d) Translate back to Original Postion

Fig. 3.14

3.8 TRANSFORMATION BETWEEN COORDINATE SYSTEMS

Till yet, we have been discussing the first point of view for describing transformation or an object. The first point of view is that the object itself moves relative to a fixed coordinate system as we did in translation, rotation, scaling, shearing and reflection. This viewpoint is described by using geometric transformation to each point of an object. Now, we discuss the second view point, that is the object is held fixed at a point, while the coordinate system is moved relative to the object. This view is beneficial when multiple objects, each one defined in its own local coordinate system, are combined, to express all these objects in a single, global coordinate system.

Let us assume $M_{p\leftarrow q}$ as the transformation that will represent a point in coordinate system p after converting its representation of coordinate system q.

Suppose $A^{(q)}$ as the representation of a point A in coordinate system q and similarly, $A^{(p)}$ as $A^{(r)}$ are the representation of a point A in coordinate system p and r, respectively.

$$A^{(p)} = M_{p\leftarrow q}.A^{(q)} \qquad ...(3.48)$$

$$A^{(q)} = M_{q\leftarrow r}.A^{(r)} \qquad ...(3.49)$$

Substituting 3.49 in 3.48, we get:

$$A^{(p)} = M_{p\leftarrow q}.A^{(q)}. = M_{p\leftarrow q}.M_{q\leftarrow r}.A^{(r)} = M_{p\leftarrow r}.A^{(r)} \qquad ...(3.50)$$

$$\text{So } M_{p\leftarrow r} = M_{p\leftarrow q}.\ M_{q\leftarrow r} \qquad ...(3.51)$$

Fig. 3.15 Shows point A and differnt Coordinate system 1, 2 and 3

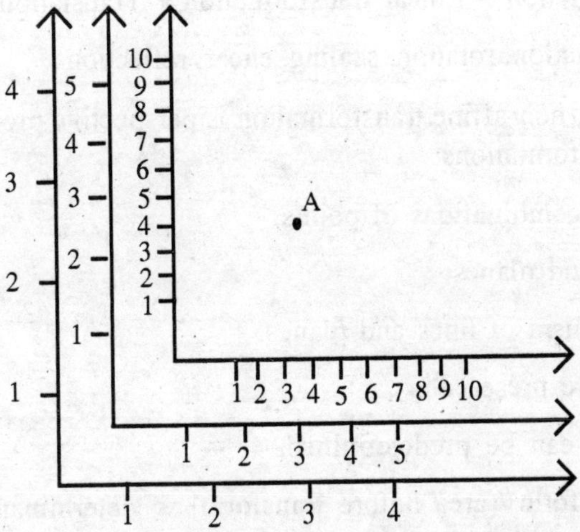

Fig. 3.15 Coordinate System 1, 2 and 3

Using equation 3.51 we can say,

$M_{1\leftarrow 3} = M_{1\leftarrow 2} \cdot M_{2\leftarrow 3}$

And $A^{(p)} = M_{p\leftarrow q} \cdot A^{(q)}$ for $1\leq p,\ q\leq 3$

Let us assume to transform an object shown in fig. 3.15 from coordinate system 1 to coordinate system 2. To map the coordinate system to 2, we have to translate the set of points that define the object 1 in coordinate system 1 by the amount T (x_1, y_1). Assuming (x_1, y_1) is the distance between two coordinate systems.

And each point of an object in coordinate system A_j is translated by T (x_1, y_1) to get mapped with the coordinate system 2.

3.9 AFFINE TRANSFORMATION

They has general properties that parallel lines are transformed into parallel lines and finite points map to finite points, i.e., the parallelism of lines is preserved. Translations, rotation, scaling, reflection and shear are all examples of two-dimensional affine transformations.

Geometric transformations that do not involve scaling or shear also preserve angles and lengths.

3.9.1 Types of Transformation

- Linear Transformation: Takes straight lines to straight lines. Example: Translation, rotation, scaling, shear, reflection.
- AFFINE: It allows us to move objects without deforming them takes parallel lines to parallel lines.

- Affine transformation = Linear transformation + Translation
- Example: Translation, rotation, scaling, shear, reflection

An example of linear non-affine transformation is perspective projection. Following are the properties of Affine transformations:

- Preserve affine combinations of points.
- Preserve lines and planes.
- Preserve parallelism of lines and planes.
- Relative ratio are preserved.
- Effect on areas can be predetermined.

  (area after transform)/(area before transform) = |determinant M|
- ORTHOGONAL: It preserves distances, move all objects as rigid bodies.

3.9.2 How it helps in Computer Graphics?

- An object will not lose its relative slope when transformed together.
- Objects will not lose their relative distances when transformation is done.

3.10 SUMMARY

Transformation means a change in position or shape or size or orientation of an graphics object like line, circle, ellipse, etc. To represent the change on an object, there are two points of view. The first point of view is that the object itself moves relative to a fix coordinate system or background. Mathematically, this viewpoint is described by applying geometric transformation to each point of an object. The second point of view states that the object is held fixed at a point, while the coordinate system is moved relative to the object. This effect is attained through the use of coordinate transformations. We can even represent 2-D coordinates by a triple, i,e., (x, y, h). Representing a (x, y) point with (x, y, h) increases the overall performance of the system by treating translation, rotation and scaling as multiplication. In this chapter, we have discussed different 2-D transformations.

3.11 GLOSSARY

- Uses of transformation:

  MODELING – Position and resize parts of a complex model.

  VIEWING – Define and positions the virtual camera.

  ANIMATION – Define how objects move or change with time.
- DENOTATION – A transformation is a single mathematical entity and as such can be denoted by a single name or symbol.

- CONCATENATION – Two transformations can be combined, or concatenated, to yield a single transformation.
- TRANSLATION - A translation is applied to a point or an object by a distance and direction, from one coordinate location to another.
- Translation is a rigid body transformation that moves objects without deformation, i.e., every point on the object is translated by the same amount.
- ROTATION – A two dimensional rotation is applied to object by repositioning it along a circular path in the xy plane.
- Direction of rotation is anticlockwise if θ positive angle, and are clockwise, i.e., from y-axis towards x-axis if θ negative angle.
- Rotating a point at position (x, y) through an angle θ about the origin:

$$x' = x\cos\theta - y\sin\theta$$
$$y' = x\sin\theta + y\cos\theta$$

- All three transformations when treated as multiplications, increases the efficiency and performance of the system.
- Successive Translations are additive.
- Successive Scalings are multiplicative.
- Successive Rotations are additive.
- Matrix multiplication is associative.

$$X.Y.Z = (X.Y).Z = X.(Y.Z)$$

- Linear Transformation: Takes straight lines to straight lines. Example: Translation, rotation, scaling, shear, reflection.
- AFFINE: It allows us to move objects without deforming them takes parallel lines to parallel lines.
- ORTHOGONAL: It preserves distances, move all objects as rigid bodies.

3.12 EXERCISE

Q1. Find the matrix that represents rotation of an object by 30^0 about the origin.

Q2. Perform a 45^0 rotation of triangle P(0,0), Q(1,1), R(5,2)

(a) about the origin

(b) about P (-1, -1)

Q3. Write the general form of a scaling matrix with respect to a fixed point Q(h, k).

Q4. The reflection along the line $y = x$ is equivalent to the reflection along the x axis followed by counter clockwise rotation by θ degrees. Find the value of θ.

Q5. Show that the 2×2 transformation matrix represents pure rotation.

Q6. How do you perform shear in two dimensions?

Q7. Describe the transformation matrix M which reflects an object about a line L.

Q8. Find the form of the matrix for reflection about a line L with slope m and y intercept (0, b).

E N D

CHAPTER 4 Curves and Surfaces

4.1 INTRODUCTION

Curve may be represented as a collection of points. Although it is an adequate representation, but an analytical representation has several advantages:

- Precision
- Compact storage
- Ease of calculation of intermediate points
- Curve properties such as slope and radius of curvature are easily determined.

Spline curve refers to any composite curve formed with polynomial sections satisfying specified continuity condition at the boundary of the pieces.

We specify a spline curve by giving a set of coordinate positions called *control points,* which indicates the general shape of the curve. We have piecewise parametric polynomial functions of pieces. When polynomial sections are fitted so that the curve passes through each control points, the resulting curve is said to interpolate the set of control points, i.e., a curve that passes through all known data points is said to fit the data.

One of the common technique for curve fitting is piecewise polynomial approximation. This technique requires determining the coefficients of a polynomial of some degree. The actual shape between data points depends on the degree of the polynomial and the imposed boundary conditions.

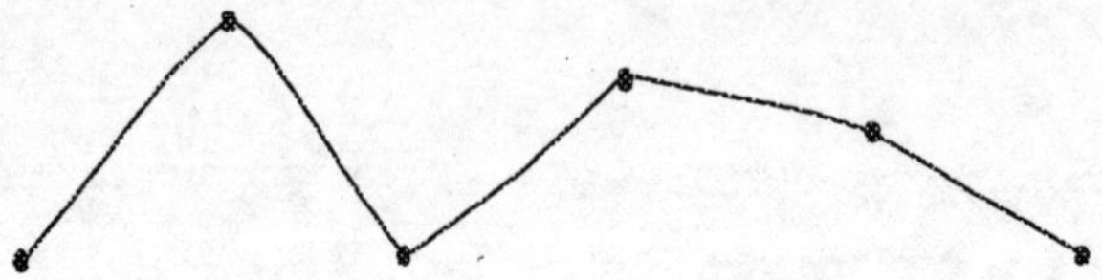

Fig. 4.1 Interpolation Curve

Alternately, if the data points are only approximations to some unknown true values, e.g., values obtained from experimental measurement or observed data, then a curve that shows the correct trend of the data is required. In general, the curve may not actually pass through any of the data points. When curve do not pass through any control points the resulting curve is said to be *approximate* as shown in fig. 4.2.

Fig. 4.2 Approximation Curve

4.2 NON-PARAMETRIC VERSUS PARAMETRIC CURVES

4.2.1 Non-parametric Curves

- *Explicit:* $y = f(x)$ ...(4.1)

  Example: $y = mx + b$ (i.e., equation of straight line)

  In this form, only one y-value is obtained for each x-value; consequently, closed or multiple value curves, e.g., a circle cannot be represented explicitly.

- *Implicit:* $f(x,y) = 0$ ...(4.2)

  The general 2nd degree implicit equation

  $ax^2 + 2bxy + cy^2 + 2dx + 2ey + f = 0$ ...(4.3)

  provides a variety of 2-D curve forms called *conic sections,* e.g., parabola, hyperbola, and ellipse. Both implicit and spline, i.e., non-parametric curves are axis-dependent. Thus, the choice of coordinate system affects the ease of use.

4.2.2 Parametric Curves

In parametric form, each coordinate of a point on a curve is represented as a function of a single parameter. The position vector of a point on the curve is fixed by the value of the parameter.

For a 2-D curve with t as the parameter, the cartesian coordinates of a point on the curve are:

$x = x(t)$

$y = y(t)$

The position vector of a point on the curve is then

$$P(t) = [x(t)\ y(t)] \qquad ...(4.4)$$

The parametric form is suitable for representing closed and multiple valued curves.

The derivative or tangent vector on a parametric curve is given by:

$$P'(t) = [x'(t)\ y'(t)] \qquad ...(4.5)$$

Where? denotes differentiation w.r.t. the parameter. The slope of the curve, dy/dx, is

$$\frac{dy}{dx} = \frac{dy/dt}{dx/dt} = \frac{y'(t)}{x'(t)} \qquad ...(4.6)$$

When $x'(t) = 0$, the slope is infinite. Hence, an infinite slope is specified by letting one component of the tangent vector be zero. Thus, computational difficulties are avoided by using the parametric derivative.

Since a point on a parametric curve is specified by a single value of the parameter, the parametric form is axis-independent.

The curve endpoints and length are fixed by the parameter range:

$$\Rightarrow 0 \le t \le 1$$

The simplest parametric curve representation is for a straight line. For two position vectors P_1 and P_2, a parametric representation of the straight line segment between them is:

$$P(t) = P_1 + (P_2 - P_1)t \qquad \Rightarrow 0 \le t \le 1 \qquad ...(4.7)$$

Since P(t) is a position vector, each of the components of P(t) has a parametric representation x(t) and y(t) between P_1 and P_2, i.e.,

$$x(t) = x_1 + (x_2 - x_1)t \qquad 0 \le t \le 1 \qquad ...(4.8)$$

$$y(t) = y_1 + (y_2 - y_1)t$$

Parametric form for circle

$$x = \cos\theta \qquad 0 \le \theta \le 2\pi$$

$$y = \sin\theta$$

Or $\quad P(\theta) = [x\ y] = [\cos\theta\ \sin\theta] \qquad 0 \le \theta \le 2\pi \qquad ...(4.9)$

Where the parameter θ is associated with the geometric angle measured counter clockwise from the positive x-axis.

Parametric representation for a curve

$$P(t) = \left[\frac{(1-t^2)}{(1+t^2)}\ \frac{2t}{(1+t^2)}\right] \qquad 0 \le t \le 1$$

$$x = \cos\theta = 1\text{-}t^2/1 + t^2 \qquad 0 \le q \le p/2 \qquad 0 \le t \le 1 \qquad ...(4.10)$$

$$y = \sin\theta = 2t/1 + t^2 \qquad 0 \le \theta \le \pi/2 \qquad 0 \le t \le 1 \qquad ...(4.11)$$

Parametric curves replace the use of geometric slopes (which may by infinite) with parametric tangent vectors (which are never infinite). Here, the curve is approximated by a pie polynomial curve instead of pie linear curve.

4.3 SPLINE REPRESENTATION

A spline surface can be described with two sets of orthogonal spline curves.

Splines are used in graphics application to:

- design curve
- surface shapes
- digitize drawings for computer storage
- specify animation paths for the objects or the camera in a scene
- typical CAD application included design of automobile bodies, design of aircraft surfaces, design of spacecraft and design of ship hulls.

Interpolation curves are commonly used to digitize drawings or to specify animation paths. Approximation curves are primarily used as design tools to structure object surfaces.

The convex polygon boundary that encloses a set of control points is called the *convex hull.* The convex hull provides a measure for the deviation of a curve or surface from the region bounding the control points some splines are bounded by the convex hull, thus ensuring that the polynomials smoothly follow the control points without veratic oscillations. Also, the polygon region inside the convex hull is useful in some algorithms as a clipping region.

4.4 HERMITE INTERPOLATION SPLINE

A Hermite spline is named after the French mathematician Charles Hermite. It is a single cubic spline piece fitted between two given points. Hermite Spline can be adjusted locally because each curve section is only dependent on its endpoint construction.

If P(u) represents a parametric cubic point function for the curve section between control point p_k and p_{k+1}, as shown in fig. 4.3, then the boundary conditions that define this Hermite curve section are:

$$\begin{aligned} P(0) &= p_k \\ P(1) &= p_{k+1} \\ P'(0) &= Dp_k \\ P'(1) &= Dp_{k+1} \end{aligned} \qquad \text{...(4.12)}$$

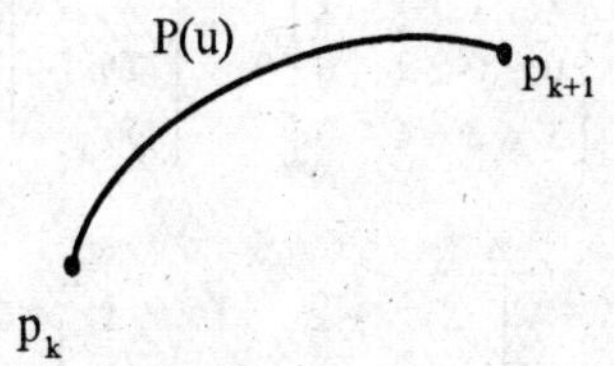

Fig. 4.3 Hermite Curve Section

With Dp_k ad Dp_{k+1} are tangents to the curve, specifying the values for the parametric derivation (slope of the curve), at control points p_k and p_{k+1}. Vector equivalent for Hermite curve section:

$P(u) = au^3 + bu^2 + cu + d, \qquad 0 \le u \le 1$ ...(4.13)

and $P(u) = (x(u), y(u), z(u))$ ...(4.14)

It means x component of P is $x(u) = a_x u^3 + b_x u^2 + c_x u + d_x$ ...(4.15)

$y(u) = a_y u^3 + b_y u^2 + c_y u + d_y$ ...(4.16)

$z(u) = a_z u^3 + b_z u^2 + c_z u + d_z$ ...(4.17)

Matrix representation of equation (4.14)

$$P(u) = [u^3 \ u^2 \ u \ 1] \cdot \begin{bmatrix} a \\ b \\ c \\ d \end{bmatrix} \qquad ...(4.18)$$

and the derivative of the point function can be expressed as:

$$P'(u) = [3u^2 \ 2u \ 1 \ 0] \cdot \begin{bmatrix} a \\ b \\ c \\ d \end{bmatrix} \qquad ...(4.19)$$

Substituting endpoint values 0 and 1 for parameter u into 4.18 and 4.19 equations.

$$\begin{bmatrix} p_k \\ p_{k+1} \\ Dp_k \\ Dp_{k+1} \end{bmatrix} = \begin{bmatrix} 0 & 0 & 0 & 1 \\ 1 & 1 & 1 & 1 \\ 0 & 0 & 1 & 0 \\ 3 & 2 & 1 & 0 \end{bmatrix} * \begin{bmatrix} a \\ b \\ c \\ d \end{bmatrix} \qquad ...(4.20)$$

$$\Rightarrow \begin{bmatrix} a \\ b \\ c \\ d \end{bmatrix} = \begin{bmatrix} 0 & 0 & 0 & 1 \\ 1 & 1 & 1 & 1 \\ 0 & 0 & 1 & 0 \\ 3 & 2 & 1 & 0 \end{bmatrix}^{-1} * \begin{bmatrix} p_k \\ p_{k+1} \\ Dp_k \\ Dp_{k+1} \end{bmatrix} \qquad ...(4.21)$$

$$= \begin{bmatrix} 2 & -2 & 1 & 1 \\ -3 & 3 & -2 & -1 \\ 0 & 0 & 1 & 0 \\ 1 & 0 & 0 & 0 \end{bmatrix} * \begin{bmatrix} p_k \\ p_{k+1} \\ Dp_k \\ Dp_{k+1} \end{bmatrix}$$

$$= M_H \begin{bmatrix} p_k \\ p_{k+1} \\ Dp_k \\ Dp_{k+1} \end{bmatrix} \qquad ...(4.22)$$

where M_H, the Hermite matrix, is the inverse of the boundary constraint matrix. Equation 4.18 can thus be written in terms of the boundary conditions as (using equation 4.22):

$$P(u) = [u^3 \ u^2 \ u \ 1] . M_H . \begin{bmatrix} p_k \\ p_{k+1} \\ Dp_k \\ Dp_{k+1} \end{bmatrix} \qquad ...(4.23)$$

Lastly, we can calculate the expressions for the Hermite *blending functions* by carrying out the matrix multiplications and collecting coefficients for the boundary constraints to obtain the polynomial form:

$$P(u) = p_k(2u^3-3u^2+1) + p_{k+1}(-2u^3 + 3u^2) + Dp_k(u^3 - 2u^2 + u) + Dp_{k+1}(u^3 - u^2)$$

$$= p_k H_0(u) + p_{k+1} H_1(u) + Dp_k H_2(u) + Dp_{k+1} H_3(u) \qquad ...(4.24)$$

The polynomials $H_k(u)$ for value of k = 0, 1, 2, 3 are known as blending functions since they blend the boundary constraint values to obtain position of each coordinate along the curve.

4.5 CONTINUITY

Hermite was a single cubic spline piece between two control points. Now we will discuss how to generate a continuous spline between an arbitrary numbers of points. Multiple cubic curve pieces are joined together. To smoothly join these parametric piecewise polynomial curves, there exists various continuity conditions.

There are two types of continuities between two adjacent piecewise curves:

1. Parametric Continuity denoted by C
2. Geometric Continuity denoted by G

Numerical superscripts are used to indicate degree of continuity, i.e., smoothness.

4.5.1 Parametric Continuity Conditions

If each section of a spline is described with a set of parametric coordinate function of the form:

$$x = x(u) \qquad y = y(u) \qquad z = z(u) \qquad u_1 \le u \le u_2$$

we set parametric continuity by matching the parametric derivatives of adjoining curve section at their common boundary.

4.5.1.1 Zero-order Parametric Continuity

It is described as C^0 continuity means simply that the curves meet, two curves share a common endpoint without regard to the shape of the curve i.e. the values of x, y and z evaluated at u_2 for the first curve section are equal, respectively, to the values of x, y and z evaluated at u_1 for the next curve section.

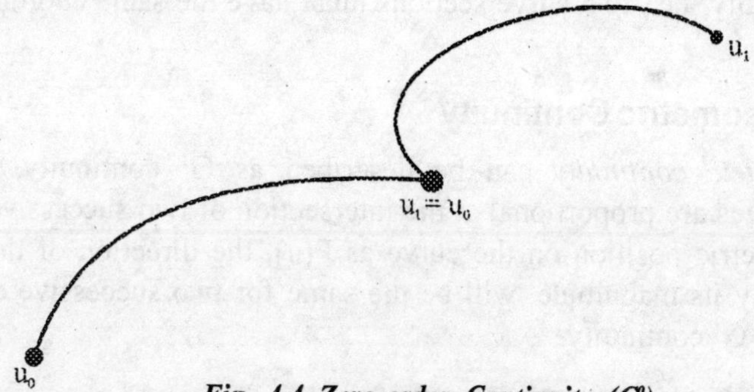

Fig. 4.4 Zero-order Continuity (C^0)

4.5.1.2 First-order Parametric Continuity

It is referred to a C^1 continuity, means that the first parametric derivatives (tangent vectors) of the two connected curve segments. For two successive curve sections, tangents are equal at their joining point.

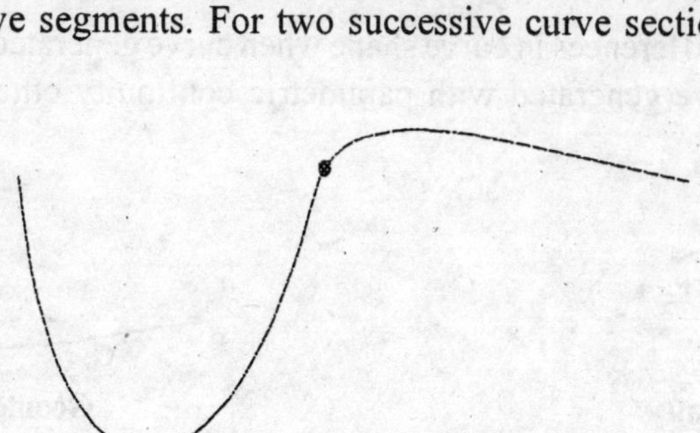

Fig. 4.5 First-order Continuity (C^1)

4.5.1.3 Second-order Parametric Continuity

It is referred to as C^2 continuity, means that both the first and second parametric derivations of the two curve sections are equal at the intersection.

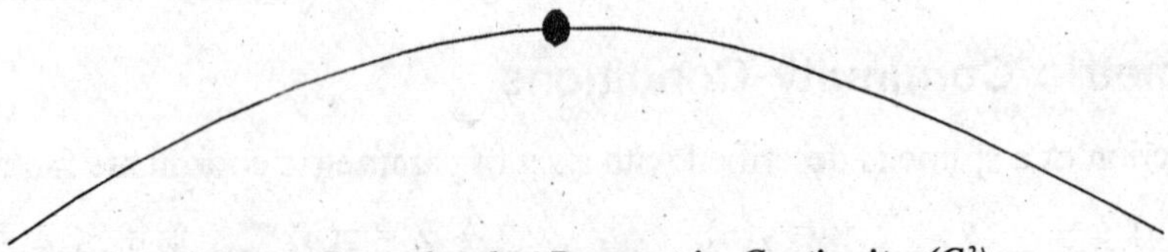

Fig. 4.6 Second-order Parametric Continuity (C^2)

4.5.2 Geometric Continuity Conditions

An alternate method for joining two successive curve sections is to specify conditions for geometric continuity. In this case, we only require that the parametric derivations of the two sections to be proportional to each other at their joining point instead of equal to each other.

4.5.2.1 Zero-order Geometric Continuity

Zero-order geometric continuity can be described as G^0 continuity is the same as zero-order parametric continuity, i.e., two curve sections must have the same coordinate positions at the joining point.

4.5.2.2 First-order Geometric Continuity

First-order geometric continuity can be described as G^1 continuity, means that the parametric first derivatives are proportional at the intersection of two successive curve sections. If we denote the parametric position on the curve as P(u), the direction of the tangent vector P′(u), but not necessarily its magnitude, will be the same for two successive curve sections at their joining point under G^1 continuity.

4.5.2.3 Second-order Geometric Continuity

Second-order geometric continuity is referred to as G^2 continuity, means that both the 1st and 2nd parametric derivatives of the two curve sections are proportional at their boundary under G^2 continuity, curvatures of two curve sections will match as the joining position.

There is only slight differences in curve shape when curve generated with geometric continuity conditions and same curve generated with parametric continuity otherwise they are similar.

Parametric Continuity **Geometric Continuity**

Fig. 4.7

With geometric continuity, the curve is pulled towards the section with the greater tangent vector (derivative).

4.6 SPLINE SPECIFICATIONS

There are three different ways for specifying a particular spline:

(i) Set of boundary conditions imposed on the spline;

(ii) Matrix functions that characterize the spline;

(iii) State the set of blending functions {or basis functions} that determine how specified geometric constraints on the curve are combined to calculate positions along the curve path.

Let us assume that the following is the parametric cubic polynomial representation for the x-component

$$x(u) = a_x u^3 + b_x u^2 + c_x u + d_x, \qquad 0 \leq u \leq 1 \qquad ...(4.25)$$

Boundary conditions would be set on the endpoint coordinates x (0) and x (1), and on the first derivative x′(0) and x′(1). These four boundary conditions are sufficient to determine the values of four coefficients a_x, b_x, c_x, d_x.

Boundary conditions representation in matrix form:-

$$x(u) = [u^3\ u^2\ u\ 1] \cdot \begin{bmatrix} a_x \\ b_x \\ c_x \\ d_x \end{bmatrix} \qquad ...(4.26)$$

$$= U.C \qquad ...(4.27)$$

where U – row matrix of power of parameter u.

C – coefficient column matrix

We can rewrite the boundary conditions and solve for coefficient matrix as:

$$C = M_{spline} \cdot M_{geo} \qquad ...(4.28)$$

where M_{geo} = boundary conditions on the spline

M_{spline} = 4 × 4 matrix to transform the geometric constraint values to the polynomial coefficient . M_{spline} is a spline matrix also known as basis matrix particularly useful for transforming from one spline representation to another.

Substituing value of C in equation 4.27

$$x(u) = U.\ M_{spline} \cdot M_{geo} \qquad ...(4.29)$$

Lastly, expand the previous equation to obtain a polynomial representation for coordinate x in terms of the geometric constraint parameters

$$x(u) = \sum_{k=0}^{n} m_k BL_k(u) \qquad ...(4.30)$$

where m_k are constraint parameters, such as the control point coordinates and slope of the curve at control points, and $BL_k(u)$ are the polynomial blending function.

4.7 BEZIER CURVES

There is another class of shape design problems that depends on both aesthetic and functional requirements apart from the technique for curve generation constrained to the curves that pass through existing data or control points (the curve fitting technique). These problems are frequently termed *ab initio* design which means without any prior knowledge of the curve shape.

This alternate method of shape description suitable for *ab initio* design of free-form curves and surface was developed by Pierre Bezier.

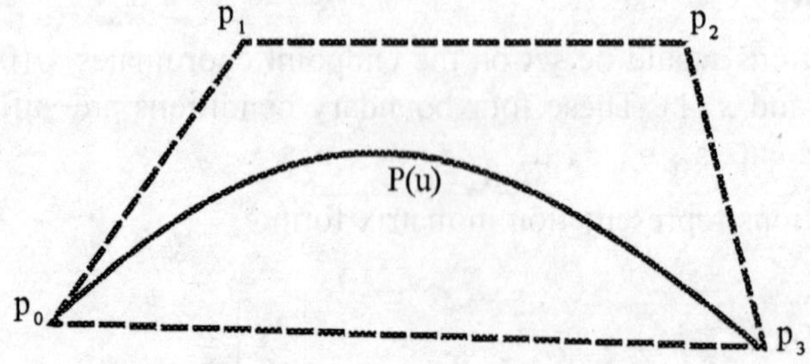

Fig. 4.8 A BEZIER Curve and its Defining Polygon

A Bezier curve is determined by a defining polygon. A Bezier curve section can be fitted to any number of control points. The number of control points with which the curve has to be approximated and their relative position determine the degree of the Bezier's polynomial.

Bezier curve too can be specified with – boundary conditions, matrix representation and blending functions. For general Bezier curves, the blending function specification is the most convenient and efficient method.

Given a set of n +1 control points position $p_0, p_1....p_n$, can be blended to produce the following position rector P(u).

$$P(u) = \sum_{j=0}^{n} p_j BZ_{j,n}(u) \quad \text{where } 0 \leq u \leq 1 \qquad ...(4.31)$$

The Bezier blending functions $BZ_{j,n}(u)$ are the Bernstein polynomials or blending functions.

$$BZ_{j,n}(u) = C(n,j)\ u^j(1-u)^{n-j} \qquad ...(4.32)$$

Where the C(n,j) are binomial coefficients:

$C(n,j)=n!/j!(n-j)!$

By expanding, we get,

$$P(u) = p_0BZ_{0,n}(u) + p_1BZ_{1,n}(u) + \ldots\ldots\ldots\ldots\ldots\ldots + p_{n-1}BZ_{n-1,n}(u) + p_{n-2}BZ_{n-2,n}(u)$$

$$= p_0\{C(n,0)u^0(1-u)^n\} + p_1\{C(n,1)u^1(1-u)^{n-1}\} + \ldots\ldots\ldots\ldots + p_{n-1}\{C(n,n-1)u^{n-1}(1-u)\} + p_n\{C(n,n)u^n(1-u)^0\}$$

Set of three parametric equations for individual curve coordinates.

$$x(u) = \sum_{j=0}^{n} x_jBZ_{j,n}(u)$$

$$y(u) = \sum_{j=0}^{n} y_jBZ_{j,n}(u)$$

$$z(u) = \sum_{j=0}^{n} z_jBZ_{j,n}(u) \qquad \ldots(4.33)$$

4.7.1 Properties of Bezier Curves

1. Bezier curve always passes through the first and last control point.
2. Degree of the polynomial curve is one less than the total number of control points.
3. First derivatives of a Bezier curve can be calculated as:

$$P'(0) = -np_0 + np_1 \qquad \ldots(4.34)$$

$$P'(1) = -np_{n-1} + np_n \qquad \ldots(4.35)$$

It shows that the direction of the tangent vector at the beginning of the curve is along the line that joins first two control points and direction of tangent at the end is along the line that joins the last two endpoints.

4. Parametric second derivates can be calculated as:

$$P''(0) = n(n-1)\,[(p_2 - p_1) - (p_1 - p_0)] \qquad \ldots(4.36)$$

$$P''(1) = n(n-1)\,[(p_{n-2} - p_{n-1}) - (p_{n-1} - p_n)] \qquad \ldots(4.37)$$

Thus, the second derivative of the Bezier curve at the initial and final points depends on the two nearest polygon span, i.e., on the nearest 3 polygon vertices. It is used to obtain maxima and minima.

5. It always lies entirely with in the convex hull of the control points.
6. All Bezier blending functions are positive and their sum is always 1.

$$\sum_{j=0}^{n} BZ_{j,n}(u) = 1 \qquad \ldots(4.38)$$

7. Bezier curve is convex hull property ensures that the polynomial smoothly follows the control points.
8. Closed Bezier curve can also be drawn by specifying first and last control point at the same position.

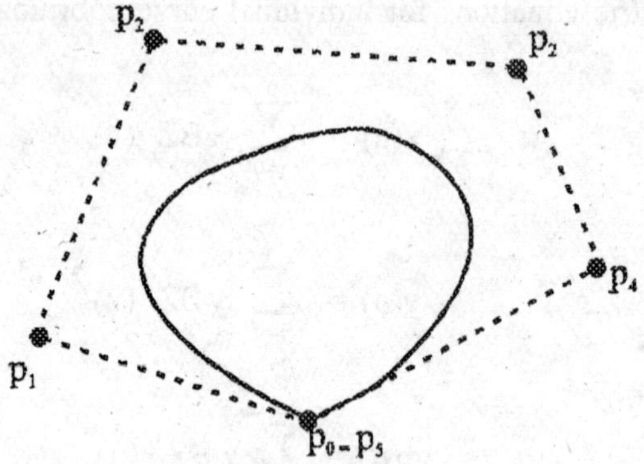

Fig. 4.9 Closed Bezier Curve

Cubic Bezier curve are generated with four control points. Cubic polynomials are most often used because lower degree polynomials give too little flexibility in controlling the shape of the curve, and higher-degree polynomials can introduce unwanted wiggles and also require more computation. Also parametric cubics are the lowest-degree curves that are non planar in 3-D. Thus, cubic Bezier curve give reasonable design flexibility while avoiding the increased calculations needed with higher-order polynomials.

Example 4.1: Draw a Bezier curve using three control points.

Solution: Let us say we have 3 control points, namely p_0, p_1, and p_2.

=> $j = 0$ to 2 where $n = 2$

$$P(u) = \sum_{j=0}^{2} p_j BZ_{j,n}(u)$$

By substituting;

$P(u) = p_0 BZ_{0,2}(u) + p_1 BZ_{1,2}(u) + p_2 BZ_{2,2}(u)$

$BZ_{j,n}(u) = C(n, j)u^j(1-u)^{n-j}$

where $C(n,j) = n!/j!(n-j)!$

By expanding, we get,

$\Rightarrow P(u) = p_0 BZ_{0,n}(u) + p_1 BZ_{1,n}(u) + \ldots\ldots\ldots\ldots + p_{n-1} BZ_{n-1,n}(u) + p_{n-2} BZ_{n-2,n}(u)$

$\Rightarrow P(u) = p_0\{C(2,0)u^0(1-u)^2\} + p_1\{C(2, 1)u^1(1-u)^{2-1}\} + p_2\{C(2,2)u^2(1-u)^0\}$

$$\Rightarrow P(u) = p_0\left[\frac{2!}{0!(2-0)!}u^0(1-u)^2\right] + p_1\left[\frac{2!}{1!(2-1)!}u(1-u)\right] + p_2\left[\frac{2!}{2!(2-2)!}u^2(1-u)^0\right]$$

$$\Rightarrow P(u) = p_0\{(1-u)^2\} + p_1\{u(1-u)^1\} + p_2\{u^2\}$$

Hence, we can now say as a rule

A Bezier curve is a polynomial of degree one less than the number of control points used.

Example 4.2: Construct a Bezier curve with two control points, i.e., p_0 and p_1.

Solution: Let us say we have two control points, namely p_0, and p_1

=> j = 0 to 1 where n = 1

$$P(u) = \sum_{J=0}^{3} p_j BZ_{j,n}(u)$$

By substituting;

$P(u) = p_0BZ_{0,1}(u) + p_1BZ_{1,1}(u)$

$BZ_{j,n}(u) = C(n, j)\ u^j(1-u)^{n-j}$

where C(n,j) = n!/j!(n-j)!

By expanding, we get,

$\Rightarrow P(u) = p_0BZ_{0,n}(u) + p_1BZ_{1,n}(u) + \ldots\ldots\ldots\ldots + p_{n-1}BZ_{n-1,n}(u) + p_{n-2}BZ_{n-2,n}(u)$

$\Rightarrow P(u) = p_0\{C(1,0)u^0(1-u)^1\} + p_1\{C(1, 1)u^1(1-u)^{1-1}\}$

$$\Rightarrow P(u) = p_0\left[\frac{1!}{0!(1-0)!}\times 1\times(u-1)\right] + p_1\left[\frac{1!}{1!(1-1)!}u(1-u)^0\right]$$

$\Rightarrow P(u) = p_0(1 - u) + p_1(u)$

=> A linear curve of degree 1.

Example 4.3: Draw the Bezier curve of degree 3, i.e., the number of control points are 4.

Solution: Cubic Bezier curves are generated with 4 control points. Let us say we have four control points, namely p_0, p_1, p_2, and p_3.

=> j = 0 to 3 where n = 3

$$P(u) = \sum_{J=0}^{3} p_j BZ_{j,n}(u)$$

By substituting;

$P(u) = p_0BZ_{0,3}(u) + p_1BZ_{1,3}(u) + p_2BZ_{2,3}(u) + p_3BZ_{3,3}(u)$

$BZ_{j,n}(u) = C(n, j)u^j(1-u)^{n-j}$

where $C(n,j) = n!/j!(n-j)!$

By expanding, we get,

$=>P(u) = p_0BZ_{0,n}(u) + p_1BZ_{1,n}(u) + \dots\dots\dots\dots + p_{n-1}BZ_{n-1,n}(u) + p_{n-2}BZ_{n-2,n}(u)$

$=>P(u) = p_0\{C(3,0)u^0(1-u)^3\} + p_1\{C(3, 1)u^1(1-u)^2\} + p_2\{C(3, 2)u^2(1-u)^1\} + p_3\{C(3, 3)u^3(1-u)^0\}$

$$=>P(u)= p_0\left[\frac{3!}{0!(3-0)!}(1-u)^3\right] + p_1\left[\frac{3!}{1!(3-1)!}u(1-u)^2\right] + p_2\left[\frac{3!}{2!(3-2)!}u^2(1-u)\right] + p_3\left[\frac{3!}{3!(3-3)!}u^3\right]$$

$=>P(u) = p_0(1-u)^3 + p_1(3u(1-u)^2) + p_2(3u^2(1-u)) + p_3(u^3)$

The 4 blending functions are:

$BZ_{0,3}(u) = C(0,3)u^0(1-u)^3 = (1-u)^3$

$BZ_{1,3}(u) = C(1,3)u^1(1-u)^2 = 3u(1-u)^2$

$BZ_{2,3}(u) = C(2,3)u^2(1-u) = 3u^2(1-u)$

$BZ_{3,3}(u) = C(3,3)u^3(1-u)^0 = u^3$

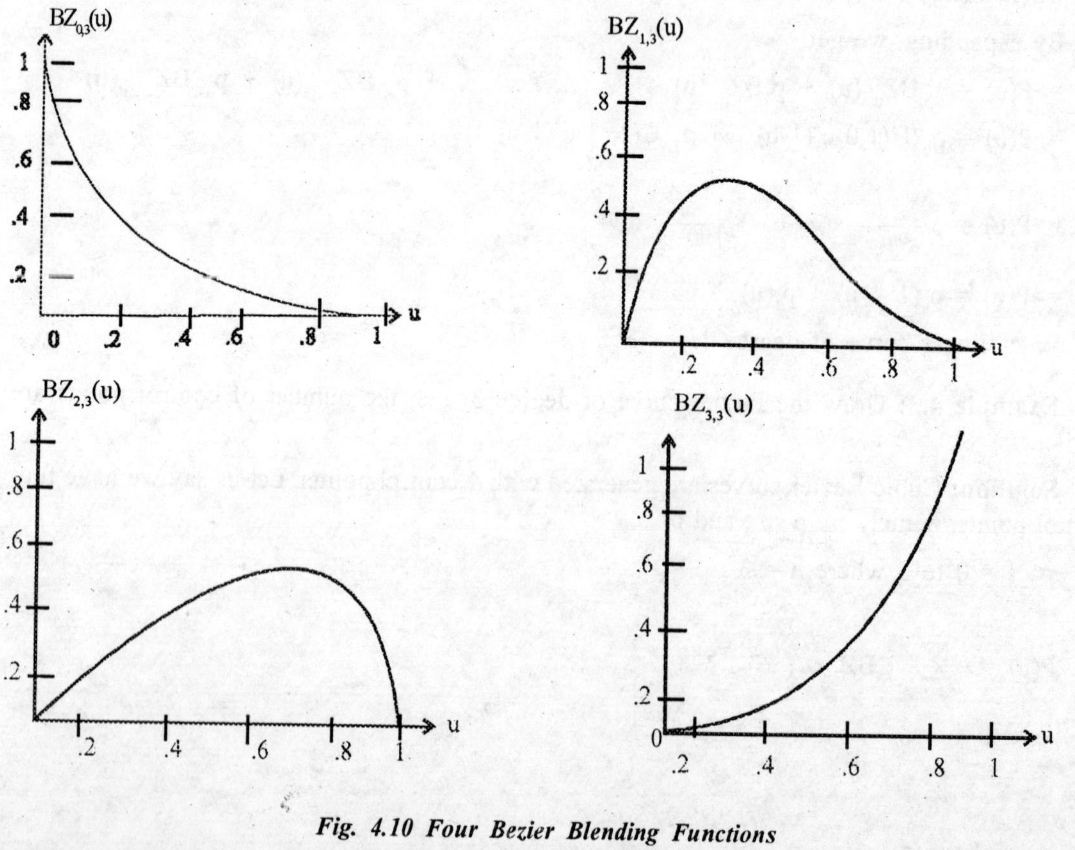

Fig. 4.10 Four Bezier Blending Functions

Plot the four cubic blending functions with the values of parameter u over the range from 0 to 1.

At u = 0, $BZ_{0,3}(u) = 1$ and at u = 1, $BZ_{3,3}(u) = 1$. Thus, the cubic Bezier curve will pass through the first and last control points, i.e., p_0 and p_3. As shown in fig. 4.10 that all the four blending functions are non-zero over the range of the parameter u from 0 to 1. It shows that in Bezier curve we don't have the local control, i.e., repositioning of any one of the control points will affect the path of the whole curve. First parametric derivatives at endprints are:

$P'(0) = 3\ (p_1 - p_0)$, $\qquad p'(1) = 3\ (p_3 - p_2)$

Second parametric derivatives are:

$P''(0) = 6\ (p_0 - 2p_1 + p_2)$, $\qquad P''(1) = 6(p_1 - 2p_2 + p_3)$

By expanding the equation of cubic blending function and representing in matrix form:

$$P(u) = [u^3\ u^2\ u\ 1]\ .\ M_{BZ}\ .\ \begin{bmatrix} p_o \\ p_1 \\ p_2 \\ p_3 \end{bmatrix}$$

$$\text{where } M_{BZ} = \begin{bmatrix} 3 & 3 & -3 & 1 \\ 3 & -6 & 3 & 0 \\ -3 & 3 & 0 & 0 \\ 1 & 0 & 0 & 0 \end{bmatrix} \qquad ...(4.39)$$

Example 4.4: Draw the Bezier curve where the number of control points are 5.

Solution: Let us say we have five control points, namely p_0, p_1, p_2, p_3 and p_4

=> j = 0 to 4 where n = 4

$$P(u) = \sum_{j=o}^{4} p_j BZ_{j,n}(u)$$

By substituting;

$P(u) = p_0BZ_{0,4}(u) + p_1BZ_{1,4}(u) + p_2BZ_{2,4}(u) + p_3BZ_{3,4}(u) + p_4BZ_{4,4}(u)$

$BZ_{j,n}(u) = C(n, j)u^j(1\text{-}u)^{n\text{-}j}$

where C(n,j) = n!/j!(n-j)!

By expanding, we get,

$$\Rightarrow P(u) = p_0 BZ_{0,n}(u) + p_1 BZ_{1,n}(u) + \ldots\ldots\ldots\ldots + p_{n-1}BZ_{n-1,n}(u) + p_{n-2}BZ_{n-2,n}(u)$$

$$\Rightarrow P(u) = p_0\{C(4,0)u^0(1-u)^4\} + p_1\{C(4,1)u^1(1-u)^3\} + p_2\{C(4,2)u^2(1-u)^2\} + p_3\{C(4,3)u^3(1-u)^1\} + p_4\{C(4,4)u^4(1-u)^0\}$$

$$\Rightarrow P(u) =$$

$$p_0\left[\frac{4!}{0!(4-0)!}(1-u)^4\right] + p_1\left[\frac{4!}{1!(4-1)}u(1-u)^3\right] + p_2\left[\frac{4!}{2!(4-2)!}u^2(1-u)^2\right] + p_3\left[\frac{4!}{3!(4-3)!}u^3(1-u)\right] + p_4\left[\frac{4!}{4!(4-4)!}u^4\right]$$

$$\Rightarrow P(u) = p_0(1-u)^4 + p_1(4u(1-u)^3) + p_2(6u^2(1-u)^2) + p_3(4u^3(1-u)) + p_4(u^4)$$

The 5 blending functions are:

$$BZ_{0,4}(u) = (1-u)^4$$
$$BZ_{1,4}(u) = 4u(1-u)^3$$
$$BZ_{2,4}(u) = 6u^2(1-u)^2$$
$$BZ_{3,4}(u) = 4u^3(1-u)$$
$$BZ_{4,4}(u) = u^4$$

$$P(u) = [u^3\ u^3\ u^2\ u1]\ .\ M_{BZ}\ .\begin{bmatrix} p_0 \\ p_1 \\ p_2 \\ p_3 \\ p_4 \end{bmatrix}$$

$$\text{where } M_{BZ} = \begin{bmatrix} 1 & -4 & 6 & -4 & 1 \\ -4 & 12 & -12 & 4 & 0 \\ 6 & 0 & 6 & -12 & 0 \\ -4 & 4 & 0 & 0 & 0 \\ 1 & 0 & 0 & 0 & 0 \end{bmatrix}$$

4.7.2 Conditions for Smoothly Joining Curve Segments

It is not possible to add more control points to smoothly extend a cubic Bezier curve, but we can select another four control points and draw the cubic Bezier curve which is then joined with the first. And if we have selected the control points carefully then it is feasible to smoothly attach the second cubic curve with the first one. Higher the order or degree of continuity, more will be the smoothness at joining point. According to the first order continuity the last control point of the first curve is equal to the first control point of the last curve.

Let two Bezier cubic curves are P(u) and Q(u) and are defined by (p_0, p_1, p_2, p_3) and (q_0, q_1, q_2, q_3) respectively, then according to zero order continuity

$$q_0 = p_3$$

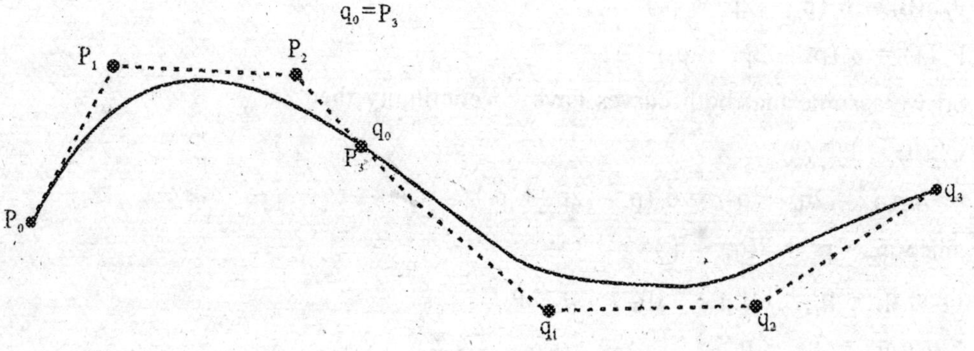

Fig. 4.11 Two Bezier Curves P(u) and Q(u)

If we want to join both P(u) and Q(u) smoothly, the tangents vector (i.e., the first derivates) to both the curves have same direction (G^1 continuity) at the joining point.

$Q'(0) = c\ P'(1) \qquad c>0$ ...(4.14)

Now $P(u) = (-u^3 + 3u^2 - 3u + 1)\ p_o + (3u^3 - 6u^2 + 3u)\ p_1 + (-3u^3 + 3u^2)\ p_2 + u^3 p_3$ ...(4.42)

then $P'(u) = (-3u^2 + 6u - 3)\ p_o + (9u^2 - 12u + 3)\ p_1 + (-9u^2 + 6u)\ p_2 + 3u^2 p_3$ ...(4.43)

put u = 0 and u = 1 in eq. 4.43

$P'(0) = -3p_0 + 3p_1 = 3(p_1 - p_0)$ i.e. $n(p_1 - p_0)$ ...(4.44)

Similarly $P'(1) = -3p_2 + 3p_3 = 3(p_3 - p_2)$ i.e. $n\ (p_n - p_{n-1})$ ...(4.45)

using equation 4.44 & 4.45 in equation 4.41

$3\ (q_1 - q_0) = c3(p_3 - p_2)$ ...(4.46)

It shows that three control points p_3, $p_3 = q_0$ and q_1 are collinear i.e. $p_3 = q_0$ lie on the line p_2 to q_1. When both magnitude and director of tangent vectors are equal at the joining point then $p_3 = q_0$ lies exactly at the mid point of line p_2 to q_1.

This shows c = 1 in equation 4.41 (C^1 continuity)

And $3(q_1 - q_0) = 3(p_3 - p_2)$ ...(4.47)

$\Rightarrow 2(p_3 = q_0) = p_2 + q_1$

$\Rightarrow p_3 = q_0 = (p_2 + q_1) / 2$

$\Rightarrow q_1 = p_3 + (p_3 - p_2)$ i.e. $p_n + (p_n - p_{n-1})$ ...(4,48)

Now $P''(0) = n\ (n-1)\ (p_0 - 2p_1 + p_2)$

$= n\ (n-1)\ \{(p_2 - p_1) - (p_1 - p_0)\}$

$\Rightarrow P''(1) = n\ (n-1)\ (p_n - 2p_{n-1} + p_{n-2})$

$= n\ (n-1)\ \{(p_{n-2} - p_{n-1}) - (p_{n-1} - p_n)\}$ ...(4.49)

For n = 3

$P''(0) = 6(p_0 - 2p_1 + p_2)$

$P''(1) = 6(p_3 - 2p_2 + p_1)$

So we assume that both curves have C^2 continuity then

$Q''(0) = P''(1)$ ... (4.50)

$\Rightarrow 6(q_0 - 2q_1 + q_2) = 6(p_3 - 2p_2 + p_1)$

since $q_2 = p_1 + 2(q_1 - q_2)$

then, $q_2 = p_1 + 2(p_3 + (p_3 - p_2) - p_2)$

Since $q_1 = 2p_3 - p_2$

$\Rightarrow q_2 = p_1 + 4(p_3 - p_2)$ ...(4.51)

i.e. $p_{n-2} + 4(p_n - p_{n-1})$ ...(4.52)

We can calculate the first three control points of the second curve with the help of the control points of first curve, by using equations discussed above. And if we calculate control points using above conditions then both the Bezier cubic curves will smoothly joined as they control have the parametric continuity of the second order, i.e., C^2.

Example 4.5: 2 Bezier curves are smoothly joined:

(i) $p_0(1,1)$; $p_1(2,2)$; $p_2(5,2)$; $p_3(7,1)$;

(ii) $q_0(a,b)$; $q_1(c,d)$; $q_2(-7,2)$; $q_3(-4,4)$;

Find out the values of a,b,c and d or q_0 and q_1.

Solution:

By zero-order parametric continuity

$p_3 = q_0$

Therefore, $q_0 = (7,1)$

Now first-order continuity gives $P'(1) = Q'(0)$

$\therefore n[p_n - p_{n-1}] = n[q_1 - q_0]$

$\Rightarrow q_1 = p_n - p_{n-1} + q_0 = p_3 - p_2 + q_0$

$= (7-1) - (5,2) + (7,1) = (14,2) - (5,2)$

$= (9,0)$

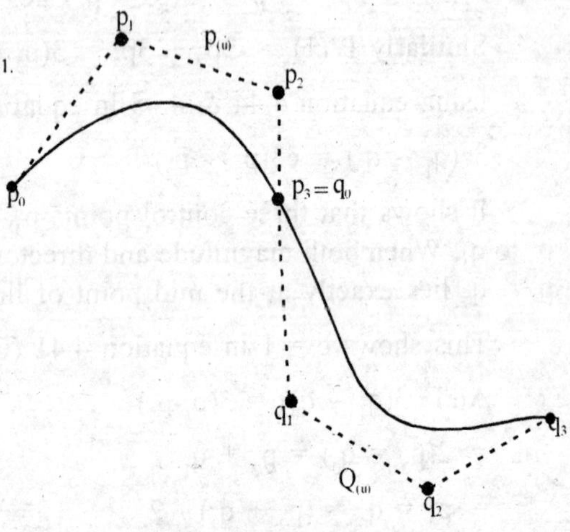

Fig. 4.12 Two Smoothly Joined Bezier Curves

Example 4.6: Given $P(u) = au^3 + bu^2 + cu + d$, where $0 \le u \le 1$. Find all Control points.

Solution:

At $u = 0$, $P(0) = d \Rightarrow p_0 = d$

At $u = 1$, $P(1) = a + b + c + d \Rightarrow p_3 = a + b + c + d$

$P'(u) = 3au^2 + 2bu + c$

$P'(1) = 3a + 2b + c$

As $P'(1) = n\,(p_n - p_{n-1}) \Rightarrow 3(p_3 - p_2)$

$\Rightarrow 3a + 2b + c = 3(p_3 - p_2)$

$$\Rightarrow p_3 - p_2 = \frac{3a + 2b + c}{3} \Rightarrow p_2 = p_3 - \left(\frac{3a + 2b + c}{3}\right)$$

But $p_3 = a + b + c + d$

putting the value of p_3

$$\Rightarrow p_2 = a + b + c + d - \left(\frac{3a + 2b + c}{3}\right)$$

$$\Rightarrow p_2 = \frac{3a + 3b + 3c + 3d - 3a - 2b - 2c}{3}$$

$$\Rightarrow p_2 = \frac{b + c + 3d}{3}$$

Also,

$P'(0) = n\,[p_1 - p_0] = 3(p_1 - p_0)$

$P'(u) = 3au^2 + 2bu + c$

$\Rightarrow P'(0) = c$

$\Rightarrow 3(p_1 - p_0) = c$

since $p_0 = d$

$$\Rightarrow p_1 = \frac{c}{3} + p_0 = \frac{c}{3} + d$$

Hence,

$$p_0 = d;\ p_1 = \frac{c}{3} + d;\ p_2 = \frac{b + c + 3d}{3};\ p_3 = a + b + c + d$$

4.7.3 Bezier Bi-cubic Surfaces

An input mesh of 4-4 control points can be used to design a bi-cubic surface. Mathematically, a general parametric function for Bezier Curve will be represented as:

$$P(u,v) = \sum_{j=0}^{n} \sum_{i=0}^{m} p_{j,k} BZ_{j,n}(v) BZ_{i,m}(u) \quad 0 \le u \le 1 \text{ and } 0 \le v \le 1 \qquad ...(4.53)$$

Where $p_{j,k}$ – location of (n + 1) by (m + 1) control points

for cubic surfaces:

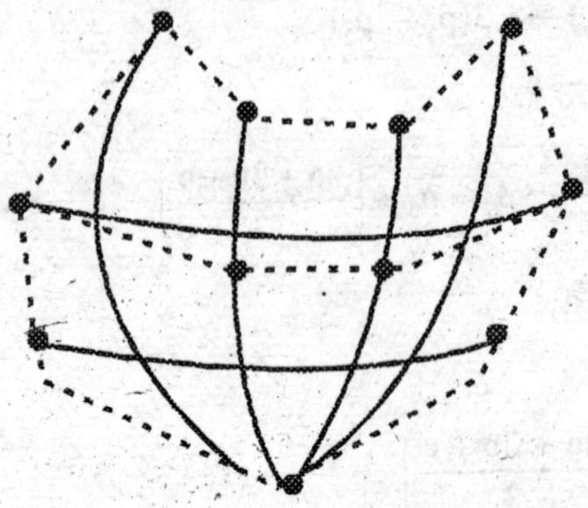

Fig. 4.13 Bezier Bi-cubic Surfaces

$$P(u,v) = \sum_{j=0}^{n} \sum_{j=0}^{m} p_{j,k} \quad BZ_{j,3}(v) \quad BZ_{i,3}(u) \quad 0 \leq u \leq 1 \text{ and } 0 \leq v \leq 1 \qquad ...(4.54)$$

The convex hull is represented by dashed lines, and solid lines shows the cubic curves. Each curve of constant u is drawn by varying v over the range from 0 to 1, with u fixed at one of its values. Similarly, the curves of constant v are constructed.

4.7.4 C Program

```
/*PROGRAM TO DRAW A BEZIER CURVE*/
#include <stdio.h>
#include <conio.h>
#include <graphics.h>
int x,y,z;
void bezier(float,int,int[][3]);
void main()
{
foat u;
int gd,gm,ymax,i,n,c[4][3];
for(i=0;i<4;i++) {c[i][0]=0; c[i][1]=0;}
printf("\n\n Enter four points p0,p1,p2,p3 : \n\n");
for(i=0; i<4; i++)
{
```

```
printf("\t X%d Y%d :",i,i);
scanf("%d %d",&c[i][0],&c[i][1]);
}
c[4][0]=c[0][0];
c[4][1]=c[0][1];
detectgraph(&gd,&gm);
initgraph(&gd,&gm, "d:\\tc\\");
ymax = 480;
setcolor(13);
for(i=0;i<3;i++)
{
line(c[i][0],ymax-c[i][1],c[i+1][0],ymax-c[i+1][1]);
}
setcolor(3);
n=3;
for(i=0;i<=40;i++)
{
u=(float)i/40.0;
bezier(u,n,c);
if(i==0)
{ moveto(x,ymax-y);}
else
{ lineto(x,ymax-y); }
getch();
}
getch();
}
void bezier(float u,int n, int p[][3])
{
int j;
float v,b;
float blendfunc(int,int,float);
```

```
x=0;y=0;z=0;
for(j=0;j<=n;j++)
{
b=blendfunc(j,n,u);
x=x+(p[j][0]*b);
y=y+(p[j][1]*b);
z=z+(p[j][2]*b);
}
}
float blendfunc(int j,int n,float u)
{
int k;
float v,blend;
v=C(n,j);
for(k=0;k<j;k++)
{v*=u;}
for(k=1;k<=(n-j);k++)
{v *= (1-u);}
blend=v;
return(blend);
}
C(int n,int j)
{
int k,a,c;
a=1;
for(k=j+1;k<=n;k++) {a*=k;}
for(k=1;k<=(n-j);k++) {a=a/k;}
c=a;
return(c);
}
```

4.8 B-SPLINES

From a mathematical point of view, a curve generated by using the vertices of a defining polygon is dependent on some interpolation or approximation scheme to establish the relationship between the curve and the polygon. This scheme is provided by the choice of basis function.

Two characteristics of the Bernstein basis, however, limit the flexibility of the resulting curves:

(i) The number of specified polygon vertices fixes the order of the resulting polynomial which defines the curve. For example, a cubic curve must be defined by a polygon with four vertices and three spans. A polygon with six vertices always produces a fifth-degree curve, i.e., a degree of Bezier curve polynomial is dependent on the number of control points.

(ii) The second limiting characteristics is due to the global nature of the Bernstein basis. This means that the value of the blending function $BZ_{j,n}(u)$ is non-zero for all parameter values over the entire curve. Since any point on a Bezier curve is a result of blending the values of all defining vertices, a change in one vertex is felt throughout the entire curve. This eliminates the ability to produce a local change within a curve. The lack of local control is detrimental in some application.

There is another basis, called the B-spline basis, which contains the Bernstein basis as a special case. Thus, B-spline offers the following two advantages over Bezier splines:

(i) The degree of a B-spline polynomial can be set independently of the number of control points,

(ii) It allows local control over the shape of a spline curve or surface; the B-spline basis is generally non-global. The non-global behaviour of B-spline curves is due to the fact that each vertex p_i is associated with a unique basis function. Thus, each vertex affects the shape of a curve only over a range of parameter values where its associated basis function is non zero.

Although there is a trade off that a B-spline is more complex than a Bezier spline. General expression of B-spline.

$$P(u) = \sum_{j=0}^{n} p_j B_{j,d}(u) \qquad u_{min} \leq u \leq u_{max}$$

p_j is the set of n+1 control points selected by the user. Here range of u depends on how to choose the B-spline parameters. B-spline blending time $B_{k,d}$ are polynomials of degree d-1, where d is a integer of range from 2 to one more than the number of control points, i.e., $2 \leq d \leq n + 1$.

Local control for B-splines is achieved by defining the blending functions over sub-intervals of the total range of u.

Blending functions for B-spline curves are defined by Cox-Deboor recursive formulas:

$$B_{j,1}(u) = \begin{cases} 1, \text{if } u_k \le u \le u_{k+1} \\ 0, \text{other wise} \end{cases}$$

$$B_{j,d}(u) = \frac{u - u_j}{u_{j+d-1} - u_j} B_{j,d-1}(u) + \frac{u_{j+d} - u}{u_{j+d} - u_{j+1}} B_{j+1,d-1}(u) \quad ...(4.56)$$

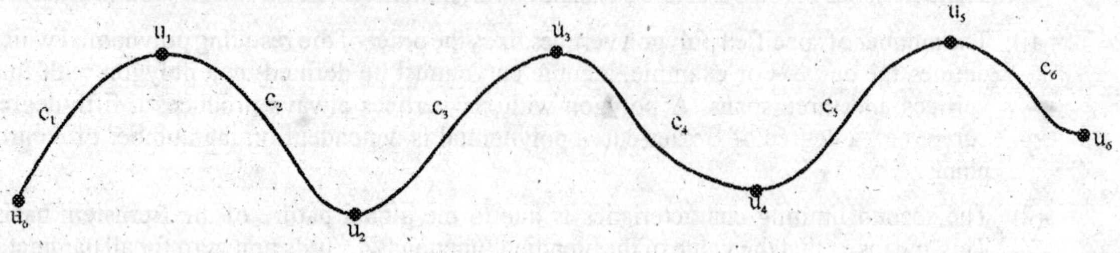

Fig. 4.14 Here $u_0, u_1, u_2, u_3, u_4, u_5, u_6$ are Knot Vectors

Where each blending function is defined over the sub-intervals of the total range of u. The selected set of sub-interval endpoints u_j is referred to as a knot vector.

Example 4.7: Let n = 2; d = 2, draw a uniform B-spline curve.

Solution: Number of Knot Vectors= n+d+1= 2+2+1=5 uniform knot vectors: {0,1,2,3,4,}. $u_0 = 0$, $u_1 = 1$, $u_2 = 2$, $u_3 = 3$, $u_4 = 4$,

$$P(u) = \sum_{j=0}^{n} p_j B_{j,d}(u)$$

$$= p_0 B_{0,2}(u) + p_1 B_{1,2}(u) + p_2 B_{2,2}(u)$$

$$= p_0 \left[\frac{u - u_0}{u_0 +_{2-1} - u_0} B_{0,2-1}(u) + \frac{u_{0+2} - u}{u_{0+2} - u_{0+1}} B_{0+1,2-1}(u) \right]$$

$$+ p_1 \left[\frac{u - u_1}{u_{1+2-1} - u_1} B_{1,2-1}(u) + \frac{u_{1+2} - u}{u_{1+2} - u_{1+1}} B_{1+1,2-1}(u) \right]$$

$$+ p_2 \left[\frac{u - u_2}{u_{2+2-1} - u_2} B_{2,2-2}(u) + \frac{u_{2+2} - u}{u_{2+2} - u_{2+1}} B_{2+1,2-2}(u) \right]$$

$$= p_0 \left[\frac{u - u_0}{u_1 - u_0} B_{0,1}(u) + \frac{u_2 - u}{u_{0+2} - u_{0+1}} B_{1,1}(u) \right]$$

$$+ p_1 \left[\frac{u - u_1}{u_2 - u_1} B_{1,1}(u) + \frac{u_3 - u}{u_3 - u_2} B_{2,1}(u) \right] + p_2 \left[\frac{u - u_2}{u_3 - u_2} B_{2,0}(u) + \frac{u_4 - u}{u_4 - u_3} B_{3,0}(u) \right]$$

for $p_0\left[\dfrac{u-u_0}{u_1-u_0}B_{0,1}(u)+\dfrac{u_2-u}{u_2-u_1}B_{1,1}(u)\right]$ we derive two intervals of curves

$u_0 \le u \le u_1$

$u_1 \le u \le u_2$

$$B_{0,1}(u)=\begin{cases}1, u_0 \le u \le u_1\\ 0, \text{otherwise}\end{cases}$$

$$B_{1,1}(u)=\begin{cases}1, u_1 \le u \le u_2\\ 0, \text{otherwise}\end{cases}$$

Similarly for $p_1\left[\dfrac{u-u_1}{u_2-u_1}B_{1,1}(u)+\dfrac{u_3-u}{u_3-u_2}B_{2,1}(u)\right]$ we derive two intervals of curves

$u1 \le u \le u_2$

$u_2 \le u \le u_3$

$$B_{1,1}(u)=\begin{cases}1, & u_1 \le u \le u_2\\ 0, & \text{otherwise}\end{cases}$$

$$B_{2,1}(u)=\begin{cases}1, & u_2 \le u \le u_3\\ 0, & \text{otherwise}\end{cases}$$

and now for $p_2\left[\dfrac{u-u_2}{u_3-u_2}B_{2,0}(u)+\dfrac{u_4-u}{u_4-u_3}B_{3,0}(u)\right]$ we derive the following two intervals

$$B_{2,0}(u)=\begin{cases}0, u_2 \le u \le u_3\\ 1, \text{otherwise}\end{cases}$$

$$B_{3,0}(u)=\begin{cases}0, u_3 \le u \le u_4\\ 1, \text{otherwise}\end{cases}$$

Put the values of knot vectors.

Following are the properties of B-spline:

(i) B-spline has degree d-1 and continuity C^{d-2} over the range of u.

(ii) For $B_{j,d}$ spline will have d intervals.

(iii) Total number of knot vectors are n+d+1.

(iv) For n+1 control points, the curve is described with n+1 blending functions.

(v) Any one control points can affect the shape of at most d curve sections.

(vi) The curve lies within the convex hull of its defining polygon and follows the shape of the defining polygon.

(vii) Convex hull property is stronger than that of Bezier curve.

(viii) The curve exhibits the variation diminishing property.

(ix) The sum of the basis function = 1.

4.8.1 Types of Kont Vectors

There are three general classifications for knot vectors:

4.8.1.1 Uniform Periodic

4.8.1.2 Non-uniform

4.8.1.3 Open Uniform

B-splines are commonly described according to the selected knot vector class.

4.8.1.1 Uniform, Periodic

When the spacing between the knot vectors is constant, the resulting curve is called a uniform B-spline.

For example,

{-1.5, -1.0, -0.5, 0.0, 0.5, 1.0, 1.5, 2.0}

Often, the knot values are normalized to the range between 0 and 1, as in

{0.0, 0.2, 0.4, 0.6, 0.8, 1.0}

Uniform B-splines have periodic blending functions, i.e., for given value values of n and d, all blending functions have the same shape.

Each successive blending function is simply a shifted version of the previous function:

$B_{j,d}(u) = B_{j+1,d}(u + \Delta u) = B_{j+2,d}(u + 2\Delta_u)$

where Δu is the interval between adjacent knot values.

4.8.1.2 Non-uniform B-splines

When the spacing between the knot vectors varies or is not constant, then the resulting curve is called non-uniform B-spline.

For example. {0,1,3,4,7,8,9}.

4.8.1.3 Open Uniform

This class of B-splines is a cross between uniform B-splines and non-uniform B-splines sometimes it is treated as a special type of uniform B-spline, and sometimes it is considered to be in the non uniform B-spline classification. For the open, uniform B-splines, or simply open B-splines, the knot spacing is uniform except at the ends where knot values are repeated d times.

For example:

{0,0,1,2,3,3} for d = 2 and n = 3

{0,0,0,0,1,2,2,2,2} for d = 4 and n = 4

4.2.2 Effects of Multiple Control Points at Same Location

Placing two or three control points in the same place forces a portion of the curve on either side of the multiple control point to be a straight line. Geometric continuity decreased as the multiplicity increases of control points at same locations.

Increasing knot multiplicity has two effects:

First, the curve becomes broken. Secondly, the multiple knots will reduce parametric continuity from C^2 to C^1 if multiplicity is 2, from C^1 to C^0 if multiplicity is 3, and from C^0 to no continuity if multiplicity is 4.

4.9 SUMMARY

Representing or storing a curve on screen is an important feature of computer graphics. In graphics, we have different types of splines. In this chapter, we have discussed about Hermite, Bezier and B-spline curves and their properties in detail.

4.10 GLOSSARY

- When polynomial sections are fitted so that the curve passes through each control points, the resulting curve is said to interpolate the set of control points, i.e., a curve that passes through all known data points is said to fit the data.
- When curve do not pass through any control points, the resulting curve is said to be approximate.
- Non-parametric curves:
  - *Explicit:* $y = f(x)$
  - *Implicit:* $f(x,y) = 0$
- Parametric curves:

  For a 2-D curve with t as the parameter, the cartesian coordinates of a point on the curve are $x = x(t)$, $y = y(t)$. The position vector of a point on the curve is then

  $P(t) = [x(t)\ \ y(t)]$

- A Hermite spline is named after the French mathematician Charles Hermite. It is a single cubic spline piece fitted between two given points.
- There are two types of continuities between two adjacent piecewise curves:
  - Parametric Continuity denoted by C
  - Geometric Continuity denoted by G
- C^0 continuity means simply that the curves meet, two curves share a common end point without regard to the shape of the curve.
- C^1 continuity, means that the first parametric derivatives (tangent vectors) of the two connected curve segments.
- C^2 continuity means that both the first and second parametric derivations of the two curve sections are equal at the intersection.
- G^0 continuity is the same as zero-order parametric continuity, i.e., two curve sections must have the same coordinate positions at the joining point.
- G^1 continuity means that the parametric first derivatives are proportional at the intersection of two successive curve sections.
- G^2 continuity means that both the 1st and 2nd parametric derivatives of the two curve sections are proportional at their boundary under G^2 continuity, curvatures of two curve sections will match as the joining position.
- Bezier curve always passes through the first and last control point.
- Degree of the polynomial curve is one less than the total number of control points.
- First derivatives of a Bezier curve can be calculated as:

  $P'(0) = -np_0 + np_1$

  $P'(1) = -np_{n-1} + np_n$
- Closed Bezier curved can also be drawn by specifying first and last control point at the same position.
- B-spline has degree d-1 and continuity C^{d-2} over the range of u.
- Total number of knot vectors are n+d+1.
- The curve lies within the convex hull of its defining polygon and follows the shape of the defining polygon.

4.11 EXERCISE

Q1. Construct a Bezier curve of order 3 and with four control points E(1,1), F(2,2), G(3,3) and H(4,4).

Q2. Draw a Bezier curve defined by the four vertices (2, 1), (3, 2), (5, 3) and (6, 4). Pick a set of control points so that the second curve is joined smoothly with the first curve.

Q3. Write short notes on:

- Bezier Curve
- B-splines
- Hermite Curve

Q4. Differentiate between:

- Interpolation and Approximation curve
- Parametric and Geometric Continuity

Q5. What are the different properties of Bezier Curve?

Q6. What are the different properties of B-Spline Curve?

Q7. Explain different spline representations.

Q8. Draw a Bezier curve with 4 control points.

E N D

CHAPTER 5 3-D Transformations

5.1 INTRODUCTION

In 2-D computer graphics, all objects have zero thickness. 3-D is an extension to 2-D, since it takes z coordinate also with x and y coordinates. In 3-D, we use a triple to represent a point (x, y, z) instead of two, i.e., (x, y), as in 2-D. We have three axis in 3-D, i.e., x-axis, y-axis and z-axis. All three axes are normal to each other.

In 3-D transformation even, we have two points of view for describing such a change on an object. In the first point of view, either the object or picture is moved, relative to a fixed coordinate system, with the geometric transformation. In the second point of view, the object held fixed at a point, while the coordinate system is moved, relative to the object, with the use of coordinate transformation.

5.2 3-D TRANSFORMATIONS

5.2.1. Translation

A translation is applied to a point or an object by repositioning it by a distance and direction, from one coordinate location to another.

In 3-D homogenous coordinate representation, we can translate point from location P= (x,y,z) to location P′ = (x′, y′, z′) with the help of the following matrix:

$$\begin{bmatrix} x' \\ y' \\ z' \\ 1 \end{bmatrix} = \begin{bmatrix} 1 & 0 & 0 & t_x \\ 0 & 1 & 0 & t_y \\ 0 & 0 & 0 & t_z \\ 0 & 0 & 0 & 1 \end{bmatrix} * \begin{bmatrix} x \\ y \\ z \\ 1 \end{bmatrix} \quad ...(5.1)$$

$P' = T(t_x, t_y, t_z) . P$ ...(5.2)

where t_x = translation distance for coordinate x

t_y = translation distance for coordinate y

t_z = translation distance for coordinate z

$x' = x + t_x, \quad y' = y + t_y, \quad z' = z + t_z$ ...(5.3)

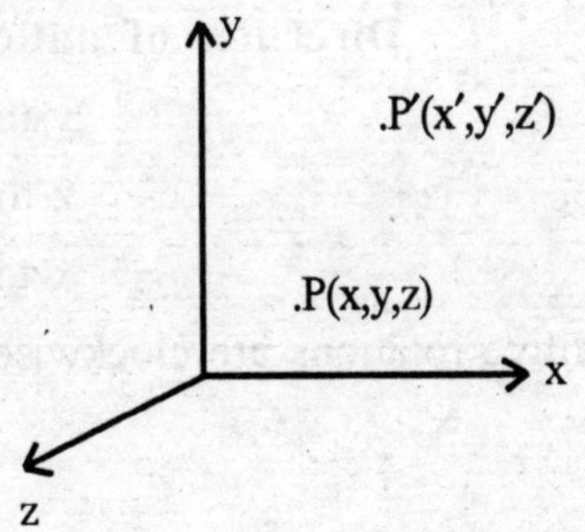

Fig. 5.1 A 3-D Translation

We can calculate the inverse of the translation matrix in equation (5.3) by negating the translation distances t_x, t_y and t_z. Now, this matrix will translate the point P in opposite direction, and the result of the product of the translation matrix and inverse is the identity matrix.

$[T] * [T]^{-1} = 1$ ...(5.4)

5.2.2 Rotation

We have already seen, that any 2-D transformation is defined by the angle of rotation and centre of rotation. But in 3-D, these two parameters are not sufficient to uniquely define rotation.

In 3-D, we have 3 different planes xy, xz and yz, in comparison to 2-D, where we have only one xy plane.

The 3-D coordinate system that we use is right-handed.

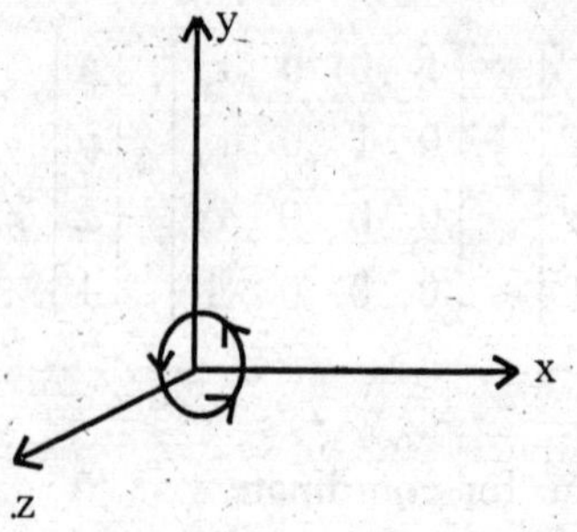

Fig. 5.2 3-D Coordinates

By convention positive rotation angles in a right-handed system produce counter-clockwise rotation such that when looking from a positive axis toward the origin, a 90° anticlockwise rotation will change one positive axis into the other. Following table from this convention:

Axis of rotation	Direction of anticlockwise rotation
x	y to z
y	z to x
z	x to y

...(5.5)

In left-handed system, positive rotations are clockwise when looking from a positive axis toward the origin.

About Z-axis

In 2-D, the rotation matrix to rotate a point P (x,y) by positive angle θ in anticlockwise direction will be:

$$\begin{bmatrix} x' \\ y' \end{bmatrix} = \begin{bmatrix} \cos\theta & -\sin\theta \\ \sin\theta & \cos\theta \end{bmatrix} * \begin{bmatrix} x \\ y \end{bmatrix} \quad ...(5.6)$$

$$x' = x \cos \theta - y \sin \theta$$

$$y' = x \sin \theta + y \cos \theta \quad ...(5.7)$$

In 3-D rotation about z-axis, z coordinate remains unchanged and both other coordinates, i.e., x and y changes after rotation in anticlockwise direction.

$$z' = z$$

$$x' = x \cos \theta - y \sin \theta$$

$$y' = x \sin \theta + y \cos \theta \quad ...(5.8)$$

In 3-D homogeneous coordinate matrix representation:

$$\begin{bmatrix} x' \\ y' \\ z' \\ 1 \end{bmatrix} = \begin{bmatrix} \cos\theta & -\sin\theta & 0 & 0 \\ \sin\theta & \cos\theta & 0 & 0 \\ 0 & 0 & 1 & 0 \\ 0 & 0 & 0 & 1 \end{bmatrix} * \begin{bmatrix} x \\ y \\ z \\ 1 \end{bmatrix}$$

$$\Rightarrow P' = R_z(\theta).P$$

About X-axis

In this, x coordinate does not change while y and z coordinates are transformed after rotation.

$x' = x$

$y' = y \cos\theta - z \sin\theta$

$z' = y \sin\theta + z \cos\theta$ ...(5.10)

In 3-D homogeneous coordinate matrix representation:

...(5.11)

$$\begin{bmatrix} x' \\ y' \\ z' \\ 1 \end{bmatrix} = \begin{bmatrix} 1 & 0 & 0 & 0 \\ 0 & \cos\theta & -\sin\theta & 0 \\ 0 & \sin\theta & \cos\theta & 0 \\ 0 & 0 & 0 & 1 \end{bmatrix} * \begin{bmatrix} x \\ y \\ z \\ 1 \end{bmatrix}$$

$\Rightarrow P' = R_x(\theta).P$ ...(5.12)

About Y-axis

In this, y-axis does not change while x and z axis changes, after rotation in anticlockwise direction.

In the use of $R_x(\theta)$ matrix with cyclic permutation of coordinate parameters, i.e., x, y and z. we replace x => y => z => x.

So $y' = y$

$z' = z \cos\theta - x \sin\theta$

$x' = z \sin\theta + x \cos\theta$ ...(5.13)

In 3-D homogeneous coordinate matrix representation:

$$\begin{bmatrix} x' \\ y' \\ z' \\ 1 \end{bmatrix} = \begin{bmatrix} \cos\theta & 0 & -\sin\theta & 0 \\ \sin\theta & 1 & \cos\theta & 0 \\ 0 & 0 & 1 & 0 \\ 0 & 0 & 0 & 1 \end{bmatrix} * \begin{bmatrix} x \\ y \\ z \\ 1 \end{bmatrix}$$ ...(5.14)

$\Rightarrow P' = R_y(\theta).P$ ...(5.15)

5.2.3 Scaling

Scaling changes the size or shape of an object scaling with respect to origin can be carried out by multiply the coordinate values (x, y, z) of each vertex of an object by scaling factors S_x, S_y and S_z respectively to produced the scaled coordinates (x′, y′, z′).

In 3-D homogeneous coordinate matrix representation:

$$\begin{bmatrix} x' \\ y' \\ z' \\ 1 \end{bmatrix} = \begin{bmatrix} S_x & 0 & 0 & 0 \\ 0 & S_y & 0 & 0 \\ 0 & 0 & S_z & 0 \\ 0 & 0 & 0 & 1 \end{bmatrix} * \begin{bmatrix} x \\ y \\ z \\ 1 \end{bmatrix} \quad ...(5.16)$$

$=> P' = S\ (S_x, S_y, S_z).\ P$ ...(5.17)

$x' = x.\ S_x, y' = y.\ S_y, z' = z.\ S_z$ ...(5.18)

5.2.4 Reflection

There are two types of reflection transformation in 3-D:

- Reflection with respect to coordinate axis
- Reflection with respect to planes

5.2.4.1. Reflection with Respect to Coordinate Axis

- **Reflection with respect to x-axis**

When we do reflection with respect to x axis, we preserve the magnitudes of all the coordinate axis, i.e., x, y and z. We only flips the signs of y and z axis.

$x' = x$

$y' = -y$

$z' = -z$

In 3-D homogeneous coordinate matrix form:

$$\begin{bmatrix} x' \\ y' \\ z' \\ 1 \end{bmatrix} = \begin{bmatrix} 1 & 0 & 0 & 0 \\ 0 & -1 & 0 & 0 \\ 0 & 0 & -1 & 0 \\ 0 & 0 & 0 & 1 \end{bmatrix} * \begin{bmatrix} x \\ y \\ z \\ 1 \end{bmatrix}$$

$=> P' = R_{ref(x)}.\ P$ ...(5.19)

- **Reflection with respect to y-axis**

When we do reflection with respect to y-axis, we preserve the magnitudes of all the coordinate axis, i.e., x, y and z. We only flips the signs of x and z axis.

$x' = -x$

$y' = y$

$z' = -z$ ...(5.20)

$$\begin{bmatrix} x' \\ y' \\ z' \\ 1 \end{bmatrix} = \begin{bmatrix} -1 & 0 & 0 & 0 \\ 0 & -1 & 0 & 0 \\ 0 & 0 & -1 & 0 \\ 0 & 0 & 0 & 1 \end{bmatrix} * \begin{bmatrix} x \\ y \\ z \\ 1 \end{bmatrix} \quad ...(5.21)$$

$$P' = R_{ref(y)} \cdot P \quad ...(5.22)$$

➲ **Reflection with respect to z-axis**

When we do reflection with respect to z-axis, we preserve the magnitudes of all the coordinate axis, i.e., x, y and z. We only flips the signs of x and y axis.

$$x' = -x$$
$$y' = -y$$
$$z' = z \quad ...(5.23)$$

$$\begin{bmatrix} x' \\ y' \\ z' \\ 1 \end{bmatrix} = \begin{bmatrix} -1 & 0 & 0 & 0 \\ 0 & -1 & 0 & 0 \\ 0 & 0 & 1 & 0 \\ 0 & 0 & 0 & 1 \end{bmatrix} * \begin{bmatrix} x \\ y \\ z \\ 1 \end{bmatrix} \quad ...(5.24)$$

$$P' = R_{ref(z)} \cdot P \quad ...(5.25)$$

5.2.4.2. Reflection with Respect to Plane

➲ **Reflection with respect to xy plane**

When we do reflection with respect to xy plane, both x and y coordinates preserve their magnitudes and sign, as well. But sign of the z coordinate gets flipped. No change in magnitude of z coordinates.

Reflection matrix would be:

$$\begin{bmatrix} 1 & 0 & 0 & 0 \\ 0 & 1 & 0 & 0 \\ 0 & 0 & -1 & 0 \\ 0 & 0 & 0 & 1 \end{bmatrix} \quad ...(5.26)$$

➲ **Reflection with respect to yz plane**

When we do reflection with respect to yz plane, both y and z coordinates preserve their magnitudes and sign, as well. But sign of the x coordinate gets flipped. No change in magnitude of y coordinates.

Reflection matrix would be:

$$\begin{bmatrix} -1 & 0 & 0 & 0 \\ 0 & 1 & 0 & 0 \\ 0 & 0 & 1 & 0 \\ 0 & 0 & 0 & 1 \end{bmatrix} \quad ...(5.26)$$

➲ **Reflection with respect to xz plane**

When we do reflection with respect to xz plane, both x and z coordinates preserve their magnitudes and sign, as well. But sign of the y coordinate gets flipped. No change in magnitude of y coordinates.

Reflection matrix would be:

$$\begin{bmatrix} 1 & 0 & 0 & 0 \\ 0 & -1 & 0 & 0 \\ 0 & 0 & 1 & 0 \\ 0 & 0 & 0 & 1 \end{bmatrix} \quad ...(5.27)$$

5.2.5 Shearing

The off-diagonal terms in the upper left 3 × 3 sub-matrix of the general 4 × 4 homogenous transformation matrix generate the effect of shear in 3-D.

$$\begin{bmatrix} x' \\ y' \\ z' \\ 1 \end{bmatrix} = \begin{bmatrix} 1 & c & e & 0 \\ a & 1 & f & 0 \\ b & d & 1 & 0 \\ 0 & 0 & 0 & 1 \end{bmatrix} * \begin{bmatrix} x \\ y \\ z \\ 1 \end{bmatrix} \quad ...(5.28)$$

$$x' = x + yc + ze$$
$$y' = ax + y + zf$$
$$z' = bx + dy + z \quad ...(5.29)$$

5.3 2-D – VIEWING

Consider a formal method of displaying view of a picture on an output device. A Cartesian coordinate system can be referred to as the *world – coordinate system*, and can be used to define the picture. For a 2-D picture, a view is selected by specifying a subarea of the total picture area. Area of the world coordinate selected to display or an area of picture selected for viewing is called a *window*. An area on the output or display device, for example, camera to which a window is mapped is called a *viewport or display*. Window is used to describe what it is to be displayed. The process of mapping a part of subarea of a world coordinate picture to device coordinates is called as a *window to viewport transformation or simply viewing transformation*. In this, we notice two types of coordinate system – *World Coordinate System (WCS)* and *Viewport Coordinate System also known as device Coordinate System*. Since we have various display devices and each has its own coordinate system. For making it simple and standardize, we introduce a concept of logical display surface. It facilitates us to transform into the required coordinate system by using same transformation. Associated to this logical display device we have the normalized device coordinate system (NDCS).

5.4 WINDOW TO VIEWPORT TRANSFORMATION

5.4.1 Viewport

(i) An area on a display device to which a window is mapped is called a viewport.

(ii) The viewport defines where it is to be displayed.

(iii) Region in the screen (device) coordinates.

(iv) It is inherent in the design of the display.

5.4.2 Window

(i) The world coordinate system for the space in which the picture is defined.

(ii) The window defines what is to be viewed.

(iii) Region in the world coordinates.

(iv) It is chosen to suit the application program.

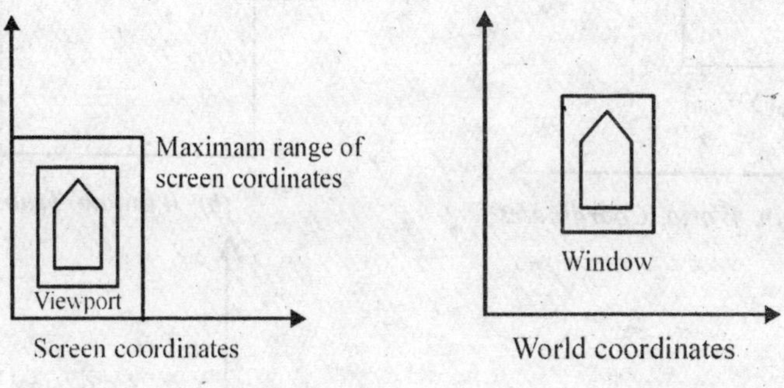

Fig. 5.3 (a) Screen Coordinates (b) World Coordinates

The mapping of a part of a world coordinate scene to device coordinates is referred to as a viewing transformation. Sometimes, the two-dimensional viewing transformation is simply referred to as the window-to-viewport transformation or the windowing transformation.

- The viewing transformation converts the picture defined in the world coordinate system into screen coordinates.
- It forms a bridge between the screen and world coordinates.

- WORLD COORDINATE SYSTEM (OBJECT SPACE) – It is a representation of some object measured in some physical units.
- WINDOW – It is a rectangle defining the part of the world we wish to display.
- SCREEN COORDINATE SYSTEM (IMAGE SPACE) – It is a space within the image is displayed.
- VIEWPORT – It is a rectangle on the raster graphic screen defining where image will appear.

5.4.3 Viewing Transformation

The process of going from a window in world coordinates to a viewport in screen coordinates consists a number of steps:

Step 1: Choose window in world coordinates.

Step 2: Clip to size of window.

Step 3: Translate to origin.

Step 4: Scale to size of viewport.

Step 5: Translate to proper position on screen.

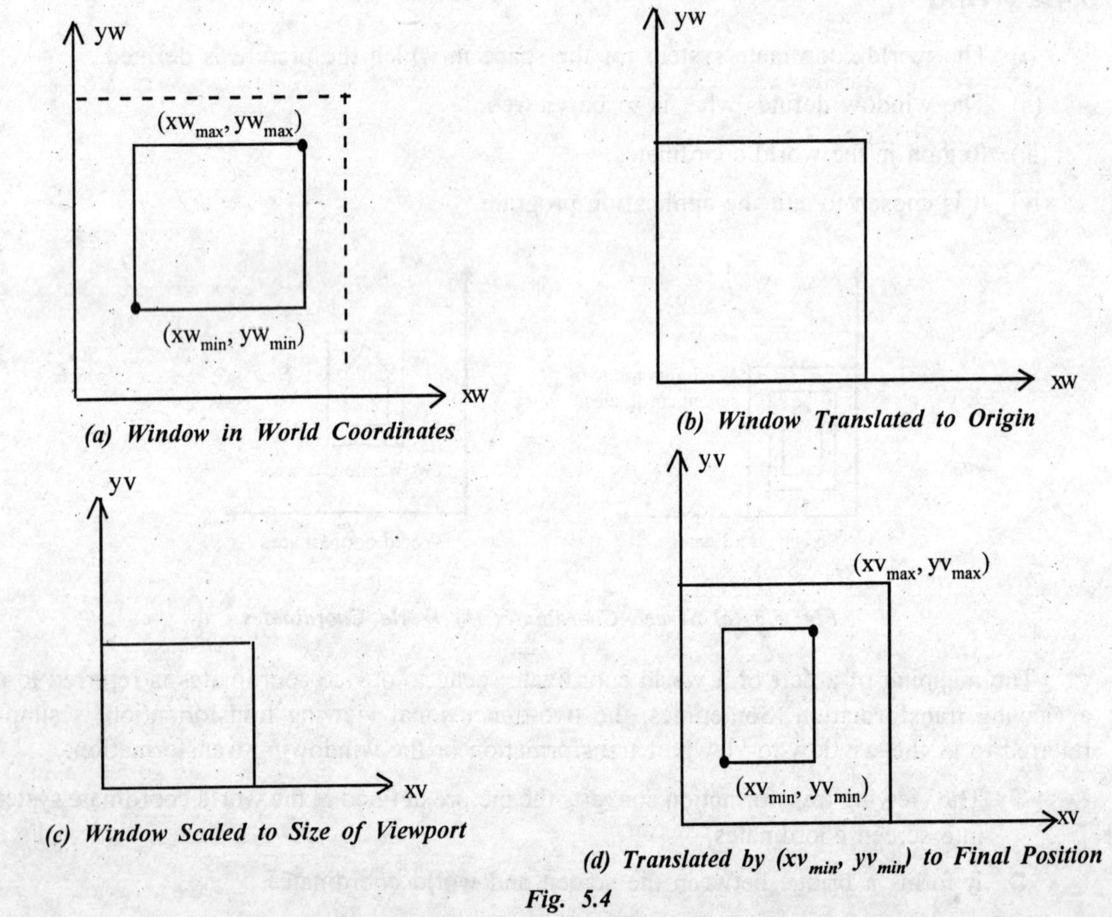

(a) Window in World Coordinates

(b) Window Translated to Origin

(c) Window Scaled to Size of Viewport

(d) Translated by (xv_{min}, yv_{min}) to Final Position

Fig. 5.4

Information outside viewport coordinates is always clipped away. Zooming is the process of reducing the window size. As window size increases, the image in viewport decreases in size, and *vice versa*. Let xw_{min} and yw_{min} and xw_{max} and yw_{max} are the lower left and upper left corners in window coordinates and xv_{min} and yv_{min} and xv_{max} and yv_{max} are viewport coordinates as shown in fig. 5.5.

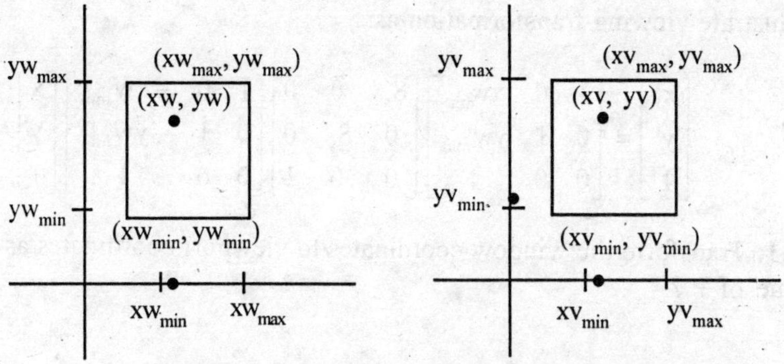

Fig. 5.5 World and Viewport Coordinates

The above figure illustrates the window-to-viewport mapping, where a point at position (xw,yw) in the window is mapped into position (xv, yv) in the associated viewport.

To maintain the same relative placement in the viewport as in the window, we require that:

$$\frac{xv - xv_{min}}{xv_{max} - xv_{min}} = \frac{xw - xw_{min}}{xw_{max} - xw_{min}} \quad ...(5.30)$$

$$\frac{yv - yv_{min}}{yv_{max} - yv_{min}} = \frac{yw - yw_{min}}{yw_{max} - yw_{min}} \quad ...(5.31)$$

Solving these expressions for the viewport position (x_v, y_v), we have:

$$xv = xv_{min} - (xw - xw_{min}).S_x \quad ...(5.32)$$

$$yv = yv_{min} - (yw - yw_{min}).S_y \quad ...(5.33)$$

Where scaling factors are:

$$S_x = \frac{xv_{max} - xv_{min}}{xw_{max} - xw_{min}}$$

and

$$S_y = \frac{yv_{max} - yv_{min}}{yw_{max} - yw_{min}} \quad ...(5.34)$$

$M_{wv} = T(xv_{min}, yv_{min})\ S(S_x, S_y).\ T(-xw_{min}, -yw_{min})$

$P' = M_{wv}\ .\ P$

Where $P' = \begin{bmatrix} x' \\ y' \\ 1 \end{bmatrix}$ and $P = \begin{bmatrix} x \\ y \\ 1 \end{bmatrix}$

Thus, we illustrate viewing transformation as:

$$\begin{bmatrix} x' \\ y' \\ 1 \end{bmatrix} = \begin{bmatrix} 1 & 0 & xv_{min} \\ 0 & 1 & yw_{min} \\ 0 & 0 & 1 \end{bmatrix} \begin{bmatrix} S_x & 0 & 0 \\ 0 & S_y & 0 \\ 0 & 0 & 1 \end{bmatrix} \begin{bmatrix} 1 & 0 & -xw_{min} \\ 0 & 1 & -yw_{min} \\ 0 & 0 & 1 \end{bmatrix} \begin{bmatrix} x \\ y \\ 1 \end{bmatrix} \quad ...(5.35)$$

Example 5.1: Transform the window coordinates to viewport coordinates as shown fig. 5.6 and find the value of P′?

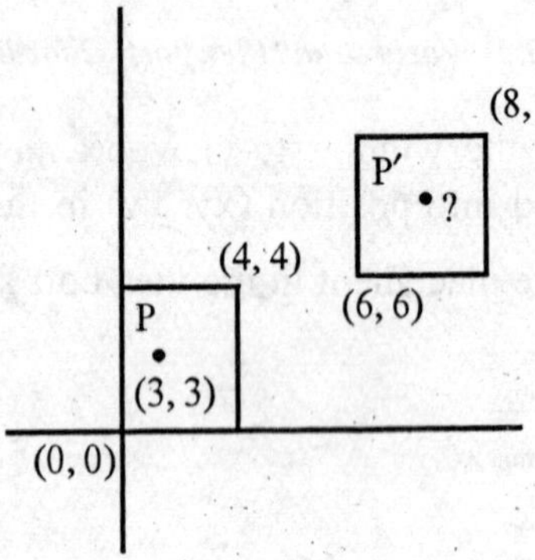

Fig. 5.6

Solution:

Here as the window is already at origin, therefore, there is no need to translate it to origin. Thus, our computation is now reduced only to two steps, namely, scaling and translate back to viewport.

Here $S_x = \dfrac{xv_{max} - xv_{min}}{yv_{max} - yv_{min}} = \dfrac{8-6}{4-0} = \dfrac{2}{4} = \dfrac{1}{2}$

$S_y = \dfrac{yw_{max} - yw_{min}}{yw_{max} - yw_{min}} = \dfrac{8-6}{4-0} = \dfrac{2}{4} = \dfrac{1}{2}$

Thus, we have:

$$\begin{bmatrix} S_x & 0 & 0 \\ 0 & S_y & 0 \\ 0 & 0 & 1 \end{bmatrix} \begin{bmatrix} 1 & 0 & xv_{min} \\ 0 & 1 & yv_{min} \\ 0 & 0 & 1 \end{bmatrix} \begin{bmatrix} x \\ y \\ 1 \end{bmatrix}$$

By substituting we get;

$$\begin{bmatrix} \frac{1}{2} & 0 & 0 \\ 0 & \frac{1}{2} & 0 \\ 0 & 0 & 1 \end{bmatrix}\begin{bmatrix} 1 & 0 & 0 \\ 0 & 1 & 6 \\ 0 & 0 & 1 \end{bmatrix}\begin{bmatrix} 3 \\ 3 \\ 1 \end{bmatrix}$$

$$\begin{bmatrix} \frac{1}{2} & 0 & 6 \\ 0 & \frac{1}{2} & 6 \\ 0 & 0 & 1 \end{bmatrix}\begin{bmatrix} 3 \\ 3 \\ 1 \end{bmatrix} = \begin{bmatrix} 7.5 \\ 7.5 \\ 1 \end{bmatrix}$$

$\Rightarrow$ P' = (7.5, 7.5)

5.5 3-D ROTATION ABOUT AN ARBITRARY AXIS

This is very much similar to 2-D rotation about an arbitrary point. The general procedure is as follows:

1. Perform transformations which align rotation axis with one of coordinate axis (x, y, z).
2. Perform rotation about the axis, to which you have aligned.
3. Perform the inverse of step 1.

Special case: The rotation axis is parallel to a principle coordinate axis. This is directly analogous to the 2-D case of rotation about a point. The steps are:

1. Translate rotation axis to coordinate axis
2. Perform rotation
3. Do inverse translation

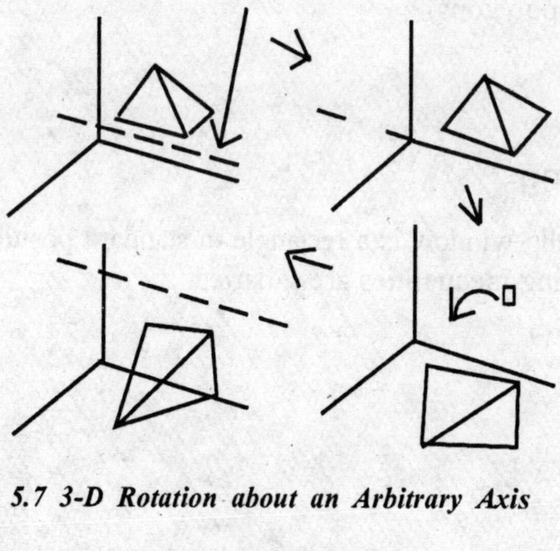

Fig 5.7 3-D Rotation about an Arbitrary Axis

5.6 CLIPPING

Any procedure that identifies those portions of a picture that are either inside or outside of a specified region of space is referred to as a *Clipping Algorithm*, or simply *Clipping*. The region against which an object is to clip is called a *Clip* Window.

Clipping, the process of extracting a portion of a database, is fundamental to several aspects of computer graphics.

Clipping provides us with a correct way to select visible information for display, i.e., a process which divides each element of the picture into its visible and invisible portions, allowing the invisible portion to be discarded.

Clipping algorithms can be implemented in hardware or software.

Following are a few applications of clipping:

- Extracting part of a defined scene for viewing.
- Identifying visible surfaces in 3-D views.
- Anti-aliasing line segments or object boundaries.
- Creating objects using solid-modeling procedures.
- Displaying a multi-window environment.
- Drawing and painting operations that allow parts of a picture to be selected for copying, moving, erasing, or duplicating.

Viewport clipping improves efficiency, as the computation dedicated to objects that appear off screen can be significantly reduced. Clipping can be applied to a variety of different types of picture element:

(a) Point clipping
(b) Line clipping (straight-line segments)
(c) Area clipping (polygons)
(d) Curve clipping
(e) Text Clipping

5.6.1 Point Clipping

Assuming that the clip window is a rectangle in standard position. We save a point P = (x, y) for display, if the following inequalities are satisfied:

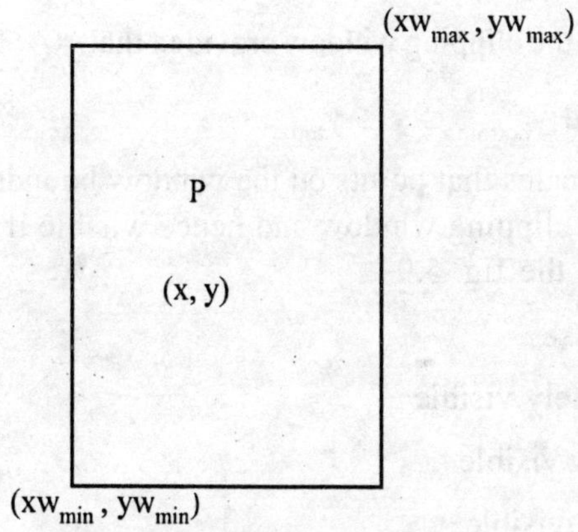

Fig. 5.8 Clipping Window

$$xw_{min}\ d \le x\ d \le xw_{max} \quad ...(5.36)$$

$$yw_{min}\ d \le y\ d \le yw_{max} \quad ...(5.37)$$

If any one of these four inequalities is not satisfied, the point is clipped (i.e., not saved for display).

Benefits and Limitations:

(i) It can be applied in viewing or device coordinates.

(ii) It works only for vertices.

(iii) It is very simple and efficient.

5.6.2 Line Clipping

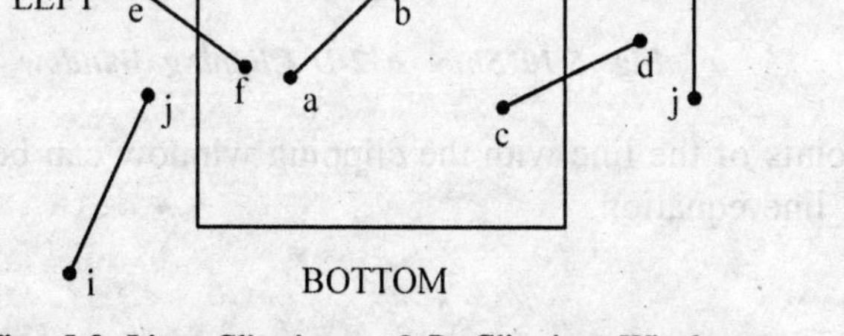

Fig. 5.9 Line Clipping – 2-D Clipping Window

The above figure shows a 2-D scene and a regular clipping window. It is defined by left (L), right (R), top (T), and bottom (B) two-dimensional edges.

Points are interior to the clipping window provided that $x_L \leq x \leq {}_R$ and $T_B \leq y \leq y_T$, i.e, ...(5.37)

$x_{left} \leq x \leq x_{right}$ and $y_{bottom} \leq y \leq y_{top}$ ...(5.38)

The equal sign indicates that points on the window boundary are included with the window. Lines are interior to the clipping window and hence, visible if both endpoints are interior to the window, e.g., line ab in the fig. 5.9.

Thus, we have:

Line ab => completely visible

Line gh => partially visible

Line kl => totally invisible

If both endpoints of a line are completely to the right of, completely to the left of, completely above, or completely below the window, then the line is completely exterior to the window and hence invisible.

5.6.3 Explicit Clipping Algorithm

In case of explicit clipping, first we need to check the type of clipping, i.e., left, right, top and bottom.

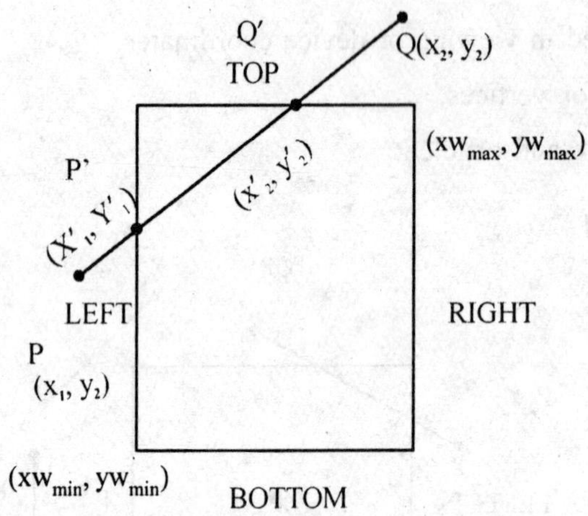

Fig. 5.10 Show a 2-D Clipping Window

Intersection points of the line with the clipping window can be calculated using the slope-intercept form of a line equation.

Let $x'_1 = xw_{min}$

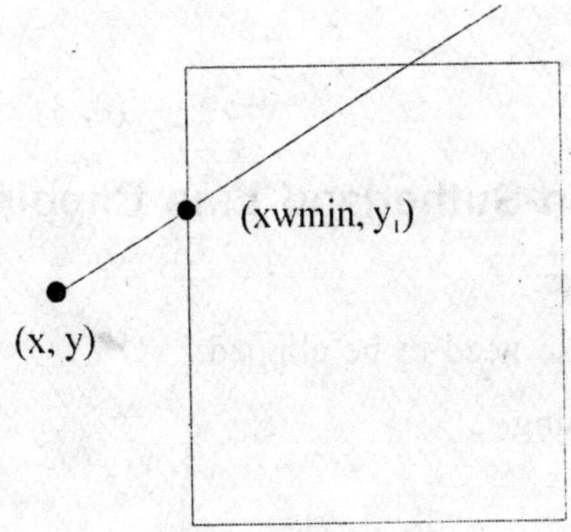

Fig. 5.11

$$\text{Slope} \quad \frac{y_1 - y}{xw_{min} - x} = m \quad \left\{ \text{Slope } m = \frac{y_2 - y_1}{x_2 - y_1} \right\} \qquad ...(5.39)$$

$$\text{Left:} \quad y_L = y + m(xw_{min} - x) \qquad ...(5.40)$$

$$\text{Right:} \quad y_R = y + m(x - xw_{max}) \qquad ...(5.41)$$

$$\text{Top:} \quad x_T = x + \frac{1}{m}(yw_{max} - y) \qquad ...(5.42)$$

$$\text{Bottom:} \quad x_B = x + \frac{1}{m}(y - yw_{min}) \qquad ...(5.43)$$

Example 5.2 To find intersection point (x, y) w.r.t. left as shown in fig. 5.12

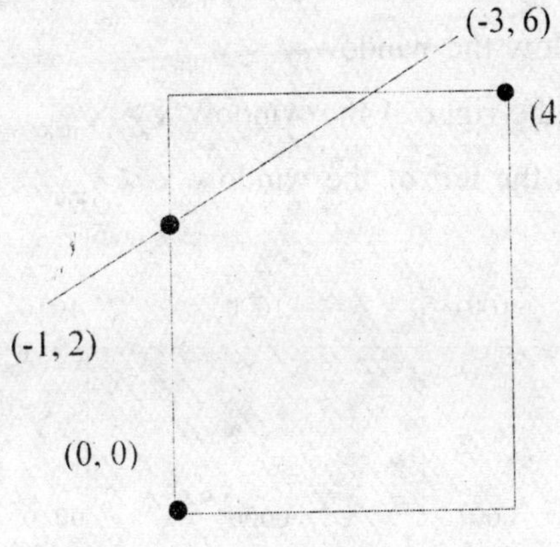

Fig. 5.12

Solution:

$$\text{Slope of the line} = \frac{6-2}{3+1} = \frac{4}{4} = 1$$

$$xw_{min} = 0 \qquad ...(5.44)$$

$x = 0$

$y_1 = 2 + 1(0-(-1))$

$= 2 + (1) = 3 \qquad \Rightarrow \qquad (0, 3)$

5.6.4 Derivation Cohen-Sutherland Line Clipping Algorithm

Algorithm has two phases:

1. Identify lines those need to be clipped.
2. Perform the clipping.

Phase 1:

To clip a line, we need to consider only its endpoints, not its infinitely many interior points.

- If both endpoints of a line lie inside the clip rectangle, the entire line lies inside the clip rectangle and can be trivially accepted.
- If both en points are outside the clip rectangle, the line may (or may not) intersect with the clip rectangle, and we need to perform further calculations to determine whether there are any intersections, and if there are, where they occur.
- If one endpoint lies inside and one outside, the line intersects the clip rectangle and we must compute the intersection point.

Method of finding the category of line:

1. Assign a 4-bit region code to each endpoint of the line.

   Bit 1: endpoint is above the window $y > y_{max}$

   Bit 2: endpoint is below the window $y < y_{min}$

   Bit 3: endpoint is to the right of the window $x > x_{max}$

   Bit 4: end point is to the left of the window $x < x_{min}$

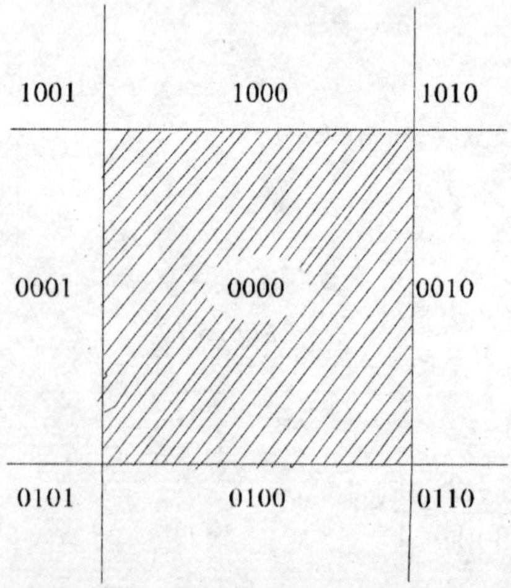

Fig. 5.13 Clipping Window with Region Codes

2. The line is visible if both region codes are 0000, not visible if the bitwise logical AND of the codes is not 0000, and a candidate for clipping if the bitwise logical AND of the region codes is 0000.

This algorithm uses a divide and conquer strategy. The line segment's endpoints are tested to see if the line is of category 1 or 2. If the line is of category 3, an intersection of the line with a window edge is determined and test is repeated. This process is continued until the line is accepted/rejected.

If bit 1 is 1, intersect with line $y = y_{max}$

If bit 2 is 1, intersect with line $y = y_{min}$

If bit 3 is 1, intersect with line $x = x_{max}$

If bit 4 is 1, intersect with line $x = x_{min}$

For a line with endpoints (x_1, y_1) and (x_2, y_2)

Intersection with a vertical boundary:

$$x_i = x_{min} \text{ or } x_{max} \quad ...(5.45)$$

$$y_i = y_1 + m(x_i - x_1) \quad ...(5.46)$$

Intersection with a horizontal boundary:

$$x_i = (y_i - y_1)/m + x_1 \quad ...(5.47)$$

$$\Rightarrow y = y_{min} \text{ or } y_{max}$$

...(5.48)

Where $m = (y_2 - y_1)/(x_2 - x_1)$ is the slope of the line. Now, we replace endpoint (x_1, y_1) with the intersection point (x_i, y_i) effectively eliminating the portion of the original line that is on the outside of the selected windows.

The Cohen-Sutherland algorithm is:

- a fast and efficient algorithm
- follows divide and conquer strategy

Example 5.3: Determine the portion of the line PQ, whose endpoints are (-1, 2) and (3, 5), that is shown in the viewport window using Cohen-Sutherland clipping.

Solution:

R-code for P = 0001

R-code for Q = 1000

And operation 0000

$\Rightarrow$ Line may pass through the window.

First, we need to find the intersection point P′.

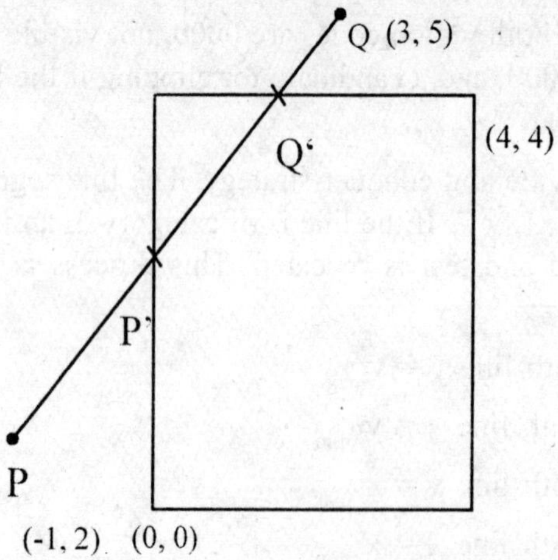

Fig. 5.14 Clipping Window with Line PQ.

which will be (x_{min}, y')

$\Rightarrow P' = (x_{min}, y')$

Here $x_{min} = 0$

We have to find y'

$$\text{Slope of line PQ} = m = \frac{y_2 - y_1}{x_2 - x_1} = \frac{5-2}{3-(-1)} = \frac{3}{4}$$

As left clipping

$\Rightarrow y' = y + m(x_{min} - x)$

By substituting the values in above equation

$$\Rightarrow y' = 2 + \frac{3}{4}(0-(-1))$$

$$= 2 + \frac{3}{4}(0-(-1)) = \frac{8+3}{4} = \frac{11}{4}$$

$\Rightarrow P' = (0, 11/4)$

Next, we determine the intersection point Q'

$Q' = (x', y_{max})$

Here $y_{max} = 4$

In case of top clipping

$$x' = x + \frac{1}{m}(y_{max} - y)$$

By substituting;

$$x' = 3 + \frac{4}{3}(4 - 5) = 3 + \frac{4}{3}(-1) = 3 - \frac{4}{3}$$

$$= \frac{9 - 4}{3} = \frac{5}{3}$$

Thus, the line will be visible from (0, 11/4) to (5/3, 4).

5.6.5 Cohen-Sutherland Algorithm

(i) Determine the outcodes of the endpoints of the line.

(ii) AND operation applied to both outcodes and result = 0000; then trivial accept.

(iii) AND operation applied to both outcodes and result ≠ 0000; then trivial reject.

(iv) For the non-trivial case, we find intersection point.

(v) Intersection with vertical boundary: $x_i = x_{min}$ or x_{max}

$y_i = y_1 + m\,(x_i - x_1)'$

(vi) Intersection with horizontal boundary: $y_i = y_{min}$ or y_{max}

$x_i = (y_i - y_1)/m + x_1$

5.6.6 C Program

```
/*PROGRAM TO CLIP A LINE USING COHEN-SUTHERLAND ALGORITHM*/
#include <stdio.h>
#include <conio.h>
#include <math.h>
#include <graphics.h>
#include <dos.h>
#include <process.h>
int pixels[2][4];
float xn1,xn2,yn1,yn2,x3,y3,m;
int xmin,ymin,xmax,ymax,x1,y1,x2,y2;
int choice,ed[20],num;
void su_co(int x1,int y1,int x2,int y2,int xmin,int ymin,int xmax,int ymax)
{
int i,j,fl;
for(i=0;i<2;i++)
```

```
for(j=0;j<4;j++)
pixels[i][j]=0;
if(y1>ymax)
pixels[0][0]=1;
if(y1<ymin)
pixels[0][1]=1;
if(x1>xmax)
pixels[0][2]=1;
if(x1<xmin)
pixels[0][3]=1;
if(y2>ymax)
pixels[1][0]=1;
if(y2<ymin)
pixels[1][1]=1;
if(x2>xmax)
pixels[1][2]=1;
if(x2<xmin)
pixels[1][3]=1;
for(j=0;j<4;j++)
{
if(pixels[0][j]==0&&pixels[1][j]==0)
continue;
if(pixels[0][j]==1&&pixels[1][j]==1)
{
fl=3;
break;
}
fl=2;
}
switch(fl)
{
case 1:
```

```
line(320+x1,240-y1,320+x2,240-y2);
break;
case 3:
printf("\n\n\a Line Is Not Visible");
break;
case 2:
m=(y2-y1)/(x2-x1);
xn1=x1;
yn1=y1;
xn2=x2;
yn2=y2;
if(pixels[0][0]==1)
{
xn1=x1+(ymax-y1)/m;
yn1=ymax;
}
if(pixels[0][1]==1)
{
xn1=x1+(ymin-y1)/m;
yn1=ymin;
}
if(pixels[0][2]==1)
{
yn1=y1+(xmax-x1)*m;
xn1=xmax;
}
if(pixels[0][3]==1)
{
yn1=y1+(xmin-x1)*m;
xn1=xmin;
}
if(pixels[1][0]==1)
```

```
{
xn2=x2+(ymax-y2)/m;
yn2=ymax;
}
if(pixels[1][1]==1)
{
xn2=x2+(ymin-y2)/m;
yn2=ymin;
}
if(pixels[1][2]==1)
{
yn2=y2+(xmax-x2)*m;
xn2=xmax;
}
if(pixels[1][3]==1)
{
yn2=y2+(xmin-x2)*m;
xn2=xmin;
}
line(320+xn1,240-yn1,320+xn2,240-yn2);
break;
}
}
void cohen()
{
clearviewport();
line(320+xmin,240-ymin,320+xmin,240-ymax);
line(320+xmin,240-ymax,320+xmax,240-ymax);
line(320+xmax,240-ymax,320+xmax,240-ymin);
line(320+xmax,240-ymin,320+xmin,240-ymin);
line (320+x1,240-y1,320+x2,240-y2);
getch();
```

```
cleardevice();
line(320+xmin,240-ymin,320+xmin,240-ymax);
line(320+xmin,240-ymax,320+xmax,240-ymax);
line(320+xmax,240-ymax,320+xmax,240-ymin);
line(320+xmax,240-ymin,320+xmin,240-ymin);
su_co(x1,y1,x2,y2,xmin,ymin,xmax,ymax);
getch();
}
void main()
{
int gd=DETECT,gm,i,j;
initgraph(&gd,&gm,"D:\\tc\\");
printf("\n\n\t\t\" Enter The Co-ordinates of the Clipping Window.");
printf("\n\n\t\t Enter X(min) & Y(min) :=");
scanf("%d %d",&xmin,&ymin);
printf("\n\t\t Enter X(max) & Y(max) :=");
scanf("%d %d",&xmax,&ymax);
printf("\n\t\t Enter The Co-ordinates of the Line.");
printf("\n\n\t\t Enter X(1) & Y(1) :=");
scanf("%d %d",&x1,&y1);
printf("\n\t\t Enter X(2) & Y(2) :=");
scanf("%d %d",&x2,&y2);
clrscr();
cohen();
}
```

Example 5.4: Determine the portion of the line PQ, whose endpoints are (-4, 3) and (2, 10), that is shown in the viewport window using Cohen-Sutherland clipping algorthim (refer fig. 5.15).

Solution:

(x_1, y_1) to (x_2, y_2)

P(-4, 3) to Q (2,10)

For P, region code is:

$x_1 < x_{min} \Rightarrow$ 1 bit = 1

$x_1 < x_{max} \Rightarrow$ 2 bit = 0

$y_1 < y_{min} \Rightarrow$ 3 bit = 0

$y_1 < y_{max} \Rightarrow$ 4 bit = 1

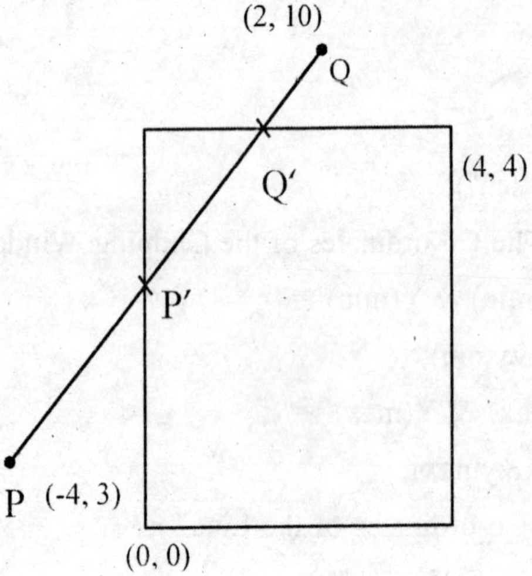

Fig. 5.15 Line PQ

$\Rightarrow$ Region code for P = 0001

For Q, region code is

$x_2 > x_{min} \Rightarrow$ 1 bit = 0

$x_2 < x_{max} \Rightarrow$ 2 bit = 0

$y_2 < y_{min} \Rightarrow$ 3 bit = 0

$y_2 > y_{max} \Rightarrow$ 4 bit = 1

Region code for Q = 1000

AND operation of the region codes = 0001 (P Region code)

AND operation of the region codes $\frac{\times 1000}{0000}$ (Q Region code)

Hence, now we proceed to find the intersection points P′ and Q′ respectively.

$P' = (x_{min}, y')$

Left clip

$y' = y + m(x_{min} - x)$ Slope $m = \frac{10-3}{2-(-4)} = \frac{7}{6}$

$= 3 + \frac{7}{6}(0-(-4))$

$= 3 + \frac{7}{6} \times 4$

$= 3 + \frac{14}{3} = \frac{9+14}{3} = \frac{23}{3}$

$\Rightarrow P' = (0, 23/3)$

$Q' = (x', y_{max})$

Here $y_{max} = 4 \Rightarrow Q' = (x', 4)$

Top clip

$\Rightarrow x' = x + \frac{1}{m}(y_{max} - y)$

$= 2 + \frac{6}{7}(4 - 10) = \frac{2 + 6 \times -6}{7} = 2\frac{-36}{7}$

$= \frac{14-36}{7} = \frac{-22}{7}$

$Q' = (-22/7, 4)$

Thus, the line is visible from (0,23/3) to (-22/7, 4).

5.6.7 Advantages of Cohen-Sutherland Line Clipping Algorithm

- Not only finds endpoints very rapidly but also rejects even more rapidly any line that is clearly invisible, even more rapidly.
- Very good algorithm for clipping pictures those are much larger than the screen.
- Inherently simply, elegant, efficient.

Example 5.5: Clip the line PQ against the window with min and max coordinates are (-1,-1) and (1,1). Refer fig. 5.16.

Solution:

$P'(x_{min}, y') \Rightarrow P'(-1, y')$

$$\text{Slope of PQ} = \left(\frac{\frac{3}{2}-\frac{1}{6}}{\frac{1}{2}-\left(\frac{-3}{2}\right)}\right) = \left(\frac{\frac{9-1}{6}}{\frac{1+3}{2}}\right) = \frac{8}{6}\times\frac{1}{2} = \frac{2}{3}$$

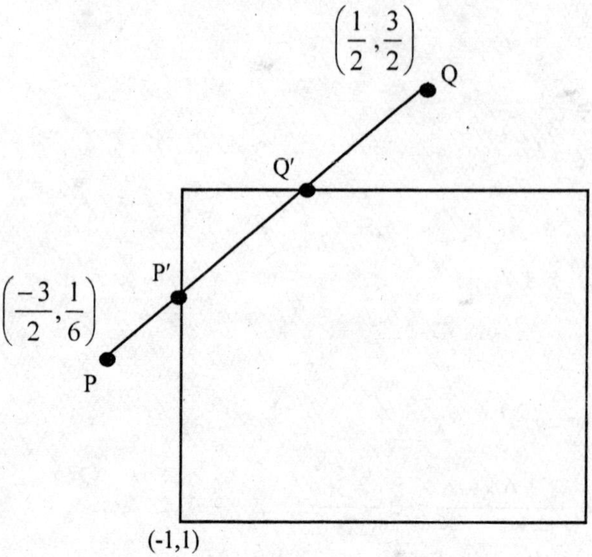

Fig. 5.16 Line PQ

Left clip:

$$y' = y + m(x_{min} - x) = \frac{1}{6} + \frac{2}{3}\left(-1+\frac{3}{2}\right)$$

$$y' = \frac{1}{6} + \frac{2}{3}\left(\frac{-2+3}{2}\right) = \frac{1}{6} + \frac{2}{3}\left(\frac{1}{2}\right)$$

$$= \frac{1}{6} + \frac{2}{3}\times\frac{1}{2} = \frac{1}{6} + \frac{1}{3} = \frac{1+2}{6} = \frac{3}{6} = \frac{1}{2}$$

$$\Rightarrow P' = \left(-1, \frac{1}{2}\right)$$

$Q' = (x', y_{max}) \Rightarrow Q' = (x', 1)$

Top clip:-

$x' = (x + 1/m(y_{max} - y))$

$$x' = \frac{1}{2} + \frac{3}{2}\left(1 - \frac{3}{2}\right) = \frac{1}{2} + \frac{3}{2}\left(\frac{2-3}{2}\right) = \frac{1}{2} - \frac{3}{2} \times \frac{1}{2}$$

$$= \frac{1}{2} - \frac{3}{4} = \frac{2-3}{4} = -\frac{1}{4}$$

$$\Rightarrow Q' = \left(\frac{-1}{4}, 1\right)$$

5.6.8 Disadvantages of Cohen-Sutherland Algorithm

1. Confined to rectangular window.
2. Requires direct calculation of the intersection of the line with the window edge. It repeatedly calculates intersections along a line path, even though the line may, i.e., completely outside the clips window and each intersection calculation requires both division and multiplication.
3. Extra calculation involved.

5.6.9 Cyrus-beck Clipping Algorithm

Cyrus-Beck algorithm is faster than Cohen-Sutherland algorithm, doesn't need to iterate. It requires the following:

- Direction of normal (n_i)
- Parametric equation of a line (P(t))
- Vertex of edges against which the clipping is tested (f_i)

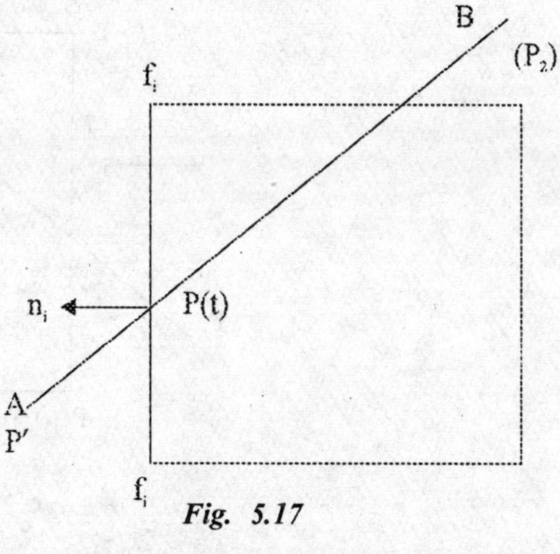

Fig. 5.17

Parametric line is useful because we are generally interested in line segment defined between the two endpoints. To find the intersection point, we need to find:

$$[P(t) - f_i].n_i = 0 \qquad ...(5.49)$$

Where n_i = outer normal, P(t) = Parametric equation of line, f_i-any vertex.

The condition that line may be visible is $0 \leq t \leq 1$

$P(t) = P_1 + (P_2 - P_1)t$ $\qquad P(t) = [x(t), y(t)]$ ...(5.50)

Entry Point $[B-A].n < 0$ $\qquad$ Leaving point $[B-A].n > 0$ ...(5.51)

$D.n < 0$ $\qquad D.n > 0$

Here D = Difference {Direction of line}

$[P(t) - f_i].n_i = 0$ ...(5.52)

$[P_1 + (P_2 - P_1)t - f_i].n_i = 0$

$[P_1 - f_i].n_i + (P_2 - P_1)t.n_i = 0$

$\Rightarrow w_i n_i + Dtn_i = 0$ ...(5.53)

where weighting function $\quad w_i = [P_1 - f_i]$ and $D = (P_2 - P_1)$

$\Rightarrow t = -w_i n_i / Dn_i$ $\qquad$ where $D \neq 0$ ...(5.54)

$D.n_i$ is zero if D = 0, which implies that $P_2 = P_1$, i.e., a point or D and n_i are perpendicular. If D and n_i are perpendicular, the line does not intersect the edge. If $P_2 = P_1$, then for

$w_i.n_i < 0$ point lies outside the region or window.

$w_i.n_i = 0$ point lies on boundary. ...(5.55)

$w_i.n_i > 0$ point lies inside the region or window.

Example 5.6: Using Cyrus-Beck algorithm, clip the line P_1, P_2 as shown in fig. 5.18

Solution:

$P_1 = (2, 2)$

$P_2 = (6, 3)$

$D = P_2 - P_1 = (4, 1)$

$t = w_i n_i / Dn_i$

$w_i = [P_1 - f_i]$

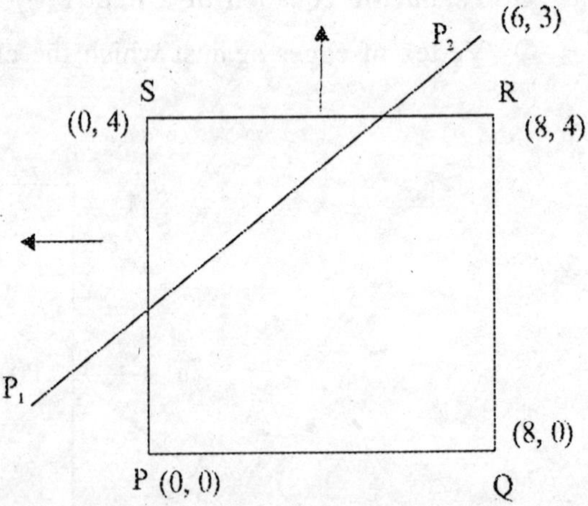

Fig. 5.18 Line P_1 P_2

Edge	n_i	f_i	w_i	$w_i.n$	D.n	t	
PQ	(0, -1)	(0, 0)	(2, 2)	-2	-1	-2	E.P.
QR	(1, 0)	(8, 4)	(-6, +2)	-6	4	+3/2	L.P.
RS	(0, 1)	(8, 4)	(-6, -2)	2	1	+2	L.P.
PS	(-1, 0)	(0, 0)	(2, 2)	-2	-4	-1/2	E.P.

Fig. 5.19

Entry Point (E.P.) with largest t value max(t) = Actual E.P.= -1/2

Leaving Point (L.P.) with smallest t value min(t) = Actual L.P. = 3/2

As E.P. < L.P. ⇒ Line lies in the window

$P(t) = P_2 + (P_2 - P_1)t$

Substituting t values in above two equations

$P(-\frac{1}{2}) = P_2 + (P_2 - P_1)(-\frac{1}{2})$, $P(3/2) = (P_2 - P_1)\ 3/2$

Cyrus-Beck Algorithm is not confined to a rectangular window; it also extends to polygons.

5.6.10 Disadvantages of Cyrus-Beck Algorithm

(i) Cannot be extended for concave polygons; only confined to convex polygons.

(ii) Direction of normal should be known.

(iii) There is no means by which we can clearly state which line is trivially rejected or accepted.

5.6.11 The Sutherland-Hodgman Polygon Clipping Algorithm

Sutherland and Hodgman polygon-clipping algorithm uses a divide-and-conquer strategy. It solves a series of simple and identical problems that, when combined solve the overall problem.

The simple problem is to clip a polygon against a single infinite clip edge. Four clip edges, each defining one boundary of the clip rectangle successively clipping a polygon against a clip rectangle.

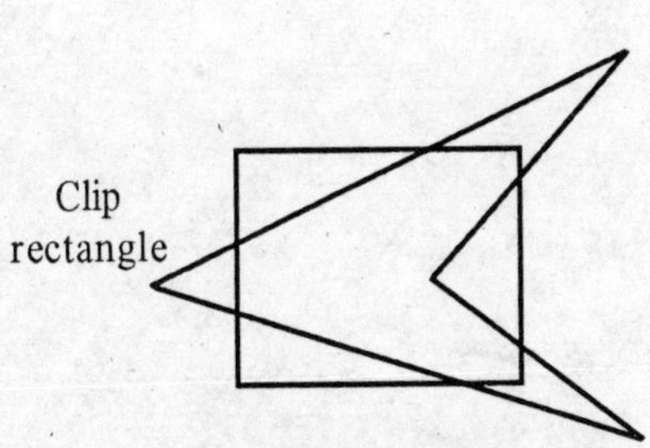

(a) Before Clipping

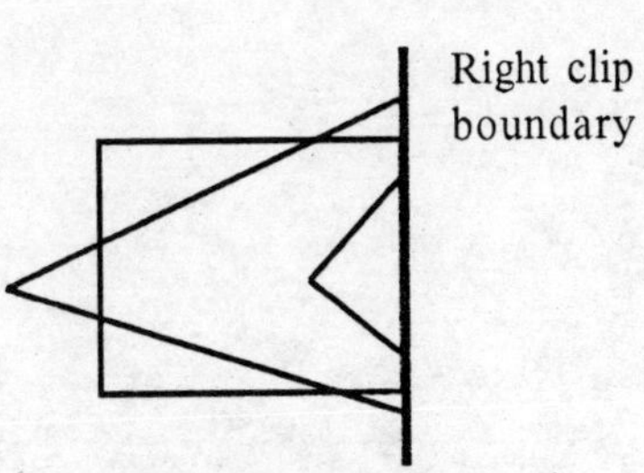

(b) Clip on right

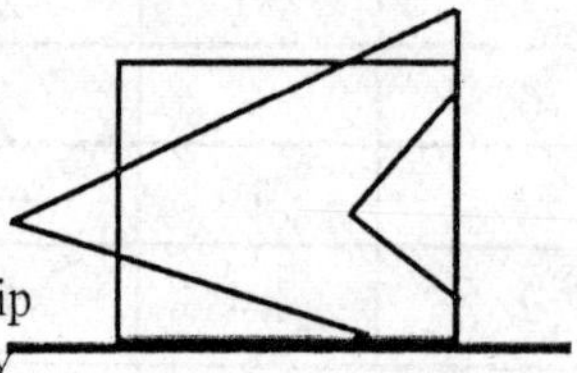

(c) Clip on bottom

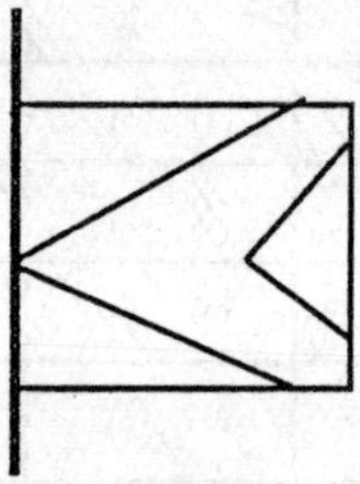

(d) Clip on left

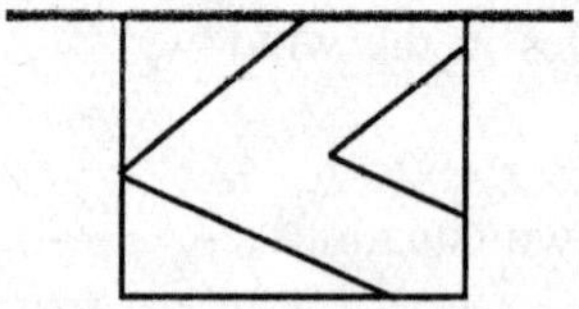

(e) Clip on top: polygon is fully clipped

Fig. 5.20 (a) to (d)

5.7 POLYGON CLIPPING

The difference between Cohen-Sutherland line clipping and this algorithm is that the polygon clipper clips against four edges in succession, whereas the line clipper test the outcode to see which edge is crossed, and clips only when necessary.

There are four possible cases when processing vertices in sequence around the perimeter of a polygon. An each pair of polygon vertices is passed to a window boundary clipper, we make the following tests:

(i) If the 1st vertex is outside the window boundary and the 2nd vertex is inside the window boundary, both the intersection point of the polygon edge with the window boundary and the 2nd vertex which is inside the window are stored to the output vertex list, i.e., R'_1 and R'_2

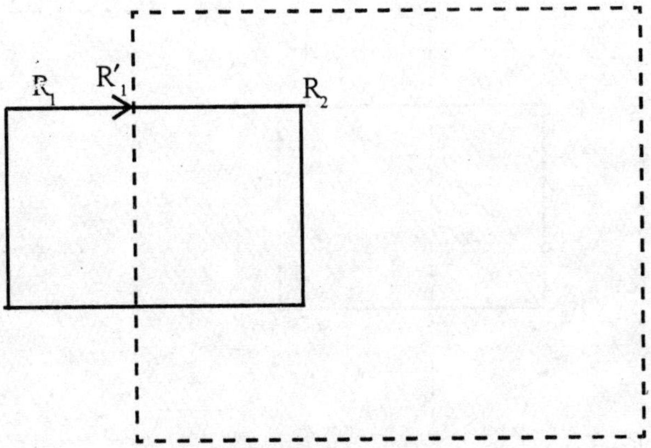

Fig. 5.21 Save R'_1 & R_2

(ii) If both input vertices, i.e., R_1 and R_2 are inside the window boundary, only the 2nd vertex is added to the output vertex list, i.e., R_2

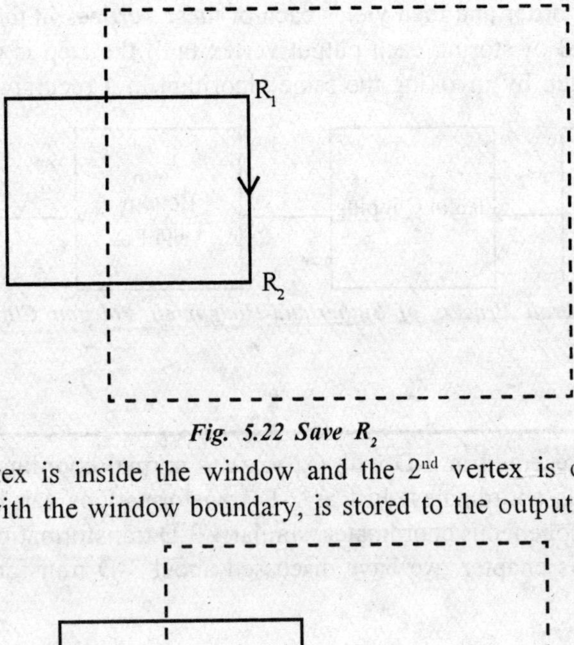

Fig. 5.22 Save R_2

(iii) If the 1st vertex is inside the window and the 2nd vertex is outside, only the edge intersection with the window boundary, is stored to the output vertex list, i.e., R'_1

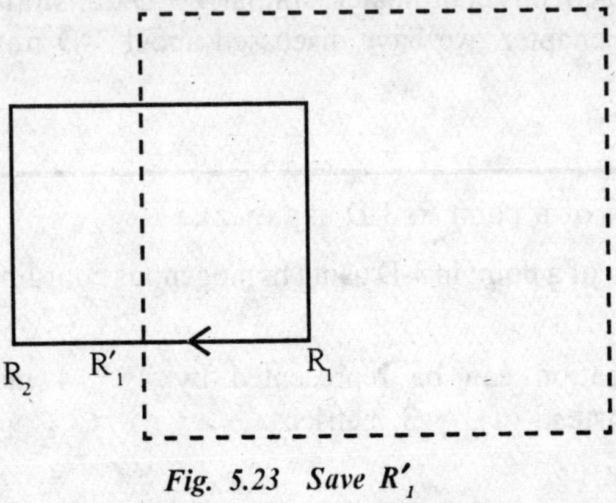

Fig. 5.23 Save R'_1

(iv) If both input vertices are outside the window boundary, nothing is stored to the output vertex list.

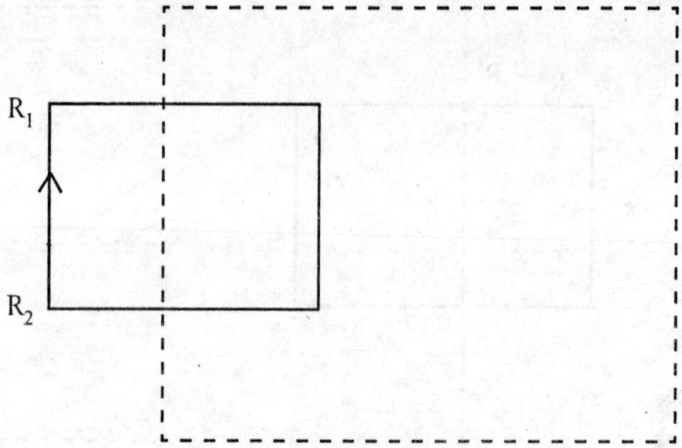

Fig. 5.24 Save NIL

It requires a large amount of storage to store intermediate polygons between steps. We can also see that such storage is unnecessary. The algorithm generates the vertices of the output polygon in sequential order and then yields each of these vertices in the same order to next step of the process. Instead of storing each output vertex until the step is complete, we can pass it directly to the next step by invoking the same algorithm in a recursive manner.

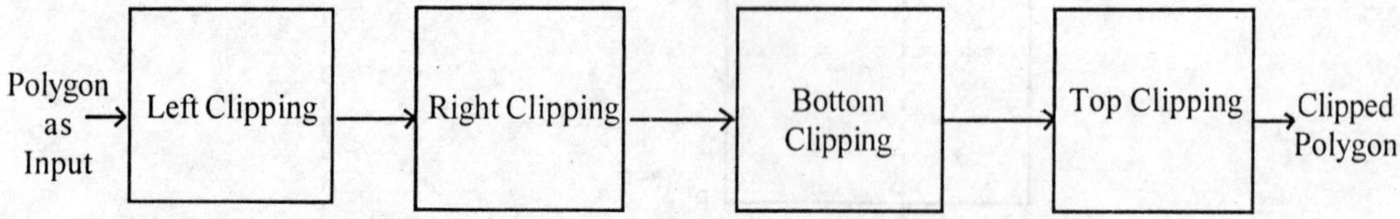

Fig. 5.25 Overall Process of Sutherland-Hodgpman Polygon Clipping Algorithm

5.8 SUMMARY

A point P is represented in 3-D with (x, y, z) as normal coordinates and with (x, y, z, h) by using homogeneous coordinates. Just as 2-D transformations can be represented by 3 × 3 matrices by using homogeneous coordinates, similarly 3-D transformations can be represented by 4 × 4 matrices. In this chapter, we have discussed about 3-D transformations.

5.9 GLOSSARY

- Representation of a point in 3-D as (x,y,z).
- Representation of a point in 3-D using homogenous coordinates (x,y,z,h) where h is equal to 1.
- 3-D transformation can be represented by 4 × 4 matrices, using homogeneous coordinates, instead of 3 × 3 metrices.

➲ 3-D Translation matrix using homogeneous coordinates:

$$\begin{bmatrix} 1 & 0 & 0 & t_x \\ 0 & 1 & 0 & t_y \\ 0 & 0 & 0 & t_z \\ 0 & 0 & 0 & 1 \end{bmatrix}$$

➲ 3-D Scaling matrix using homogeneous coordinates is:

$$\begin{bmatrix} S_x & 0 & 0 & 0 \\ 0 & S_y & 0 & 0 \\ 0 & 0 & S_z & 0 \\ 0 & 0 & 0 & 1 \end{bmatrix}$$

➲ 3-D Rotation matrices with respect to x, y and z axis are:

About x-axis

$$\begin{bmatrix} x' \\ y' \\ z' \\ 1 \end{bmatrix} = \begin{bmatrix} 1 & 0 & 0 & 0 \\ 0 & \cos\theta & -\sin\theta & 0 \\ 0 & \sin\theta & \cos\theta & 0 \\ 0 & 0 & 0 & 1 \end{bmatrix} * \begin{bmatrix} x \\ y \\ z \\ 1 \end{bmatrix}$$

$$\Rightarrow P' = R_x(\theta).P$$

About y-axis

$$\begin{bmatrix} x' \\ y' \\ z' \\ 1 \end{bmatrix} = \begin{bmatrix} \cos\theta & 0 & \sin\theta & 0 \\ 0 & 1 & 0 & 0 \\ -\sin\theta & 0 & \cos\theta & 0 \\ 0 & 0 & 0 & 1 \end{bmatrix} * \begin{bmatrix} x \\ y \\ z \\ 1 \end{bmatrix}$$

$$\Rightarrow P' = R_y(\theta).P$$

About z-axis

$$\begin{bmatrix} x' \\ y' \\ z' \\ 1 \end{bmatrix} = \begin{bmatrix} \cos\theta & 0 & -\sin\theta & 0 \\ \sin\theta & 1 & \cos\theta & 0 \\ 0 & 0 & 1 & 0 \\ 0 & 0 & 0 & 1 \end{bmatrix} * \begin{bmatrix} x \\ y \\ z \\ 1 \end{bmatrix}$$

$$\Rightarrow P' = R_z(\theta).P$$

- *Clipping*, the process of extracting a portion of a database, is fundamental to several aspects of computer graphics.
- The region against which an object is to clip is called a *Clip Window*.

5.10 EXERCISE

Q.1. Consider the effect of a translation in the x, y, z direction by -2, -4 and -6 respectively on the homogeneous coordinate positive vectors [1,6,4].

Q.2. Given a parallelogram which is unit distance of z-axis, 2 distance on x-axis and 3 distance on y-axis. What is the effect of scaling factor, $S_x = ½$, $S_y = 1/3$ and $S_z = 1$?

Q.3. Perform reflection of a unit cube about the xy plane.

Q.4. Prove that the multiplication of 3-D transformation metrices for each of the following sequence of operation is commutative.

a. Any 2 successive translations.

b. Any 2 successive scaling operations.

c. Any 2 successive rotations with respect to any of the coordinate axis.

Q.5. Use Cohen-Sutherland algorithm to clip line P_1(70, 20) and P_2(100, 10) against a window lower left-hand corner (50, 10) and upper right-hand corner (80, 40).

Q.6. Perform a 45^0 rotation of triangle A(0,0), B(2,1), C(3,3,)

(a) about the origin and

(b) about point (-1, -1)

Q7. The coordinates of a clipping window are A(20, 20), B(60, 20), C(60, 40), D(20, 40). Using Cohen-Sutherland algorithm, find the visible portion of the line segment joining the points P(40, 80) and Q(120, 30).

Q8. Use the Cohen-Sutherland algorithm to clip line P(70,20) and Q(100,10) against a window whose lower left-hand corner (50,10) and upper right-hand corner (80,40).

Q9. Explain Cohen-Sutherland Line clipping algorithm with example.

Q10. What is Clipping? Explain briefly Sutherland-Hodgman polygon clipping in detail.

E N D

CHAPTER 6 Projection

6.1 VIEWING IN 3 DIMENSIONS

In 2-D, we specify a window and a viewport on 2-D view surface. Objects are clipped and then displayed on viewport. Extra complexity of 3-D viewing is caused in part of added dimension and fact that display devices are only 2-D. Mismatch between 3-D and 2-D is accomplished using projections which transform 3-D objects onto a 2-D plane. Thus, projectioners off the required solution.

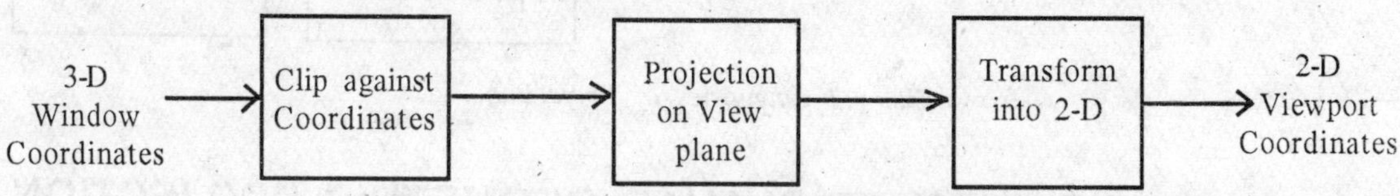

Fig. 6.1 Basic Model of the 3-D Viewing Process

6.2 PROJECTION

Projection transforms points in a coordinate of n-dimension into points in coordinate system of dimension less than n. The class of projections we deal with is known as planar geometric projections because of two reasons:

- Projection is onto a plane rather than a curved surface.
- It uses straight rather than curved projectors.

Plane geometric projections of objects are formed by the intersection of projection plane with projection rays (projectors).

Projectors are lines from an arbitrary point called the *centre of projection* (COP), passing through each point of an object.

Applications of plane geometric projections:

(i) Artists and architects to yield realistic pictures.

(ii) Basis of descriptive geometry

Applications of non-planar/non-geometric projection:

(i) Extensively used in cartography.

6.2.1 Categories of Projection

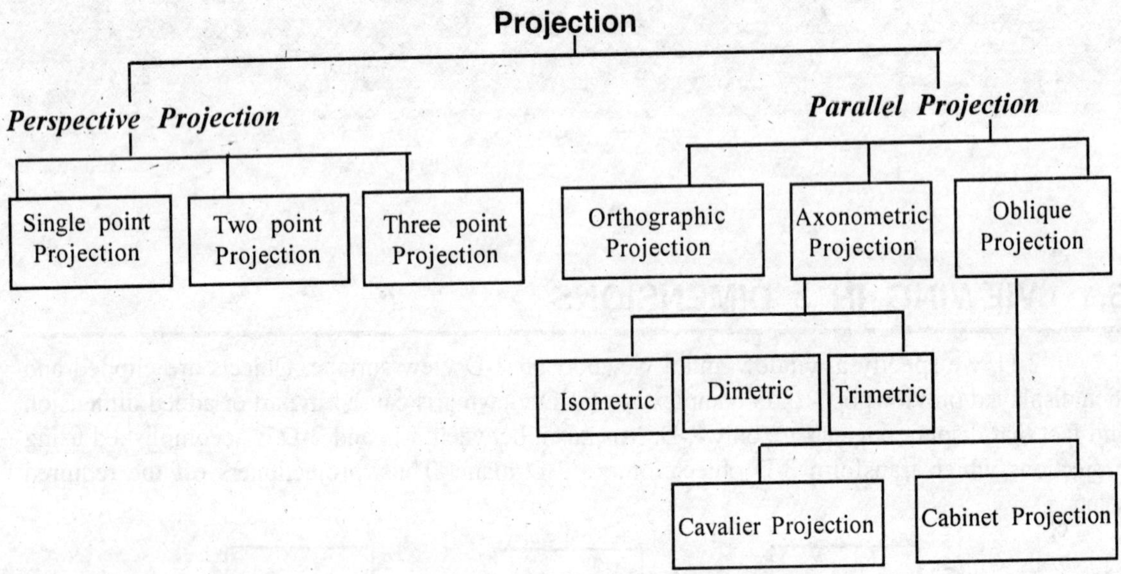

Fig. 6.2 Categories of Projection

6.3 CLASSIFICATION OF PLANAR GEOMETRIC PROJECTION

Planar geometric projections can be divided into two basic classes:

6.3.1 Perspective Projection

If center of projection (COP) is located at a finite point in three space, the result is a perspective projection. In this, objects are transformed to the view plane along the line that converges to a point, known as center of projection or projection reference point.

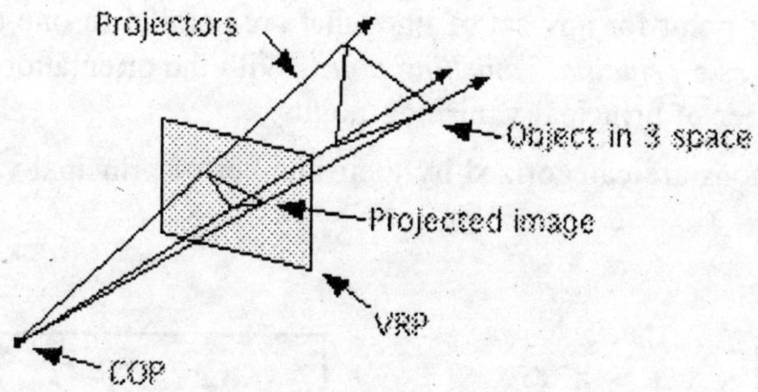

Fig. 6.3 Perspective Projection

When any of the first three elements of the 4th row of the general 4×4 homogeneous coordinate transformation matrix is non-zero, a perspective projection results

Single point perspective projection

$$\begin{bmatrix} x' \\ y' \\ z' \\ 1 \end{bmatrix} = \begin{bmatrix} 1 & 0 & 0 & 0 \\ 0 & 1 & 0 & 0 \\ 0 & 0 & 1 & 0 \\ 0 & 0 & r & 1 \end{bmatrix} * \begin{bmatrix} x \\ y \\ z \\ 1 \end{bmatrix} = \begin{bmatrix} x \\ y \\ z \\ rz+1 \end{bmatrix} \quad ...(6.1)$$

In perspective transformations:

- parallel lines converge.
- object size is reduced with increasing distance from COP.
- non-uniform foreshortening of lines in the object as a function of orientation and distance of the object from the centre of projection occurs.
- aid in depth perception of human visual system.
- shape of object is not preserved.

Have discussed that perspective projection is similar to that of photographic systems and of the human visual system and is known as *perspective foreshortening*.

- Size of perspective projection of object varies inversely with the distance of that object from COP (Center of Projection).
- It is not realistic.

Perspective foreshortening is the illusion. The illusion that certain set of parallel lines appear to meet at a point is another feature of perspective drawings. When we project a 3-D object onto a view plane using perspective transformation equations, set of parallel lines in the object that are not parallel to the plane, are projected into converging lines. Parallel lines, that are parallel to the view plane, will be projected as parallel lines. The point at which a set of projected parallel lines appear to converge is called ***vanishing points.***

A scene can have *'n'* number of vanishing points, if there are *'n'* sets of parallel lines in the scene. The vanishing point for any set of lines that are parallel to one of the principal axes of an object is known to as a *principal vanishing point*. With the orientation of projection plane, we can control the number of principal vanishing points.

Perspective projections are categorized by their number of principal vanishing points.

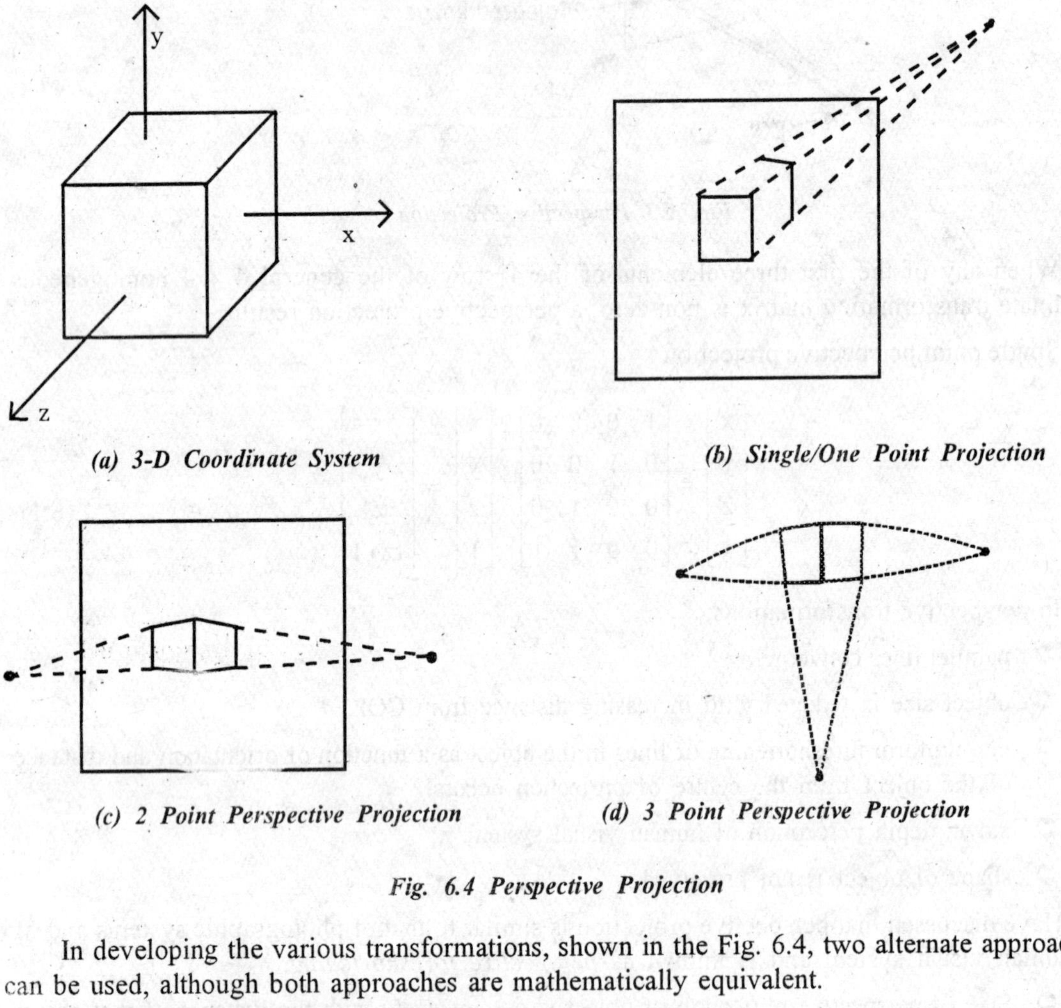

(a) 3-D Coordinate System *(b) Single/One Point Projection*

(c) 2 Point Perspective Projection *(d) 3 Point Perspective Projection*

Fig. 6.4 Perspective Projection

In developing the various transformations, shown in the Fig. 6.4, two alternate approaches can be used, although both approaches are mathematically equivalent.

(i) Assume, COP = Eye = fixed ...(6.2)

Plane of projection per to viewing direction.

The object is manipulated to get any required view.

Example: Human observer, asked to describe an object, he picks it up, rotates and translates it in order to view all sides and aspects of the object, i.e., COP is fixed and object manipulated, eg, book.

(ii) Assume, object = fixed ...(6.3)

COP is free to move anywhere in three space plane of projection is not necessarily 1 to the viewing direction.

Example: Human observer when asked to describe a large object, e.g., an automobile. The observer walks around the object to view the various sides, climbs up on a ladder to view the top, kneels down to look at bottom, i.e., object fixed and COP and eye point moves.

While generating the perspective project of an object on a view plane, the lines that are not parallel to the view plane converge on a vanishing point. Based on number of vanishing points the perspective projection can be divided into following three categories:

6.3.1.1 Single/One Point Projection

When two principal axis of object are parallel to view plane, there is only one vanishing point, since only one axis is not parallel to the view plane. In this type generally z-axis is not parallel so the vanishing point is called z-vanishing point. There are different types of one point perspective projection.

When COP is located at x-axis, it is given by:

$$\begin{bmatrix} x' \\ y' \\ z' \\ 1 \end{bmatrix} = \begin{bmatrix} 1 & 0 & 0 & 0 \\ 0 & 1 & 0 & 0 \\ 0 & 0 & 1 & 0 \\ a & 0 & 0 & 1 \end{bmatrix} * \begin{bmatrix} x \\ y \\ z \\ 1 \end{bmatrix} = \begin{bmatrix} x \\ y \\ z \\ ax+1 \end{bmatrix} \quad ...(6.4)$$

Since ax +1 ! = 1, then

$$\begin{bmatrix} x/(ax+1) \\ y/(ax+1) \\ z/(ax+1) \\ 1 \end{bmatrix} \quad ...(6.5)$$

It has COP at $\begin{bmatrix} -1/a \\ 0 \\ 0 \\ 1 \end{bmatrix}$ and a vanishing point is located on x-axis is at $\begin{bmatrix} 1/a \\ 0 \\ 0 \\ 1 \end{bmatrix}$.

When COP is located at y-axis, it is given by:

$$\begin{bmatrix} x' \\ y' \\ z' \\ 1 \end{bmatrix} = \begin{bmatrix} 1 & 0 & 0 & 0 \\ 0 & 1 & 0 & 0 \\ 0 & 0 & 1 & 0 \\ 0 & b & 0 & 1 \end{bmatrix} * \begin{bmatrix} x \\ y \\ z \\ 1 \end{bmatrix}$$

$$= \begin{bmatrix} x \\ y \\ z \\ by+1 \end{bmatrix} \quad ...(6.6)$$

Since, by +1 !=1, then

$$\begin{bmatrix} x/(by+1) \\ y/(by+1) \\ z/(by+1) \\ 1 \end{bmatrix} \qquad ...(6.7)$$

It has COP at $\begin{bmatrix} 0 \\ -1/b \\ 0 \\ 1 \end{bmatrix}$ and a vanishing point is located on y-axis is at $\begin{bmatrix} 0 \\ 1/b \\ 0 \\ 1 \end{bmatrix}$.

When COP is located at z-axis, it is given by:

$$\begin{bmatrix} x' \\ y' \\ z' \\ 1 \end{bmatrix} = \begin{bmatrix} 1 & 0 & 0 & 0 \\ 0 & 1 & 0 & 0 \\ 0 & 0 & 1 & 0 \\ 0 & 0 & c & 1 \end{bmatrix} * \begin{bmatrix} x \\ y \\ z \\ 1 \end{bmatrix} \qquad ...(6.8)$$

$$\begin{bmatrix} x \\ y \\ z \\ cz+1 \end{bmatrix} \qquad ...(6.9)$$

Since, cz +1 !=1, then

$$\begin{bmatrix} x/(cz+1) \\ y/(cz+1) \\ z/(cz+1) \\ 1 \end{bmatrix} \qquad ...(6.10)$$

It has COP at $\begin{bmatrix} 0 \\ 0 \\ -1/c \\ 0 \end{bmatrix}$ and a vanishing point is located on y-axis is at $\begin{bmatrix} 0 \\ 0 \\ 1/c \\ 0 \end{bmatrix}$.

6.3.1.2 Two Point Perspective Projection

When one principal axis of object are parallel to view plane then, there are two vanishing points, since two axis are not parallel to the view plane. In this generally z-axis and x-axis are not parallel, so there are two vanishing points, the z-vanishing point and x-vanishing point.

$$\begin{bmatrix} x' \\ y' \\ z' \\ 1 \end{bmatrix} = \begin{bmatrix} 1 & 0 & 0 & 0 \\ 0 & 1 & 0 & 0 \\ 0 & 0 & 1 & 0 \\ a & 0 & c & 1 \end{bmatrix} * \begin{bmatrix} x \\ y \\ z \\ 1 \end{bmatrix} \quad ...(6.11)$$

$$\begin{bmatrix} x \\ y \\ z \\ ax+cz+1 \end{bmatrix} \quad ...(6.12)$$

Since, ax + cz +1 !=1, then

$$\begin{bmatrix} x/(ax+cz+1) \\ y/(ax+cz+1) \\ z/(ax+cz+1) \\ 1 \end{bmatrix} \quad ...(6.13)$$

Two point perspective used in architectural, engineering, industrial design and advertising design. There are two methods of determining vanishing points:

- One, intersection of transformed lines to find vanishing points.
- Second, numerically, more accurate but more complex.

Two point perspective projection can also be obtained by concatenation of two single point perspective transformation.

6.3.1.3 Three Point Perspective Projection

When no principal axis of object is parallel to view plane, there are three vanishing points, i.e., z-vanishing point, x-vanishing point, y-vanishing point. This type of project is of not much use in real life. It is mostly used to reconstruct the shape of a 3-D object. Matrix representation of three point perspective projection:

$$\begin{bmatrix} x' \\ y' \\ z' \\ 1 \end{bmatrix} = \begin{bmatrix} 1 & 0 & 0 & 0 \\ 0 & 1 & 0 & 0 \\ 0 & 0 & 1 & 0 \\ a & b & c & 1 \end{bmatrix} * \begin{bmatrix} x \\ y \\ z \\ 1 \end{bmatrix} \quad ...(6.14)$$

$$\begin{bmatrix} x \\ y \\ z \\ ax+by+cz+1 \end{bmatrix} \quad ...(6.15)$$

Since, ax + by + cz + 1!=1, then

$$\begin{bmatrix} x/(ax+by+cz+1) \\ Y/(ax+by+cz+1) \\ z/(ax+by+cz+1) \\ 1 \end{bmatrix} \quad ...(6.16)$$

Three point perspective projections can also be obtained by concatenation of three single point perspective transformations.

6.3.2 Parallel Projection

In parallel projection, coordinate positions are transformed to the view plane along parallel lines. If centre of projection is located at infinity, all projectors are parallel and the result is parallel projection.

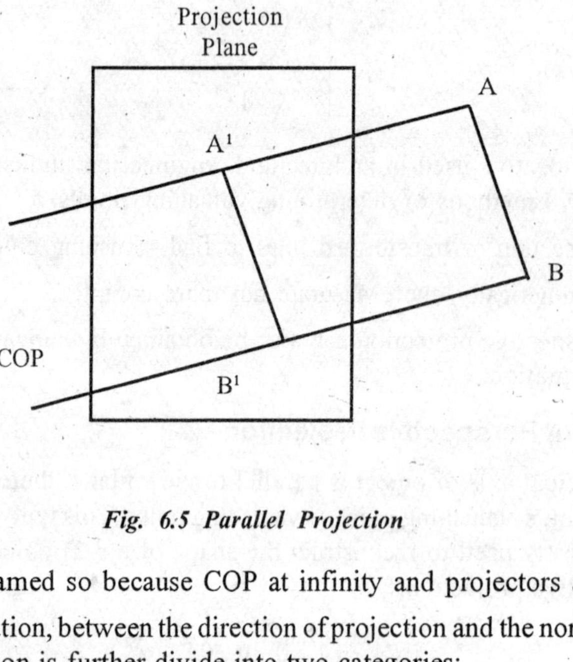

Fig. 6.5 Parallel Projection

Parallel projection named so because COP at infinity and projectors are parallel.

Depending on the relation, between the direction of projection and the normal to the projection plane, the parallel projection is further divide into two categories:

6.3.2.1 Orthographic Parallel Projection

In orthographic parallel projection, the direction of projection and the normal to the projection plane are in same direction or reverse and hence exact size and shape of a single plane face of an object is obtained. In orthographic projection, length of line segments which are parallel to projection plane does not change. Length of other lines gets reduced. It is the projection on one of the coordinate planes i.e. x=0, y=0, z=0. This type of projection based on relation between the direction of projection and the normal to the projection plane, categorized into four types:

***(a) Side Elevation*:** When x-axis of object is perpendicular to projection plane, it is said to be side elevation, i.e., x = 0. The matrix representation for projection onto x = 0 plane is

$$P_{orth(x)} = \begin{bmatrix} 0 & 0 & 0 & 0 \\ 0 & 1 & 0 & 0 \\ 0 & 0 & 1 & 0 \\ 0 & 0 & 0 & 1 \end{bmatrix} \quad ...(6.17)$$

In the above matrix, x-column is set to zero. The effect of this would be that the x coordinate will set to zero.

(b) Top Elevation: When y-axis is perpendicular to projection plane, it is said to be Top Elevation. The matrix representation for projection onto y = 0 plane is

$$P_{orth(y)} = \begin{bmatrix} 1 & 0 & 0 & 0 \\ 0 & 1 & 0 & 0 \\ 0 & 0 & 1 & 0 \\ 0 & 0 & 0 & 1 \end{bmatrix} \quad ...(6.18)$$

(c) Front Elevation: When z-axis is object is perpendicular to projection plane, it is said to be front elevation. The matrix representation for projection onto z = 0 plane is

$$P_{orth(z)} = \begin{bmatrix} 1 & 0 & 0 & 0 \\ 0 & 1 & 0 & 0 \\ 0 & 0 & 0 & 0 \\ 0 & 0 & 0 & 1 \end{bmatrix} \quad ...(6.19)$$

6.3.2.2 Axonometric Parallel Projection

When none of the principal axis of object is perpendicular to projection plane, then it is said to be axonometric orthographic parallel projection. It is divided into three categories:

(i) Isometric: When all principal axis of object makes equal angles with projection plane, then it is said to be isometric parallel projection.

(ii) Dimetric: When two principal axis of object makes equal angles with projection plane, then it is said to be dimetric parallel projection.

(iii) Trimetric: When none of principal axis of object makes equal angles with projection plane, then it is said to be trimetric parallel projection.

Example 6.1: Write down the coordinates of a unit cube in orthographic projection about x=0, y = 0 and z = 0.

Solution: Coordinates of the unit cube in matrix representation as per the figure.

$$M_{cube} = \begin{matrix} P \\ Q \\ R \\ S \\ T \\ U \\ V \\ W \end{matrix} \begin{bmatrix} 0 & 0 & 1 & 1 \\ 1 & 0 & 1 & 1 \\ 1 & 1 & 1 & 1 \\ 0 & 1 & 1 & 1 \\ 0 & 0 & 0 & 1 \\ 1 & 0 & 0 & 1 \\ 1 & 1 & 0 & 1 \\ 0 & 1 & 0 & 1 \end{bmatrix}$$

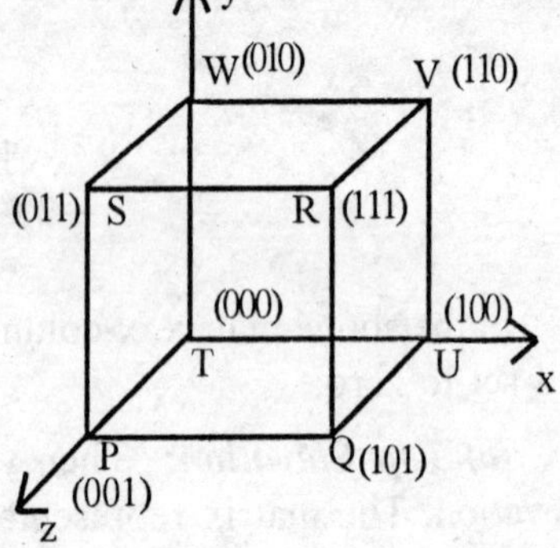

According to the equation 6.17, the matrix represesentaion for projection onto x = 0 plane is:

$$P_{orth\,(x)} = \begin{bmatrix} 0 & 0 & 0 & 0 \\ 0 & 1 & 0 & 0 \\ 0 & 0 & 1 & 0 \\ 0 & 0 & 0 & 1 \end{bmatrix}$$

then the projection would be:

$$M_{cube} \cdot P_{orth(x)} = \begin{bmatrix} 0 & 0 & 1 & 1 \\ 1 & 0 & 1 & 1 \\ 1 & 1 & 1 & 1 \\ 0 & 1 & 1 & 1 \\ 0 & 0 & 0 & 1 \\ 1 & 0 & 0 & 1 \\ 1 & 1 & 0 & 1 \\ 0 & 1 & 0 & 1 \end{bmatrix} \cdot \begin{bmatrix} 0 & 0 & 0 & 0 \\ 0 & 1 & 0 & 0 \\ 0 & 0 & 1 & 0 \\ 0 & 0 & 0 & 1 \end{bmatrix} = \begin{bmatrix} 0 & 0 & 1 & 1 \\ 0 & 0 & 1 & 1 \\ 0 & 1 & 1 & 1 \\ 0 & 1 & 1 & 1 \\ 0 & 0 & 0 & 1 \\ 0 & 0 & 0 & 1 \\ 0 & 1 & 0 & 1 \\ 0 & 1 & 0 & 1 \end{bmatrix}$$

Similarly, according to equation 6.18 and 6.19 for projection onto y = 0 and z = 0 plane is

$$P_{orth(y)} = \begin{bmatrix} 1 & 0 & 0 & 0 \\ 0 & 0 & 0 & 0 \\ 0 & 0 & 1 & 0 \\ 0 & 0 & 0 & 1 \end{bmatrix}$$

Projection onto y = 0 plane would be:

$$M_{cube} \cdot P_{orth(y)} = \begin{bmatrix} 0 & 0 & 1 & 1 \\ 1 & 0 & 1 & 1 \\ 1 & 1 & 1 & 1 \\ 0 & 1 & 1 & 1 \\ 0 & 0 & 0 & 1 \\ 1 & 0 & 0 & 1 \\ 1 & 1 & 0 & 1 \\ 0 & 1 & 0 & 1 \end{bmatrix} \cdot \begin{bmatrix} 1 & 0 & 0 & 0 \\ 0 & 0 & 0 & 0 \\ 0 & 0 & 1 & 0 \\ 0 & 0 & 0 & 1 \end{bmatrix} = \begin{bmatrix} 0 & 0 & 1 & 1 \\ 1 & 0 & 1 & 1 \\ 1 & 0 & 1 & 1 \\ 0 & 0 & 1 & 1 \\ 0 & 0 & 0 & 1 \\ 1 & 0 & 0 & 1 \\ 1 & 0 & 0 & 1 \\ 0 & 0 & 0 & 1 \end{bmatrix}$$

Similarly,

$$P_{orth(z)} = \begin{bmatrix} 1 & 0 & 0 & 0 \\ 0 & 1 & 0 & 0 \\ 0 & 0 & 0 & 0 \\ 0 & 0 & 0 & 1 \end{bmatrix}$$

Projection onto z = 0 plane would be:

$$M_{cube} \cdot P_{orth(z)} = \begin{bmatrix} 0 & 0 & 1 & 1 \\ 1 & 0 & 1 & 1 \\ 1 & 1 & 1 & 1 \\ 0 & 1 & 1 & 1 \\ 0 & 0 & 0 & 1 \\ 1 & 0 & 0 & 1 \\ 1 & 1 & 0 & 1 \\ 0 & 1 & 0 & 1 \end{bmatrix} \cdot \begin{bmatrix} 1 & 0 & 0 & 0 \\ 0 & 1 & 0 & 0 \\ 0 & 0 & 0 & 0 \\ 0 & 0 & 0 & 1 \end{bmatrix} = \begin{bmatrix} 0 & 0 & 0 & 1 \\ 1 & 0 & 0 & 1 \\ 1 & 1 & 0 & 1 \\ 0 & 1 & 0 & 1 \\ 0 & 0 & 0 & 1 \\ 1 & 0 & 0 & 1 \\ 1 & 1 & 0 & 1 \\ 0 & 1 & 0 & 1 \end{bmatrix}$$

6.3.2.3 Oblique Parallel Projection

When the direction of projection and normal to view plane, are not in same direction or reverse, or we can say, when the angle between the direction of projection and the normal to the projection plane is not equal to 90°. Thus, projection and projection plane are not perpendicular to each other. For example, projection is seen in the form of shadow of any object due to sunlight. Thus, we use this type of projection to display shadows of the object, not the original object.

The most common Oblique Projections are:

1. Cavalier Projection
2. Cabinet Projection

1. **Cavalier:** This type of project is generated at 45^0 angle between the direction of projection and normal to projection plane, the special property of cavalier projection is that length of all principal axis of object are preserved and hence are very useful in Computer Aided Design (CAD).

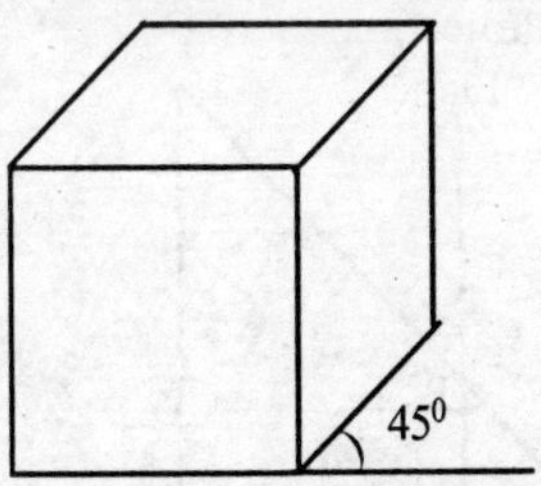

Fig. 6.6 Cavalier Projection

2. **Cabinet:** This is similar to cavalier projection only difference is that z-axis of object is printed with half of its length, or we can say, the foreshortening factor for edge perpendicular to the projection plane, makes the view more realistic.

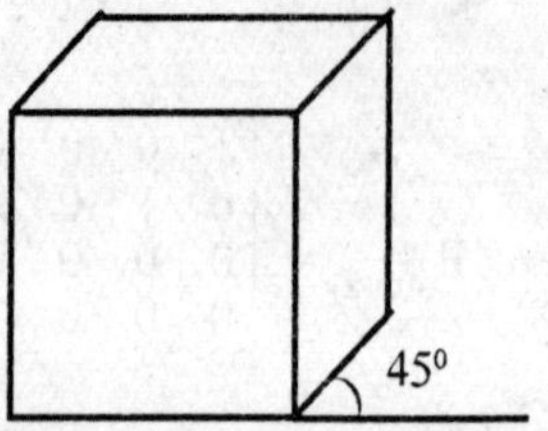

Fig. 6.7 Cabinet Projection

6.4 MATHEMATICS OF PLANAR GEOMETRIC PROJECTION

To transform points in 3-D into 2-D we need 4 × 4 matrix just like other transformations (translation, scaling etc.). There are following 2 ways of deriving this matrix.

6.4.1 When COP is at origin

In this case, we presume that the COP is at origin and view plane (projection plane) is at d distance from the origin on the z-axis.

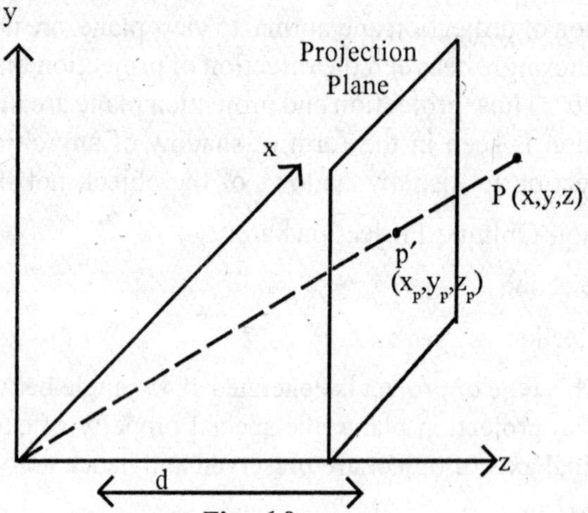

Fig. 6.8

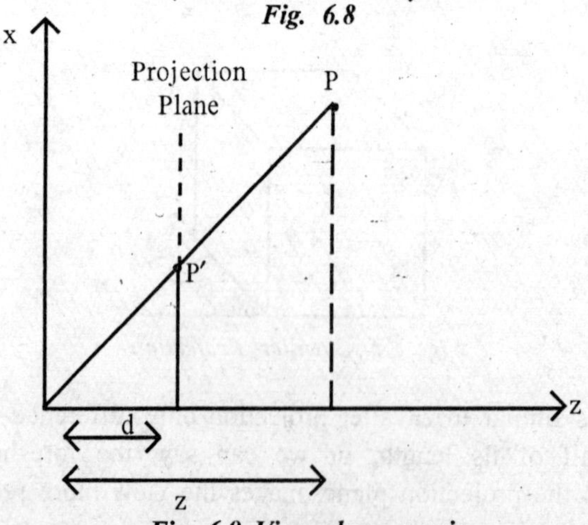

Fig. 6.9 View along y-axis

We have the point P(x,y,z) given in 3-D and its projection on view plane is $P'(x_p, y_p, z_p)$ since view plane is at 'd' distance, we have $z_p = d$. If we view along y-axis, and there are two similar triangles, and we know that ratio of two similar triangles is equal. Since, we have:

$$\frac{x_p}{d} = \frac{x}{z} \Rightarrow x_p = \frac{x.d}{z} \Rightarrow x_p = \frac{x}{\left(z/d\right)} \qquad ...(6.20)$$

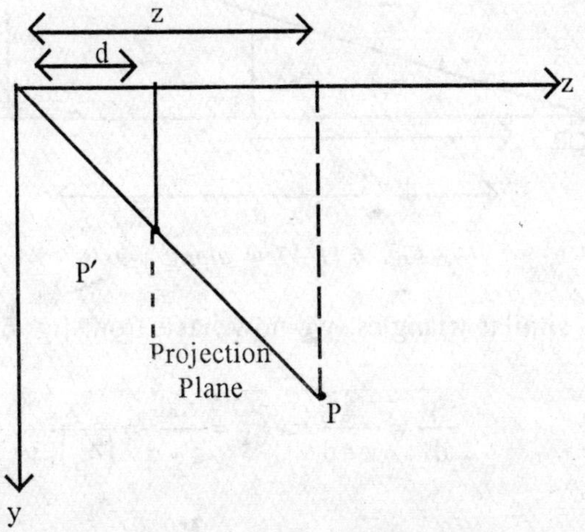

Fig. 6.10 View along x-axis

Similarly, we can calculate y_p:

$$\frac{y_p}{d} = \frac{y}{z} \Rightarrow y_p = \frac{y.d}{z} \Rightarrow y_p = \frac{y}{\left(z/d\right)} \qquad ...(6.21)$$

It can be represented using homogeneous coordinates as:

$$\begin{bmatrix} x' \\ y' \\ z' \\ w \end{bmatrix} \Rightarrow \begin{bmatrix} x_p \\ y_p \\ z_p \\ w \end{bmatrix} = \begin{bmatrix} 1 & 0 & 0 & 0 \\ 0 & 1 & 0 & 1 \\ 0 & 0 & 1 & 0 \\ 0 & 0 & 1/d & 0 \end{bmatrix} \begin{bmatrix} x \\ y \\ z \\ 1 \end{bmatrix} \qquad ...(6.22)$$

$x' \Rightarrow x_p = x$

$y' \Rightarrow y_p = y$

$z' \Rightarrow z_p = z$

$w \Rightarrow w = z/d \qquad ...(6.23)$

Since in homogeneous coordinate system we always work on w=1 plane. So, we have

$$x' = \frac{x}{\left(z/d\right)}, y' = \frac{y}{\left(z/d\right)}, z' = \frac{z}{\left(z/d\right)} = d, w = 1 \qquad ...(6.24)$$

6.4.2 When Projection Plane is at Origin and COP is at d Distance

In this case, we have projection plane at origin (z=0) and COP at z = -d distance.

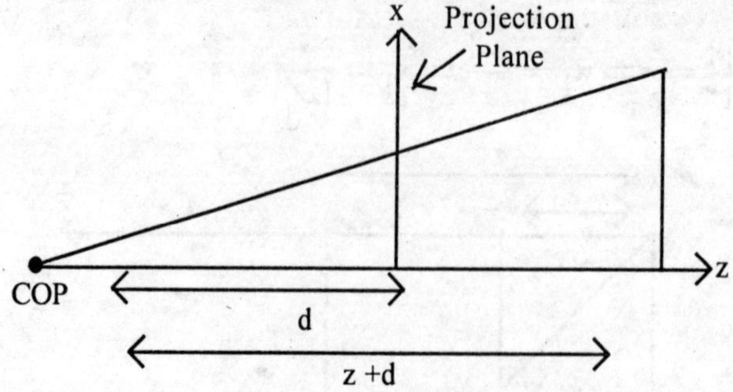

Fig. 6.11 View along y-axis

Using the ratio of similar triangles, we now have from fig. 6.11

$$\frac{x_p}{d} = \frac{x}{z+d} \Rightarrow x_p = \frac{x.d}{z+d} = \frac{x}{\left(z/d\right)+1} \quad ...(6.25)$$

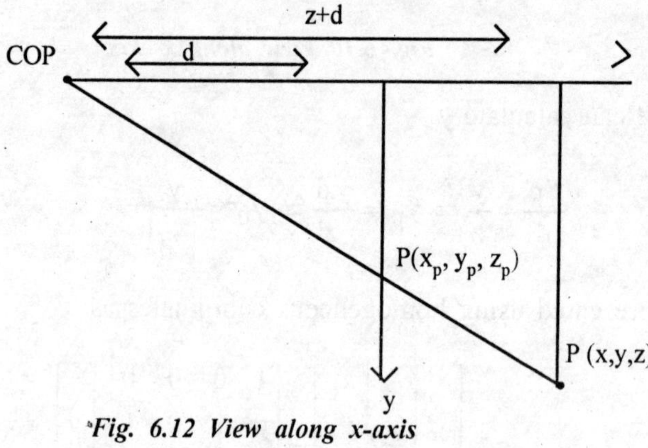

Fig. 6.12 View along x-axis

Similarly, we can calculate y_p from fig. 6.12

$$\frac{y_p}{d} = \frac{y}{z+d} \Rightarrow y_p = \frac{y.d}{z+d} = \frac{y}{\left(z/d\right)+1} \quad ...(6.26)$$

Above relationship can be rewritten in matrix from as follows:

$$M_{per} = \begin{bmatrix} 1 & 0 & 0 & 0 \\ 0 & 1 & 0 & 0 \\ 0 & 0 & 0 & 0 \\ 0 & 0 & 1/d & 1 \end{bmatrix} \quad ...(6.27)$$

Multiplying point with this matrix

$$\begin{bmatrix} x' \\ y' \\ z' \\ 1 \end{bmatrix} = \begin{bmatrix} 1 & 0 & 0 & 0 \\ 0 & 1 & 0 & 0 \\ 0 & 0 & 0 & 0 \\ 0 & 0 & 1/d & 1 \end{bmatrix} \cdot \begin{bmatrix} x \\ y \\ z \\ 1 \end{bmatrix} \quad ...(6.28)$$

We get

$x' = x$

$y' = y$

$z' = 0$

$w = (z/d) + 1$ ...(6.29)

Since in homogeneous coordinate system we always work on w = 1 plane so we have

$$x' = \frac{x}{(z/d)+1},\ y' = \frac{y}{(z/d)+1},\ z' = 0,\ w = 1 \quad ...(6.30)$$

Example 6.2: Find out perspective projection of a line $P_0(4,5,10)$ and P_1 (12,16,15) onto square screen of size 10 units which is placed at a distance 20 units from the origin of centre of sight.

Solution: In this case, we have view plane of 10 × 10 size place on 20 units from COP which is on origin (i.e. d=20), to we will refer to 6.4.1 and can use the following matrix to calculate the projection:-

$$M_{per} = \begin{bmatrix} 1 & 0 & 0 & 0 \\ 0 & 1 & 0 & 0 \\ 0 & 0 & 0 & 0 \\ 0 & 0 & 1/d & 1 \end{bmatrix} \quad ...(6.31)$$

Putting value of d and multiplying it with object matrix $P_0(4,5,10)$ and P_1 (12,16,15) arranged in columns, we get the projected points as follows:

$$\begin{matrix} P'_0 & P'_1 \end{matrix} \quad M_{per} \quad \begin{matrix} P_0 & P_1 \end{matrix}$$

$$\begin{bmatrix} 4 & 12 \\ 5 & 16 \\ 10 & 15 \\ 10/20 & 15/20 \end{bmatrix} = \begin{bmatrix} 1 & 0 & 0 & 0 \\ 0 & 1 & 0 & 0 \\ 0 & 0 & 1 & 0 \\ 0 & 0 & 1/20 & 0 \end{bmatrix} \cdot \begin{bmatrix} 4 & 12 \\ 5 & 16 \\ 10 & 15 \\ 1 & 1 \end{bmatrix} \quad ...(6.32)$$

Converting point P'_0 and P'_1 back into w=1 plane we get:

P'_0 – (4/ (10/20), 5/ (10/20), 10/ (10/20) = (8, 10, 20)

P'_1 – (12/ (15/20), 16/ (15/20), 15/ (15/20) = (16, 21.33, 20)

In this case only point P'_0 (8, 10, 20) will be projected on to screen whereas P'_1 (16, 21.33, 20) is outside the screen.

Example 6.3: Given point P_1(1, 2, 0), P_2(3, 6, 20), P_3(2, 4, 6) and view point C(0, 0, -10). Determine which points obscure others when viewed from C.

Solution: In this case, COP at 10 unit distance on negative z-axis, so we will refer section 6.4.2 and will use following matrix to calculate the projection and determine whether any point is obscuring any other point, or not:

$$M_{per} = \begin{bmatrix} 1 & 0 & 0 & 0 \\ 0 & 1 & 0 & 0 \\ 0 & 0 & 0 & 0 \\ 0 & 0 & 1/d & 1 \end{bmatrix}$$

Putting value of d and multiplying it with object matrix P_1(1, 2, 0) and P_2(3, 6, 20) and P_3 (2, 4, 6) arranged in columns, we get the projected points as follows:

$$\begin{matrix} P'_1 & P'_2 & P'_3 \end{matrix} \qquad M_{per} \qquad \begin{matrix} P_0 & P_2 & P_3 \end{matrix}$$

$$\begin{bmatrix} 1 & 3 & 2 \\ 2 & 6 & 4 \\ 0 & 0 & 0 \\ 0/10+1 & 20/10+1 & 6/10+1 \end{bmatrix} = \begin{bmatrix} 1 & 0 & 0 & 0 \\ 0 & 1 & 0 & 0 \\ 0 & 0 & 1 & 0 \\ 0 & 0 & 1/10 & 0 \end{bmatrix} \cdot \begin{bmatrix} 1 & 3 & 2 \\ 2 & 6 & 4 \\ 0 & 20 & 6 \\ 1 & 1 & 1 \end{bmatrix}$$

Converting point $P'_{1,}$ P'_2 and P'_3 back into w=1 plane we get

$$\begin{matrix} P'_1 & P'_2 & P'_3 \end{matrix} \qquad \begin{matrix} P'_1 & P'_2 & P'_3 \end{matrix}$$

$$\begin{bmatrix} 1 & 3/3 & 2/1.6 \\ 2 & 6/3 & 4/1.6 \\ 0 & 0 & 0 \\ 1 & 1 & 1 \end{bmatrix} = \begin{bmatrix} 1 & 1 & 2/1.6 \\ 2 & 2 & 4/1.6 \\ 0 & 0 & 0 \\ 1 & 1 & 1 \end{bmatrix}$$

So, from this result we can conclude that point P_1 will be obscured by P_2.

6.5 SUMMARY

In 3-D, angle from which we are watching an object is very important, since from different angles we will see a different portion of an object. The mapping between 3-D to 2-D is done by a process called *Projection*. It is classified into two categories: perspective and parallel projection. In perspective, the size of a projected object is less than the size of the original object, whereas, in parallel projection the size will remains the same. In this chapter, we have discussed different types of projections.

6.5 GLOSSARY

- Projection transforms points in a coordinate of n-dimension into points in coordinate system of dimension less than n.
- PERSPECTIVE PROJECTION: If centre of projection is located at a finite point in three space, the result is a perspective projection.
- PARALLEL PROJECTION: In parallel projection, coordinate positions are transformed to the view plane along parallel lines. If centre of projection is located at infinity, all projectors are parallel and the result is parallel projection.
- The point at which a set of projected parallel lines appear to converge is called, *vanishing points.*
- The vanishing point for any set of lines that are parallel to one of the principal axes of an object is known to as a *principal vanishing point.*
- One point perspective projection: When two principal axis of object are parallel to view plane, there is only one vanishing point, since only one axis is not parallel to the view plane.
- Two point perspective projection: When one principal axis of object are parallel to view plane, there are two vanishing points, since two axis are not parallel to the view plane.
- Three point perspective projection: When no principal axis of object is parallel to view plane, there are three vanishing points, i.e., z-vanishing point, x-vanishing point, y-vanishing point.
- In orthographic parallel projection, the direction of projection and the normal to the projection plane are in same direction or reverse.
- *Side Elevation*: When x-axis of object is perpendicular to projection plane, it is said to be side elevation.
- *Top Elevation:* When y-axis is perpendicular to projection plane, it is said to be top Elevation.
- *Front Elevation:* When z-axis is object is perpendicular to projection plane, it is said to be front elevation.
- *Axonometric*: When none of the principal axis of object is perpendicular to projection plane, it is said to be axonometric orthographic parallel projection.
- *Isometric:* When all principal axis of object makes equal angles with projection plane, it is said to be isometric parallel projection.
- *Dimetric:* When two principal axis of object makes equal angles with projection plane, it is said to be dimetric parallel projection.
- *Trimetric:* When none of principal axis of object makes equal angles with projection plane, it is said to be trimetric parallel projection.
- *Oblique parallel projection:* When the direction of projection and normal to view plane, are not in same direction or reverse.
- The most common oblique projections are:
  - Cavalier projection
  - Cabinet projection

6.7 EXERCISE

Q1. What is Projection? Explain briefly the classification of projection.

Q2. What is the difference between perspective and parallel projection?

Q3. Explain Orthographic parallel projection with its types.

Q4. What are vanishing points and how to calculate them?

Q5. To find orthographic projection of a unit cube onto the x = 0, y = 0.

Q6. What is 3-D viewing? Explain the steps in 3-D viewing.

Q7. What is oblique projection? Give example.

E N D

CHAPTER 7 Solid Modelling

7.1 INTRODUCTION

The need to model objects are solid has resulted in the development of a variety of specialized ways to represent them.

Following are the properties desirable in a solid representation scheme:

(i) The DOMAIN of representation should ideally be large enough to allow a useful set of physical objects to be represented.

(ii) The representation should be UNAMBIGUOUS; so that it should be COMPLETE. There should be no confusion as to what is being represented and given representation should represent only one solid.

(iii) It should be UNIQUE, i.e., the representation should be different from all others and if encoded gives solid in only one way. If representation has unique property, then operations can be performed on them for testing the equality of two objects.

(iv) Representation should be ACCURATE, i.e., allow an object to be represented without approximation.

(v) A representation scheme should make it possible to create a valid representation (i.e., one that does correspond to solid). On the other hand, it should not be difficult TO CREATE A VALID REPRESENTATION, by using different solid modelling representation system.

(vi) Solid objects should maintain CLOSURE under different transformations, like rotation, translation and other operations. This means that if we perform these operations on valid solids then result should be valid solids only.

(vii) The representation should be COMPACT to save the storage space, which in turn may save communication time and increase the performance and deficiency in a distributed system.

(viii) Representation should allow the use of EFFICIENT algorithms to compute the physical properties of an object, which is important for us while representing them as pictures.

7.2 REGULARIZED BOOLEAN SET OPERATIONS

No matter how we have represented the objects, we would like to be able to combine them in order to makes new ones. One of the most popular methods of combining objects to make new ones is by Boolean set operations, such as union, difference, and intersection. Applying an ordinary set operation to two solid objects, however, do not necessarily yield a solid object. So, rather than using the ordinary boolean set operators, we instead use the regularized boolean set operators, denoted as U*, and – * such that operations on solids always yields solids.

Regularized Boolean set operators have been used in:

- User-interface technique to build complex objects from simple ones.
- Used in constructive solid geometry.

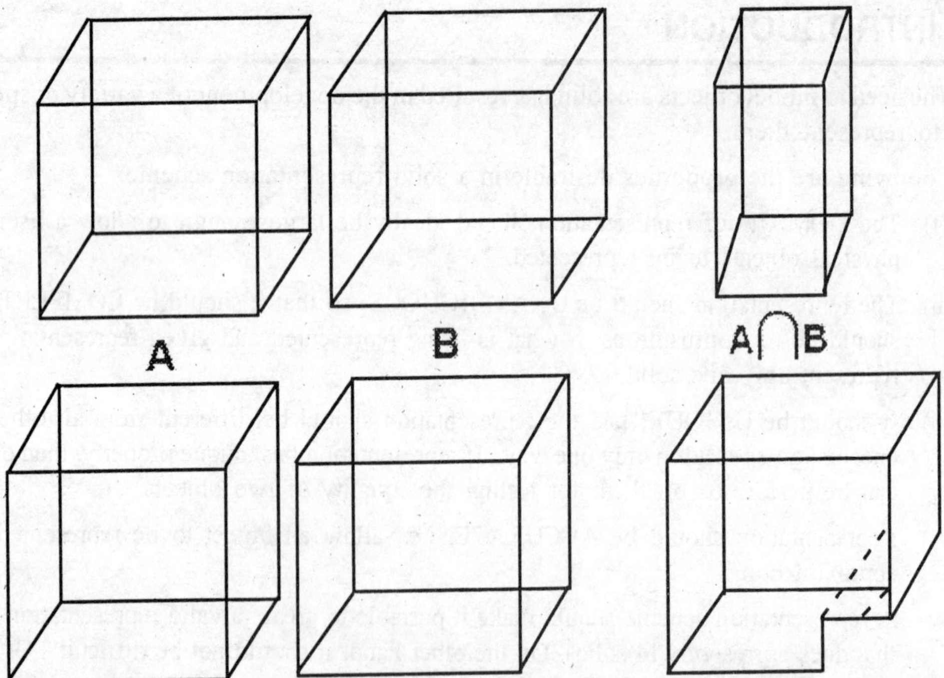

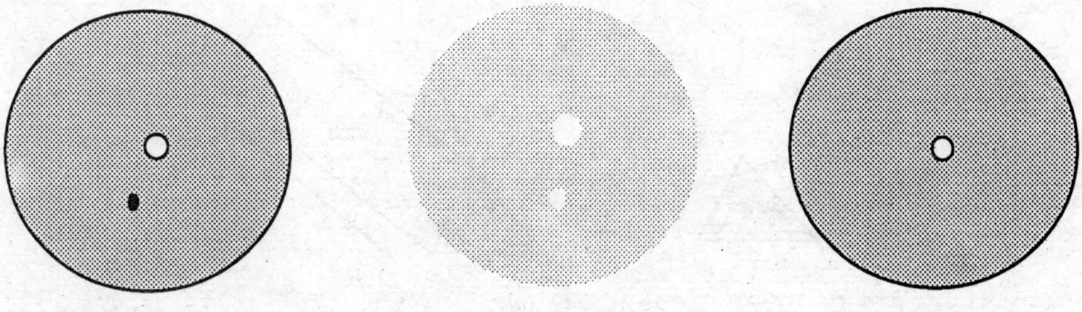

A op^*B = closure (interior (A opB))

Fig. 7.1 (a) and (b) Solid Objects using Boolean set operators; (c) Solid Objects using Regularized Boolean set operations

7.3 PRIMITIVE INSTANCING

In this modelling system, we define a set of primitives of 3-D solid shapes which are relevant to the kind of applications have to be represented as solids. These primitives are typically parameterized on the basis of transformations and certain but on other properties as well. They are mostly used for relatively complex objects such as gears and solids for those solids that are very difficult to represent using other techniques like Boolean set operations etc.

7.4 SWEEP REPRESENTATION

Sweep representation is useful for constructing 3-D objects by using 2-D (mostly) object and basic transformations. A 3-D surface is also obtained by traversing an entity, e.g., line, polygon or curve, along a path in space. The resulting surfaces are called *sweep surfaces,* and the representation is known as *sweep representation*. Sweeping an object along a trajectory through space defines a new object, called a *sweep*.

We can represent such objects by specifying a 2-D shape and a sweep, i.e. translation or rotation that moves the shape through a region of space.

In different graphics systems, a set of 2-D primitives, such as circles and rectangles can be provided for sweep representation as menu options. There are also other methods for obtaining 2-D figures that includes closed spline-curve construction and cross-sectional slices of solid objects.

With a 2-D object representation, we perform translational sweep along a straight-line path perpendicular to the plane. In between along this path, we repeat the shape and draw a set of connecting lines in the direction of the sweep to obtain the wireframe representation.

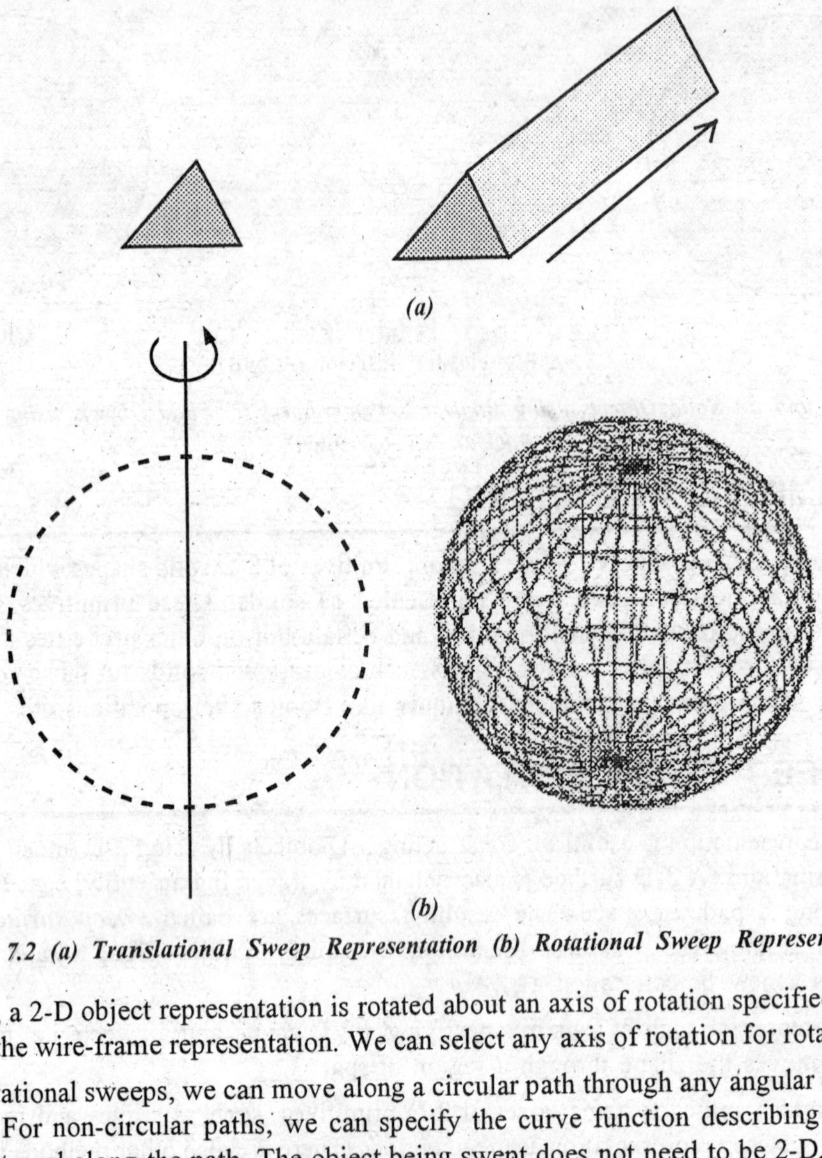

Fig. 7.2 (a) Translational Sweep Representation (b) Rotational Sweep Representation

In this, a 2-D object representation is rotated about an axis of rotation specified in the plane to produce the wire-frame representation. We can select any axis of rotation for rotational sweep.

For rotational sweeps, we can move along a circular path through any angular distance from 0° to 360°. For non-circular paths, we can specify the curve function describing the path and distance of travel along the path. The object being swept does not need to be 2-D, we can even change the shape or size of the cross-section, or we could make changes in the orientation of the cross-section corresponding to the sweep path as we move the shape through a region of space. Sweeps in solids are useful in modelling the region swept out by a machine tool cutting head or robot following a path.

Sweeps whose generating area or volumes changes in size, shape or orientation as they are swept along the sweep path and that follow an arbitrary curved trajectory are called general sweeps. There are few disadvantages of representing general sweeps like:

- General sweeps are particularly difficult to model efficiently.
- Not always able to represent solids.

If the sweep transformation contains only translations or overall scaling, the resulting surface is planar. If the sweep transformation contains rotations, the result surface is non-planar.

7.5 SPATIAL PARTITIONING REPRESENTATIONS

In Spatial Partitioning Representations, a solid is decomposed into a collection of adjoining, non intersecting solids. One of the types of spatial partitioning representation is octrees, that are designed to take care of demanding storage requirements.

7.5.1 Quadtree and Octrees

These are hierarchical tree structures, used to represent solid objects in various graphics systems. Medical imaging and various other applications that demands high storage space commonly use octree representations.

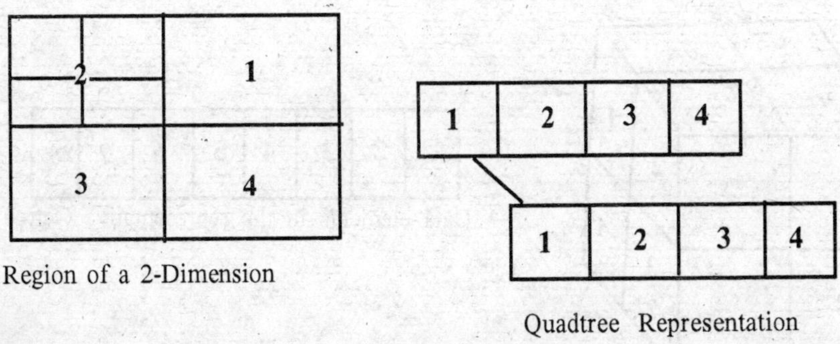

Fig 7.3

The octree representation for a 3-D space is an extension of a 2-D representation scheme, called quadtree. The fundamental idea behind both the quadtree and octree is the divide and-conquer strategy. The quadtrees are derived by successively subdividing the 2-D region into quadrants. Each node in the quadtree have 4 data elements. Each quadrant may be full (F), empty (E), or partially full (P). Each quadrant may be called homogenous, or full or empty, depending on how much of the quadrant intersects the area, or we can say, quadrant is said to be homogenous if all pixels within a quadrant have the same color, the associated data element in the node stores that color. In addition to this, a flag is also used in the data element to indicate that the quadrant is homogeneous.

A partially full quadrant is called a heterogeneous quadrant. It is then further successively subdivided into subquadrant. The corresponding data element in the node now flags the quadrant as heterogeneous and stores the pointer to the next node in the quadtree. In partially full or heterogeneous quadrant, subdivision continues until all quadrants are homogeneous (either full or empty) or until a predetermined cut-off depth is reached.

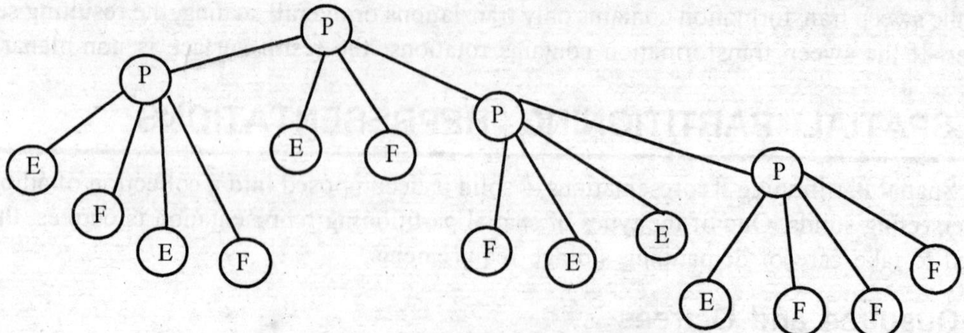

Fig. 7.4 Quadtree Data Structure

The octree is similar to the quadtree, except that its 3 dimensions are successively subdivided into octants, and stores information in corresponding data elements of each node of the tree.

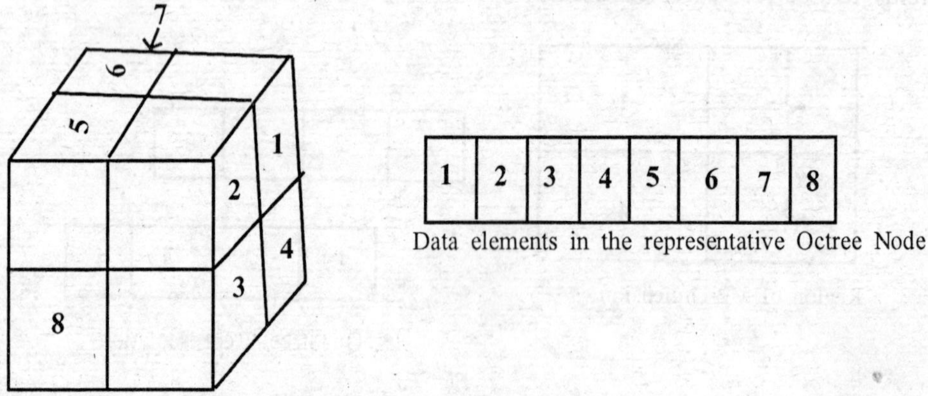

Region of a 3-Dimensional Space

Fig. 7.5 Octree

Quadtree: Number of nodes α Object's perimeter.

Octree: Number of nodes α Object's surface.

These relations hold because node subdivision arises only from the need to represent the boundary of the object being enclosed. The only internal nodes that are split are those through which part of the boundary passes. Thus, any operation on one of these data structures that is linear in the number of nodes it contains also executes in time properties to the size of its perimeter or area.

Once an octree representation has been established for a solid object, a number of procedures can be applied to the represented solid. An algorithm for performing set operations can be applied to two octree representations for the same region of space.

For a union operation, a new octree is constructed with the combined regions for each of the input objects. Similarly, intersection and difference operations are performed by looking into the regions that are overlapping, in the two octrees. The new octree is then formed by either storing the octants where the two objects overlap or the region occupied by one object but not the other. Octree is even used in visible-surface detection, by searching the octants from front to back. First, we detect the visible part of an object, and then transfer that information to a quadtree representation for display.

7.6 CONSTRUCTIVE SOLID-GEOMETRY METHODS (CSG)

In CSG, we use a technique to combine the volumes that are occupied by overlapping three-dimensional objects using Boolean set operations.

An object is stored as a tree with operators at the interval node and simple primitives, or volumes or objects, at the leaves. To determine the physical properties of the root, we must be able to combine the properties of the leaves. CSG creates a new volume or object by applying different Boolean set operations like union, intersection, or difference operation to two specified volumes.

A CSG representation starts with an initial set of 3-D objects (primitives) such as blocks, pyramids, cylinders, cones and spheres. These primitives can be selected as menu options in different CSG packages. Follow the steps to combine the volumes to create a new one:

- To create a new 3-D shape using CSG, we first select two primitives and drag them into position in a region of space.
- Then we select an operation like union, intersection, or difference for combining the volumes of the two primitives.

We keep on repeating the above steps until we get the desired volume. An object designed using the above method is represented with a binary tree.

CSG can be implemented by ray-casting method when objects are described with boundary representations.

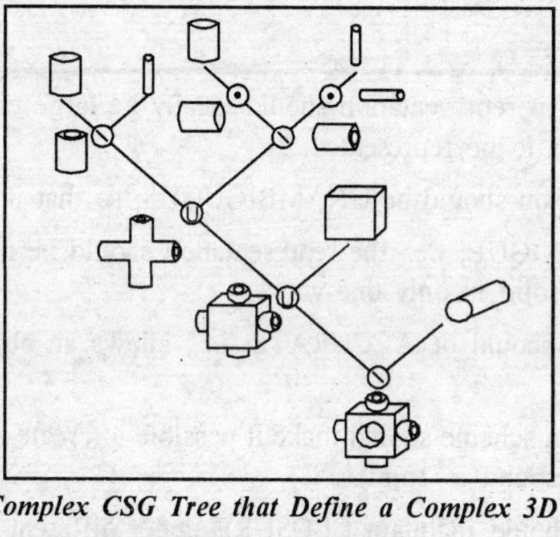

Fig. 7.6 A Complex CSG Tree that Define a Complex 3D Object

7.7 BOUNDARY REPRESENTATIONS

Boundary Representations (also known as b-reps) describe an object in terms of its surface boundary, vertices, edges, and faces. Some of b-reps are restricted to planar polygonal boundaries.

Polyhedra and Euler's Formula

A polyhedron is a solid that is bounded by a set of polygons whose edges are each a member of an even number of polygons. A b-rep of simple polyhedron satisfies Euler's formula, which expresses an invariant relationship among the number of vertices, edges and faces of a simple polyhedron:

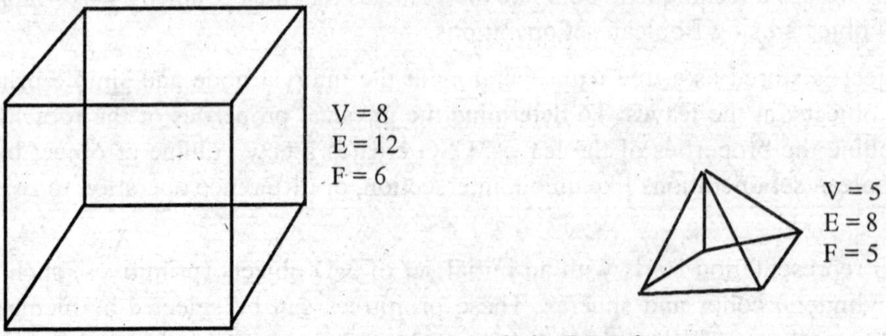

Fig. 7.7 Verifying Euler's Formula

$$V - E + F = 2$$

Where V is number of vertices, E is number of edges and F is the number of faces. B-reps may be combined using regularized Boolean set operators to create new b-reps.

7.8 SUMMARY

In this chapter, we have discussed the different properties that are desired to represent solids and a number of ways of representing solids.

7.9 GLOSSARY

- The DOMAIN of representation should ideally be large enough to allow a useful set of physical objects to be represented.
- The representation should be UNAMBIGUOUS; so that it should be COMPLETE.
- It should be UNIQUE, i.e., the representation should be different from all others and if encoded gives solid in only one way.
- Representation should be ACCURATE, i.e., allows an object to be represented without approximation.
- A representation scheme should make it possible to create a valid representation (i.e., one that does correspond to solid).
- Solid objects should maintain CLOSURE under different transformations, like rotation, translation and other operations.
- The representation should be COMPACT to save the storage space, which in turn may save communication time and increase the performance and deficiency in a distributed system.

- Representation should allow the use of EFFICIENT algorithms to compute the physical properties of an object, which is important for us while representing them as pictures.
- Regularized Boolean set operators have been used in:
  - User-interface technique to build complex objects from simple ones.
  - Used in Constructive Solid Geometry.
- Sweep representation is useful for constructing 3-D objects by using 2-D (mostly) object and basic transformations. A 3-D surface is also obtained by traversing an entity, e.g., line, polygon or curve, along a path in space.
- **OCTREES:** These are hierarchical tree structures, used to represent solid objects in various graphics system.
- B-reps may be combined using regularized Boolen set operators to create new b-reps.

7.10 EXERCISE

Q1. Write short notes on:

- Constructive Solid Geometry
- Primitive Instancing
- Boundary representations

Q2. What are homogeneous nodes in quadtree and octree?

Q3. Differentiate between octree and quadtree.

Q4. What are the desirable properties in solid representation scheme.

Q5. What is sweep representation? Give some examples.

E N D

CHAPTER 8 Illumination Model

8.1 INTRODUCTION

Realistic display, refer to a picture that consists most of the natural lighting effects while interacting with all real physical objects. One example of realistic display is *Photographic System or photorealism.* Producing realistic images involves physics and psychology, as well. After interacting with the physical environment, light, i.e., electromagnetic energy, reaches the eye. In the eye, physical and chemical changes takes place that generates electrical pulses that are interpreted, i.e., perceived, by the brain. Perception is a learned characteristic. The psychology of visual perception thus exist.

Realistic displays of a scene are obtained by generating perspective projections of objects and by applying natural lighting effects to all surfaces which are visible. A basic difficulty in achieving total realism is the complexity of the real world. Observe the richness of our environment. There are various surfaces with different optical and material properties, different types of light and light sources, different textures, color gradations, reflections, shadows, etc.

An *illumination model*, is used to calculate the intensity of light at a given point on a specific surface of an object. It is also known as *lighting model* or *shading model.*

Rendering is the process of producing realistic images or pictures. The term *rasterization,* is also used to refer specifically to those methods that involve in finding pixel values from input geometric primitives. A *surface rendering algorithm* uses the intensity calculated by illumination model to find the light intensity for all the projected pixels of different surfaces in the scene.

8.2 LIGHT SOURCE

Light source refers to an object that is emitting radiant energy, such as a light bulb or the sun. These are also referred to as *light-emitting sources.*

A luminous object can both be a light source and a light reflector. Example: A plastic lamp with a light bulb inside both emits and reflects light from the surface of the lamp.

Light that illuminates object are of two types light-emitting sources and light-reflecting sources. Light-emitting sources are like bulb, tubes and sun. Light-reflecting sources includes, all objects except light emitting sources, walls of a room, ceiling, door etc.

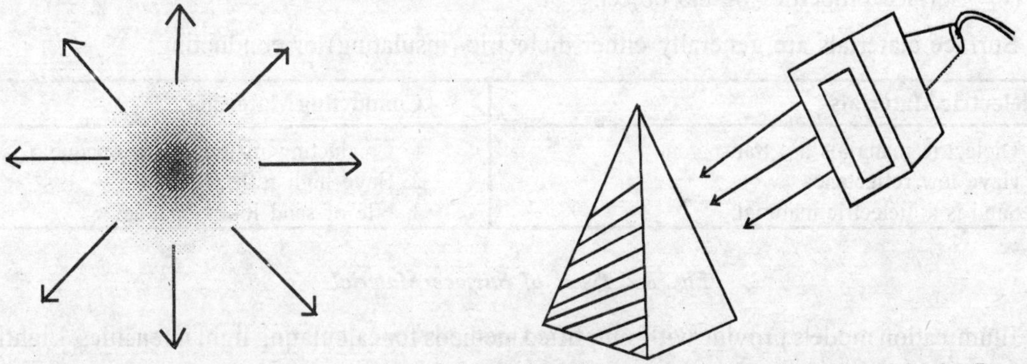

(a) Point Light Source *(b) Object Illuminated with a Distributed Light Source*

Fig. 8.1

The simplest model for a light emitter is a *point source.* The size or dimension of the light-emitting source is smaller in comparison to the object or area, we are referring or want to illuminate. In this case, the light-emitting source is known as *point source.* The another model for a light emitter is a *distributed light source.* In this case, size or dimension of the light-emitting source is bigger in comparison to the object or area we are referring or want to illuminate. In this case, the light-emitting source is known as *distributed light source.*

8.3 ILLUMINATION MODELS

As discussed earlier, an illumination model is used to calculate the intensity of the light that we should see at a given point on a specific surface of an object. Here, we take care of the following things:

1. Location of the light source that falls on an object.
2. Quality of the light source that falls on an object.
3. Interaction of the object with the light on the basis of its physical properties.

When light energy falls on a surface, it can be absorbed, reflected, or transmitted. Some of the light energy incident on a surface is absorbed and converted to heat; the rest is either reflected or transmitted. It is the reflected or transmitted light that makes an object visible.

Part of incident light on an object gets reflected, while rest is absorbed. The ratio of the light reflected from the surface to the total incident light on the surface is called *coefficient of reflection* i.e. k. The value of k varies from 0 to 1. The amount of incident light reflected by a surface depends on the type of material. If the surface is of shiny material, it will reflect more of the incident light (k closer to 1), and if it is a dull surface, it will absorb more of incident light (k closer to 0). The characteristics of the light reflected from or transmitted through the surface of an object depends on:

(i) Composition of the light source.

(ii) Direction of the light source.

(iii) Geometry of the light source.

(iv) Surface orientation of the object.

(v) Surface properties of the object.

Surface materials are generally either dielectric (insulating) or conducting

Dielectric Materials	Conducting Materials
1. Dielectric materials are transparent. 2. Have low reflectance. 3. Sand is a dielectric material.	1. Conducting materials are opaque. 2. Have high reflectance. 3. Pile of sand looks opaque.

Fig. 8.2 Types of Surface Material

Illumination models provide with simplified methods for calculating light intensities. Lighting calculations are based on:

- Optical properties of a surface, i.e., glossy, matte, transparent or opaque.
- Relative position of the surface with respect to light sources.
- Background lighting conditions.
- Light source specifications.

8.3.1 Ambient Light

If there is diffuse, indirect source of light, then the product of multiple reflections of light from many surfaces present in the environment or a surface that is not exposed directly to a light source still will be visible if nearby objects are illuminated, i.e., nearby objects will act as light-reflecting sources. Ambient light is also known as the *background light.* Ambient light has no spatial or directional characteristics. The amount of ambient light incident on each object is constant for all surfaces and over all directions. If we assume that background light, i.e., ambient light, falling equally on all surfaces from all directions, then illumination equation would be:

$$I = I_a k_a \qquad ...(8.1)$$

where, I_a = Intensity of ambient light incident on a surface, assumed to be constant for all objects.

k_a = ambient-reflection coefficient, ranges from 0 to 1. It determines the amount of ambient light reflected from an object's surface. It is a material property (from which the surface is made).

8.3.2 Diffuse Reflection

Diffusely reflected light is scattered equally in all directions and as a result, position of the observer is unimportant. Rough, or grainy surface tend to scatter reflected light in all directions. Dull, matte surfaces (grainy), such as chalk, exhibit diffuse reflection, also known as *lambertian reflection.*

These surfaces reflect light with equal intensity in all directions, and hence appear equally bright from all viewing angles. Such source are sometimes referred as *ideal diffuse reflectors.*

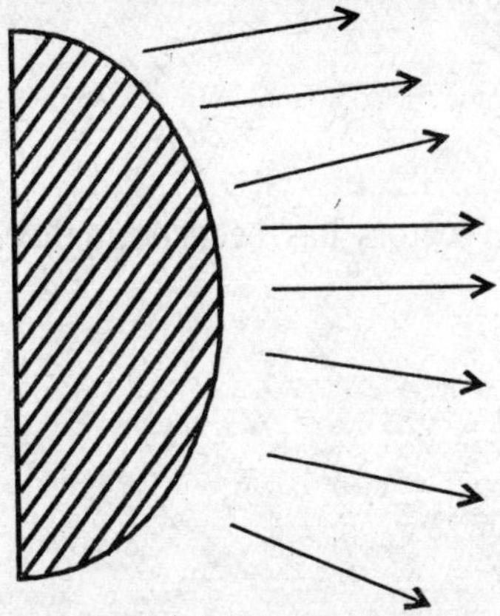

Fig. 8.3 Diffuse Reflection

Lambert's cosine law states that the intensity of the reflected light depends on the angle of illumination. According to *Lambert's law,* the intensity of light reflected from a perfect diffuser is proportional to the cosine of the angle between the light direction and the normal to the surface.

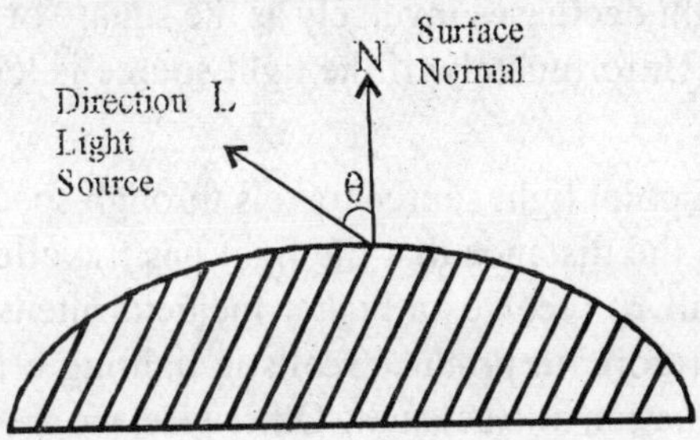

Fig. 8.4 Lambertian Cosine Law

$I_{diff} \alpha \cos\theta$

If light source at normal, i.e., if $\theta = 0$, the object is illuminated to its maximum.

Thus, the amount of light seen by the viewer is independent of the viewer's direction and proportional only to $\cos\theta$, the angle of incidence of light.

The diffuse illumination equation is given by:

$$I_{diff} = I_p k_d \cos\theta \quad ...(8.2)$$

Where, I_p = point light source intensity.

k_d = material's diffuse reflection coefficient ranges from 0 to 1.

$\cos\theta$ = angle between 0° to 90° if the light source is to have any direct effect on the point being shaded.

For angles greater then 90°, light source is behind the object and thus no reflected light directly reaches an observer.

Dot product $L.N = |L|\,|N| \cos\theta$

$$\Rightarrow \cos\theta = \frac{\vec{L}.\vec{N}}{|L||N|}$$

Let |L| and |N| = 1 since the vectors has been normalized.

$$\Rightarrow \cos\theta = L.N \qquad ...(8.3)$$

By substituting in equation 8.2

$$I = I_p k_d (N.L) \qquad ...(8.4)$$

Total intensity $I = I_{ambient} + I_{diff}$

$$= I_a k_a + I_p k_d (N.L) \qquad ...(8.5)$$

$0 \le \theta \le 90°$, $k_a + k_d = 1$; and k_a and k_d both depend on surface material.

If this illumination model is used to determine the intensity of light reflected from two objects with the same orientation to the light source but at different distances, the same intensity for both objects results.

If the objects overlap, then it is not possible to distinguish between them. However, it is well known that the intensity of light decreases inversely as the square of the distance from the source; farther away appear dimmer. Unfortunately, if the light source is located at infinity, the distance to the object is infinite.

As radiant energy from a point light source travels through space, its amplitude is attenuated by the factor $1/d^2$, where *d* is the distance that the light has travelled. This means that a surface close to the light source (small *d*) receives a higher incident intensity from the source than the distant surface (large *d*). Therefore, to produce realistic lighting effects, our illumination model should take this intensity attenuation into account. Otherwise, we are illuminating all surfaces with the same intensity. No matter how far they might be from the light source. Overlapping surfaces hence may be indistinguishable from each other, i.e., the two surfaces will be displayed as one surface.

If we use the factor $1/d^2$ to attenuate intensities, we do not always produce realistic pictures. The factor $1/d^2$ produces too much intensity variations when d is small, and it produces very little variation when d is large. Warnock's suggested that more realistic results are obtained by using a linear, $1/d$ attenuation law, the simple illumination model is then:

$$I = I_a k_a + I_p k_d \cos\theta/(d + k)$$

where k is an arbitrary constant and $0 \le p \le 2$.

When the viewpoint is at infinity, the distance d is frequently determined relative to the location of the object closet to the viewpoint. This has the effect of illuminating the object closest to the viewpoint with the full intensity of the point light source, and all objects farther from the viewpoint at lower intensities.

8.3.3 Specular Reflection

Specular reflection can be observed on any shiny surface. When we look at an illuminated shiny surface, such as an apple, we see a bright spot, at certain viewing directions. This is due to the total, or near to total, reflection of the incident light in a specific range. This phenomenon is called *specular reflection.* At the bright spot, the object appears to be of white color, the color of incident light. The specular reflection angle is equal to the angle of the incident light, with two angles measured on opposite sides of the unit normal vector **N**. As per figure 8.5, **R** is the unit vector in the direction of ideal specular reflection, **L** is used to represent the unit vector directed toward the point light source and **S** is used to represent the unit vector pointing to the viewer from the surface position. Angle between **S** and **R** i.e. $Ø$ is called *viewing angle.* Specular reflection of light is directional. For a perfect reflecting surface (mirror), incident light is reflected only in the specular reflection direction. Thus, only an observer located at **R,** sees any specularly reflected light, i.e., sight vector, S is coincident with the reflection vector R, i.e., the angle $Ø$ is zero.

Phong Specular Reflection Model

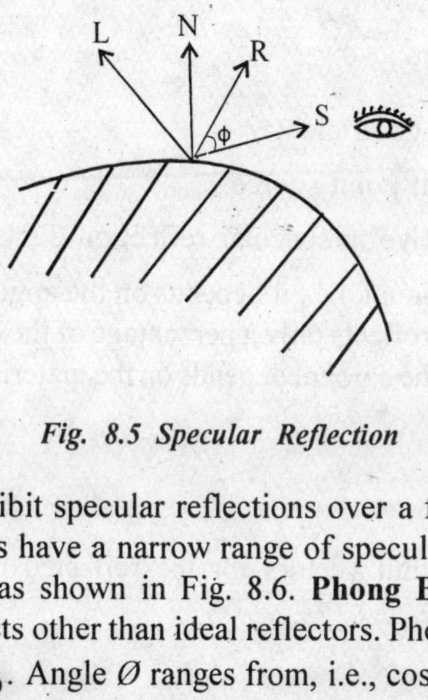

Fig. 8.5 Specular Reflection

Non-perfect reflectors exhibit specular reflections over a finite range of viewing positions around vector **R**. Shiny surfaces have a narrow range of specular reflection, while dull surfaces have a wider reflection range as shown in Fig. 8.6. **Phong Bui-Tuong** developed a popular illumination model for the objects other than ideal reflectors. Phong sets the intensity of specular-reflection proportional to $\cos^{n_s}\phi$. Angle $Ø$ ranges from, i.e., cos $Ø$ varies from 0 to 1. The value assigned to specular-reflection parameter n_s is depends upon the type of surface that we want to display. If a very shiny surface has to be modelled, a large value for n_s (say, 100 or more), and if duller surfaces has to be modelled, a smaller values of n_s (down to 1), are used. For a perfect reflector, n_s is infinite. For a rough surface, such as chalk, n_s would be assigned a value near 1.

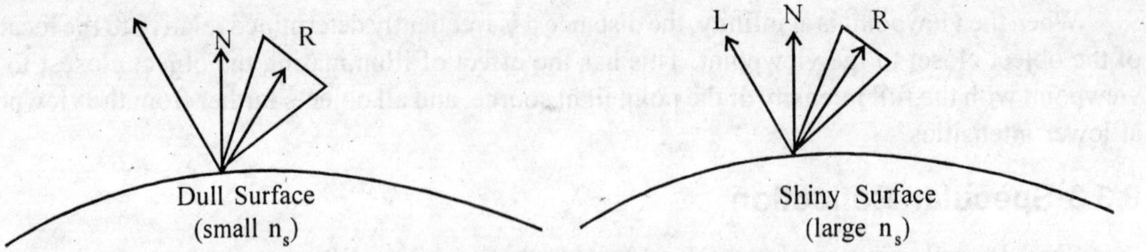

Fig. 8.6 Specular Reflection

The intensity of specularly reflected light based on:

- the angle of incidence,
- material properties.
- polarization and color of incident light.

This model is approximated for determining the monochromatic specular intensity variations by using W(θ), a *specular reflection coefficient* for every surface. Specular reflection coefficient ranges from 0° to 90°. W(θ) tends to increase as the angle of incidence increases. At θ = 90°, W(θ) = 1 and there is total reflection (all incident light is reflected). The variation of specular intensity with angle of incidence is governed by *Fresnel's Laws of reflection.* Using W(θ), we can write the specular reflection equation as:

$$I_{spec} = W(\theta) I_p \cos^{n_s} \phi \qquad \text{...(8.7)}$$

Where,

W(θ) = Specular-reflection coefficient

I_p = Intensity of the light point source

Ø = Viewing angle relative to specular reflection direction **R**, and between 0° to 90°.

Specular reflection is directional, i.e., it depends on the angle of the incident light. Light that strikes a surface perpendicularly reflects only a percentage of the light specularly; the rest is either absorbed or reflected diffusely. The amount depends on the material properties and the wavelength.

$$\cos\alpha = \frac{R.S}{|R||S|} = \hat{R}\,\hat{S} \qquad \text{...(8.8)}$$

Where $\hat{R}$ and $\hat{S}$ are the unit vectors for the reflected ray and line-of-sight directions, respectively.

$$I_{spec} = k_s I_l (\hat{R}.\hat{S})^{n_s} \qquad \text{...(8.9)}$$

Here we have replaced W(θ) with a constant specular-reflection coefficient k_s;

$$\text{Thus, } I = I_a k_a + \frac{I_l}{d+k}(k_d \cos\theta + k_s \cos^{n_s}\phi) \text{ Where } 0 \le k_s \le 1 \qquad \text{...(8.10)}$$

In case of specular reflection, light sources create highlights or bright spots. The highlighting effect is more pronounced on shiny surfaces than on dull surfaces.

8.4 POLYGON RENDERING METHODS

Models of *reflection/scattering* and *shading* are used to describe the appearance of a surface. Shading can be broken down into two orthogonal issues, which are often studied independently:

- **Reflection/Scattering** – How light interacts with the surface *at a given point.*
- **Shading** – How material properties vary across the surface.

Each polygon can be rendered with a single intensity, or the intensity can be obtained at each point using interpolation scheme.

8.4.1 Constant Shading

The simplest shading model for a polygon is constant shading also known as faceted shading and flat shading.

In this method, only once a single intensity is calculated for each polygon. Whole polygon is then displayed with the same intensity over the surface. Constant shading can be useful for quickly displaying a complex surface.

In general, flat shading provides an accurate rendering for an object or polygon only if all of the following assumptions are valid:

- The polygon is not an approximation of an object with a curved surface.
- All light sources that illuminate the object are sufficiently far from the surface so that N.L is constant over the surface.
- The viewer is at infinity, so that S.R is constant over the surface.

If either of the assumptions is not true, even then, we can approximate the constant light intensity using small polygon facets.

8.4.2 Gouraud Shading

This intensity-interpolation scheme, developed by Henri Gouraud and generally referred to as Gouraud shading. The polygon is rendered by linearly interpolating intensity values across the surface. Calculated intensity of one surface is matched with the intensity of adjacent polygons along the common edges.

Following calculations are performed on each polygon surface when rendered using Gouraud shading:

- Determine the average unit normal vector at each polygon vertex.
- Apply an illumination model on each vertex to determine the vertex intensity.
- Linearly interpolate the vertex intensities over the surface of the polygon.

Normal vector can be obtained at each polygon vertex, by averaging the surface normals of all polygons sharing that vertex.

$$N_v = \frac{\sum_{k=1}^{n} N_k}{|\sum_{k=1}^{n} N_k|} \qquad ...(8.11)$$

Where *n* is the number of surface normals sharing that vertex.

According to the next step, now determine the intensity on each vertex by applying an illumination model to it. After this step, now we know the intensity at each vertex. Finally, we linearly interpolate the intensities of vertex over the surface of the polygon.

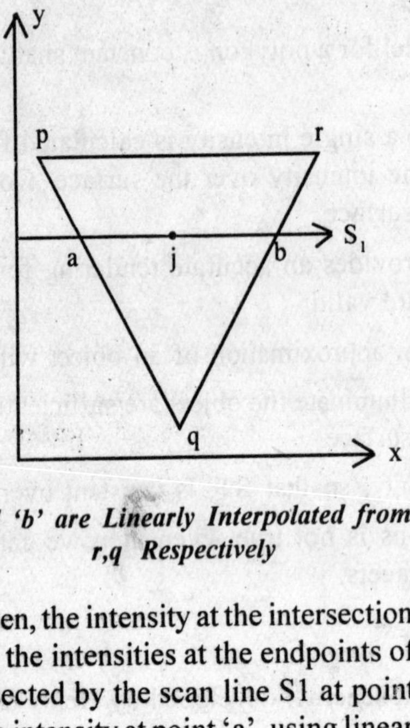

Fig. 8.7 Intensity at Point 'a' and 'b' are Linearly Interpolated from Intensities at Vertices p,q and r,q Respectively

For each scan line on the screen, the intensity at the intersection of the scan line with a polygon edge is linearly interpolated from the intensities at the endpoints of the edge. For example, in fig. 8.7, the polygon edge pq is intersected by the scan line S1 at point 'a'. Let the intensity at p and q are denoted by I_p and I_q. Then the intensity at point 'a', using linear interpolation of the intensities at p and q, we get:

$$I_a = \frac{y_a - y_q}{y_p - y_q} I_p + \frac{y_p - y_q}{y_p - y_q} I_q \qquad ...(8.12)$$

Similarly, we can determine the intensity at point b using the linear interpolation of I_r and I_q.

$$I_b = \frac{y_b - y_q}{y_r - y_q} I_r + \frac{y_r - y_b}{y_r - y_q} I_q \qquad ...(8.13)$$

Intensity at point j will be determined as:

$$I_j = \frac{x_b - x_j}{x_b - x_a} I_a + \frac{x_j - x_a}{x_b - x_a} I_b \qquad ...(8.14)$$

Incremental calculations are used to obtain successive edge intensity values:

$$I = \frac{y - y_q}{y_p - y_q} I_p + \frac{y_p - y}{y_p - y_q} I_q \qquad ...(8.15)$$

Then we can obtain the intensity along this edge for the next scan line y – 1, as

$$I' = I + \frac{I_q - I_p}{y_p - y_q} \qquad ...(8.16)$$

8.4.2.1 Advantages of Gouraud Shading

Following are the advantages of Gouraud Shading:

- Can be combined with a hidden surface algorithm to fill in the visible polygons along each scan line.
- Removes the intensity discontinuities existing in flat shading.
- Very simple.

8.4.2.2 Difficulties in Gouraud shading

Following are the difficulties faced in Gouraud Shading:

- Linear shading interpolation may induce the match band effect; can cause bright and dark intensity streaks.
- Highlights on the surface are sometimes displayed with anomalous shapes.

We can shade any surface by calculating the surface normal at each visible point and applying the desired illumination model at that point.

8.4.3 Phong Shading

An accurate method for rendering a polygon surface is to interpolate normal vector, and then apply the illumination model to each surface point. This method, developed by **Phong Bui-Tuong,** is called *Phong shading or normal vector interpolation shading.*

It displays more realistic highlights on the surface.

The polygon surface is rendered using Phong shading by covering out the following steps:

- Determine the average unit normal vector at each polygon vertex.
- Linearly interpolate the vertex normals over the surface of the polygon.
- Apply an illumination model to calculate projected pixel intensities for the surface points along each scan line.

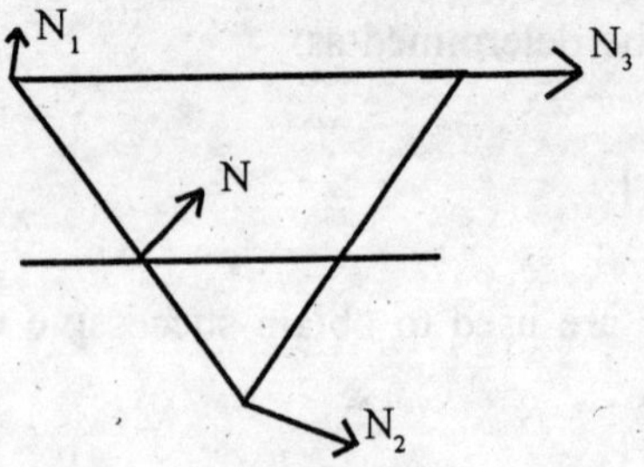

Fig. 8.8

Interpolation of surface normals along a polygon edge between two vertices is illustrated below.

$$N = \frac{y-y_2}{y_1-y_2}N_1 + \frac{y_1-y}{y_1-y_2}N_2 \quad ...(8.17)$$

The normal vector N for the scan line intersection point along the edge between vertices 1 and 2 can be obtained by vertically interpolating between edge endpoint normals.

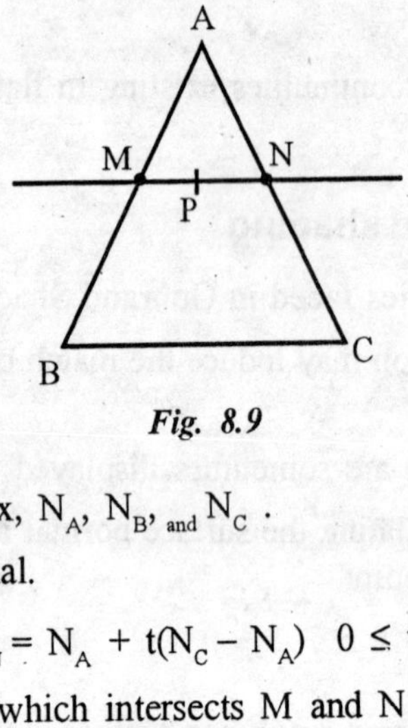

Fig. 8.9

(i) Find normal at each vertex, N_A, N_B, and N_C .

(ii) Find interpolation of normal.

$$N_M = N_A + t(N_B - N_A) \; N_N = N_A + t(N_C - N_A) \quad 0 \le t \le 1$$

(iii) Draw a scan line over P which intersects M and N on the edge.

(iv) Find normal at P.

$$N_P = N_M + (N_A - N_M)w \quad 0 \le w \le 1$$

(v) Find intensity at P.

Incremental methods are used to evaluate normal between scan lines and along each individual scan line. At each pixel position along a scan line, the illumination model is applied to determine the surface intensity at that point.

Phong's method greatly reduces:

- the disturbing mach bands
- removes frame-to-frame discontinuities

- produces more realistic highlights
- more accurate.

8.4.3.1 Advantages

This technique gives a better:

- local approximation to the surface curvature
- rendering of the surface
- specular highlights appear more realistic.

8.4.3.2 Disadvantages

- Requires more computation
- Discrepancy in normal vectors will cause shading discontinuity.

Intensity calculations using an approximated normal vector at each point along the scan line produce more accurate results.

GOURAUD SHADING	PHONG SHADING
• Calculation is less.	• Intensity is more accurate.
• Intensity is approximate and less accurate.	• Specular reflection.
• No specular reflection.	

Fig. 8.10 Gouraud and Phong Shading

8.5 COLOR CONSIDERATIONS

Most graphics displays of realistic scenes are in color. But the illumination model we have described so far considers only monochromatic lighting effects.

To incorporate color, we need to write the intensity equation as a function of the color properties of the light sources and object surfaces.

For an RGB description, each color in a scene is expressed in terms of red, green and blue components. We then specify the RGB components of light source intensities and surfaces color, and the illumination model calculates the RGB components of the reflected light.

We represent the object's diffuse color by 1 value of O_d for each component

=> For the red component

$$I_R = I_{aR}k_aO_{dR} + f_{att}I_{pR}k_dO_{dR}(N.L) \quad ...(8.18)$$

where f_{att} = attenuation factor.

In the original specular reflection model, Phong set parameter k_s to a constant value independent of the surfaces color. This produces specular reflections that are the same color as the incident light (usually while) which gives surface a plastic appearance. For a non-plastic material, the color of the specular reflection is a function of surface properties and may be different from both the color of the incident light and the color of the diffuse reflections.

8.6 TRANSPARENCY

A transparent surface, in general, not only reflect light but also allow some part of the incident light to pass through it.

The total contribution of the transmitted light depends on level of transparency of the surface, is whether any light sources or illuminated surfaces are behind the transparent surfaces.

When we have to model a transparent surface, we should always take care about the contribution of the light passing through the surface. Physical transparency is neither a necessary nor a sufficient condition for the perception of transparency.

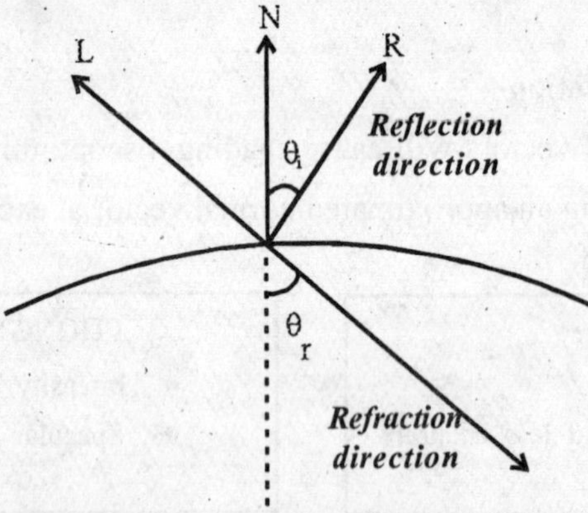

Fig. 8.11 Angle of Reflection and Refraction

Realistic transparency effects are modelled by considering light refraction, who changes the direction when crosses the boundary between two media. When a light is incident upon a transparent surface like a glass, a part of it is reflected by the surface and part of it is refracted by the surface. Since different materials or media have different speed of light, resulting different path when crosses the boundary. According to the ***Snell's Law***

$$\sin\theta_r = \frac{n_i}{n_r}\sin\theta_i \tag{8.19}$$

where n_i = index of refraction of the "incident" materials; n_r = index of refraction of the refracting material.

Inter-object reflections: Occurs when a surface reflects other surfaces in its environment.

Pseudo-transparency: Called screen door transparency offers an inexpensive technique for achieving a transparency effect with the z buffer algorithm. It is frequently implemented in hardware.

8.6.1 Application of Transparency

Visualization of the interior of complex objects and spaces.

8.7 SHADOWS

When the observer's position is coincident with the light source, no shadows are seen. As the positions of the observer and the light source separated, shadow appears.

8.7.1 Applications of shadows

(i) contribute considerably to the realism of the scene of increasing depth perception.

(ii) are important in simulation, for example, a specific area of interest may be invisible because it is in shadow.

(iii) significantly influence heating, air-conditioning and solar power calculations for building and spacecraft design applications.

8.7.2 Types of Shadows

- *Umbra* is the central dense, black, darkest part of the shadow, where the light source is completely blocked by the body.
- *Penumbra* is the lighter area surrounding the umbra, or the region in which only a portion of the light source is obscured by the body.

The point light sources generate only umbra shadows and the distributed light sources generate umbra and penumbra both. While light is totally excluded from the umbra shadow, the penumbra receives light from part of the distributed light source. Because of the computational expense, in many applications, only the shadow umbra generated by point light source is considered.

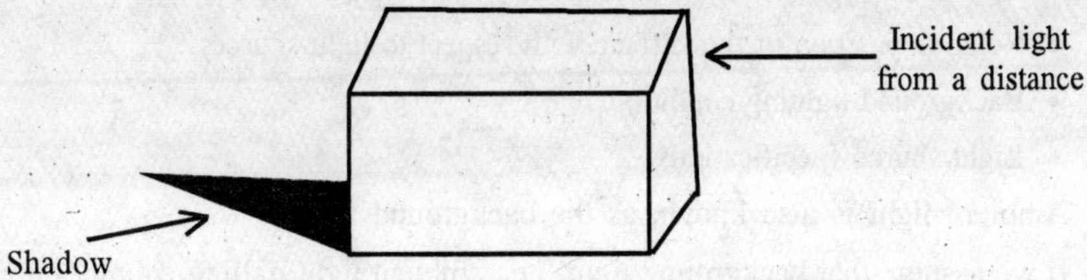

Fig. 8.12 Object Modelled with Shadow Region

Visible surface algorithms determine which surfaces can be seen from the viewpoint; shadow algorithms determine which surfaces can be seen from the light source. Thus, visible surface algorithms and shadow algorithm are essentially the same. The surfaces that are visible from the light source are not in shadow; those that are not visible from the light source are in shadow.

8.8 SUMMARY

Light is an electromagnetic wave and has wave properties like frequency and wavelength. In this chapter, we have discussed different illumination models and shading techniques. Also briefly discussed about colors, transparency and shadows.

8.9 GLOSSARY

- Producing realistic images involves physics and psychology, as well.
- An *illumination model*, is used to calculate the intensity of light at a given point on a specific surface of an object.
- *Rendering* is the process of producing realistic images or pictures.
- A *surface rendering algorithm* uses the intensity calculated by illumination model to find the light intensity for all the projected pixels of different surfaces in the scene.
- Light source refers to an object that is emitting radiant energy, such as a light bulb or the sun. These are also referred to as light-emitting sources.
- Light that illuminates object are of two types light-emitting sources and light-reflecting sources.
- The size or dimension of the light-emitting source is smaller in comparison to the object or area we are referring or want to illuminate. In this case, the light-emitting source is known as *point source.*
- Size or dimension of the light-emitting source is bigger in comparison to the object or area we are referring or want to illuminate. In this case, the light-emitting source is known as *distributed light source.*
- Lighting calculations are based on:
  - Optical properties of a surface, i.e., glossy, matte, transparent or opaque.
  - Relative position of the surface with respect to light sources.
  - Background lighting conditions.
  - Light source specifications.
- Ambient light is also known as the background light.
- If we assume that backgroung light, i.e., ambient light, falling equally on all surfaces from all directions, then illumination equation would be:

$$I = I_a k_a$$

- Surfaces reflect light with equal intensity in all directions, and hence appear equally bright from all viewing angles. Such source are sometimes referred as *ideal diffuse reflectors.*
- *Lambert's cosine law* states that the intensity of the reflected light depends on the angle of illumination.
- The diffuse illumination equation is given by:

$$I_{diff} = I_p k_d \cos\theta$$

- When we look at an illuminated shiny surface, such as an apple, we see a bright spot, at certain viewing directions. This phenomenon is called *specular reflection.*

8.10 EXERCISE

Q1. What is illumination model? Explain briefly with its types.

Q2. Write short notes on:

- Ambient Light
- Diffuse Reflection
- Specular Reflection

Q3. Explain the Lambertian cosine law in detail.

Q4. What is Gouraud Shading? State its advantages and disadvantages.

Q5. What is Phong Shading? State its advantages and disadvantages.

Q6. Define the terms:

- Transparency
- Shadows
- Light Source
- Rendering

E N D

CHAPTER 9 Visible Surface Determination

9.1 INTRODUCTION

One of the most challenging problems in computer graphics is removal of hidden parts from images of solid objects. This is sometimes also referred to as *visible surface detection*, although there can be subtle differences between identifying visible surfaces and eliminating hidden surfaces.

Visible surface detection algorithms/hidden surface elimination algorithms are broadly classified according to whether they deal with object definitions directly or their projected images. These two approaches are called *object space methods* and *image space methods*, respectively.

Object-space Algorithm/Object Precision	Image-space Algorithm/Image Precision
(i) The object space algorithm concentrates on the geometrical relationships among the objects in the scene definition in order to determine which parts of which objects are visible.	(i) Image space algorithm concentrates on the final image and asks what is visible within each raster pixel, i.e., visibility is decided point by point at each pixel position on the projection plane.
(ii) It performs geometric calculation with as much precision as possible, usually the precision available, in floating-point hardware of the computer. Since the precision of the solution is much greater than of a display device, the image can be displayed enlarged many times without loosing accuracy.	(ii) It performs calculations with only enough precision to match the resolution of the display screen used to present the image. These algorithms simply calculate an intensity for each of the 2,50,000 or 1 million distinct dots on the screen.
(iii) The computation time of an object space algorithm will tend to grow with the number of objects in the scene whether visible or not.	(iii) The image-space computation tends to grow with the complexity of the visible parts of the image.

(iv) As complexity of scene increases, cost of object space algorithm increases.	(iv) As complexity of scene increases, cost of image space algorithm grows more slowly.
(v) Object space methods are used primarily in line display algorithms (hidden-line algorithms).	(v) Image space methods are used primarily in visible surface/hidden surface algorithms.

Although there are major differences in the basic approach taken by the various visible surface detection algorithms, most use sorting and coherence methods to improve performance.

9.1.1 Sorting

Use some form of geometric sorting to distinguish visible parts of an object from those that are hidden. Geometric sorting locates objects that lie near to observer and are therefore visible.

9.1.2 Coherence

Hidden line and hidden surface algorithms also capitalize on various forms of coherence in order to reduce the computing required to generate the regularities in a scene, to generate the image. It is the degree to which parts of an environment or its projection exhibit local similarities. Different forms of coherence are related to different forms of order, or regularity, in the image.

(a) **Scan-line coherence:** It arises because the display of a scan line in a raster image is usually very similar to the display of the preceding scan line.

(b) **Frame coherence:** In a sequence of images designed to show motion, recognizes that successive frames are very similar. So, the calculations can be reused of one frame for another similar frame in the sequence.

(c) **Object coherence:** It is the results from relationships or comparisons between different objects or between separate parts of the same object.

(d) **Depth coherence:** Depth coherence expresses the fact that the depth or distance to the viewer at some surface point changes gradually. Adjacent parts of a surface are usually close in depth. Therefore, the depth at some surface point can be efficiently calculated by incrementally updating the depth information of an already processed nearby surface point.

9.2 EXPLOITING COHERENCE

9.2.1 Incremental Techniques

Incremental techniques are best suited to exploit coherence properties. In few situations only, incremental calculations leads you to the desired result. In coherent situations, as discussed above, using incremental calculations algorithm increases the performance and efficiency of the system, in comparison to the algorithms that do not reuse previous results. Incremental methods try to reduce the cost of calculating complex operations during iteration.

Some examples in computer graphics where it is very beneficial to use incremental computations are: scan conversion of lines, circle, ellipses, Gouraud shading, and Phong shading.

Even we can do data compression through incremental storage, i.e., storing only the small differences to previous data sets, is another example of incremental method.

Incremental techniques reduce both computation cost and storage cost. Instead of doing an expensive complex calculation of a result from scratch, you can use the previous result stored by slightly modifying it.

9.2.2 Bounding Volumes

The core idea of bounding volumes is that it is cheaper to process a number of simple objects (bounds) instead of a complex object. A complex object is approximated by a simple bounding volume. This strategy reduces most of the complex calculations and only few calculations must be done with the complex object.

This strategy can only helps us in reducing the computation expense, but there would be no improvement on the linear time complexity (in the number of objects).

9.2.3 Subdivision Techniques

The divide-and-conquer approach is often used to subdivide a complex problem into simple subproblems that are easier to process. The solution of the complex problem is then derived from the solutions of the simple subproblems.

In computer graphics, subdivision is done to make use of the principle of locality that mostly exists in coherent situations. By doing subdivision, we try to obtain coherent homogeneous regions that can be manipulated efficiently. With the help of subdivision, faster calculation, parallel processing and reduction in storage space requirements are achievable.

9.3 VISIBLE SURFACE DETECTION ALGORITHMS

9.3.1 Z-Buffer Method

The Z-buffer or depth-buffer image precision algorithm is one of the simplest visible surface detection algorithms. A depth buffer works by associating a depth, or distance from the viewpoint, with each pixel on the window. It can easily be implemented in either software or hardware. It was proposed by Catmull in 1974.

Z-buffer is used to store the intensity of each pixel in an image, very much like frame buffer. Frame buffer is used to store the attributes (intensity/shade/color) of each pixel in the image space. The Z-buffer is a separate depth buffer used to store the z coordinate, or depth of every visible pixel in the image space. Number of entries in Z-buffer is equal to the number of entries in frame buffer. We are assuming that the viewing direction is positive z-axis.

The Z-Buffer Algorithm

1. Initially, initialize both Z-buffer (Z_b) and frame buffer (I). Set Z-buffer to zero and frame buffer to the background color.

   => $Z_b(x, y) = 0$, $I(x, y) = I_{bg}$

   for all buffer positions (x, y)

2. For each (x, y) pixel, compare the new z to previously stored value in the depth buffer to determine the highest depth.

   Calculate the depth Z for each (x, y) position on the polygon surface.

   If calculated $Z > Z_b\ (x, y)$, then

   $Z_b(x, y) = z, \quad I(x, y) = I_{surf}(x, y)$

   where $I_{surf}(x, y)$ is the projected intensity value for the surface at pixel position (x, y).

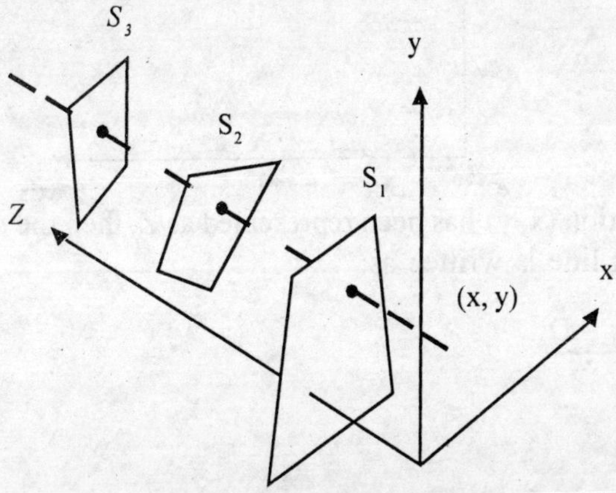

Fig. 9.2 Z-Buffer Method

3. After all the processing, the depth buffer (Z_b) contains the depths of the surfaces that are visible, and the refresh buffer contains the associated intensity values of all those surfaces, in the scene.

It works on the principle of 'Depth coherence', i.e., adjacent parts of the same surface are typically close in depth whereas different surfaces at the same screen location are typically separated farther depth. Once the depth at one point of the surface is calculated, the depth of points on the rest of the surface can often be determined by a simple difference equation.

By using the fundamental of depth coherence, we can simplify the calculation of Z for each point on a scan line by exploiting the fact that the polygon is planar.

We have the plane equation of the following form

$$Ax + By + Cz + D = 0 \qquad ...(9.1)$$

$$\Rightarrow Z = \frac{-D - Ax - By}{C} \qquad ...(9.2)$$

For any scan line, adjacent to the horizontal positions and a difference of 1, and a vertical y value on an adjacent scan line with a difference of 1.

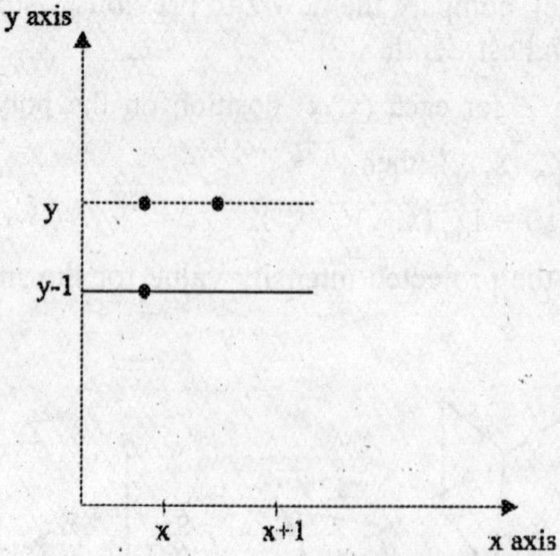

If the depth at position (x, y) has been represented as Z, then the depth Z′ at the next position (x+1, y) along the scan line is written as:

$$Z' = \frac{-A(x-1) - By - D}{C}$$

Or $$Z' = Z - \frac{A}{C}$$

The ratio A/C is constant for each surface, so succeeding depth values across the scan line can be obtained by just doing a single addition to the previous stored values.

If we are processing down a vertical edge, we obtain:

$$Z' = Z + \frac{B}{C}$$

9.3.1.1 Advantages of Z-buffer algorithm

(i) No presorting is necessary.

(ii) No object-object comparisons are required; the entire process is no more than a search.

(iii) Simplicity is its greatest advantage.

(iv) It handles the visible surface problem and the display of complex surface intersections trivially.

(v) Applicable for any object for which depth and shading characteristics can be calculated.

(vi) Since elements of a scene or picture are written to the frame or Z-buffer in arbitrary order, they need not be sorted into depth priority order and hence the computation time associated with the depth sort is eliminated.

(vii) Does not require that objects to be polygons.

9.3.1.2 Disadvantages of Z-buffer Algorithm

(i) The storage required is the principal disadvantage of the algorithm, i.e., it requires a second buffer in addition to the refresh buffer.

One way to reduce storage requirements is to process one section of the scene at a time, using a small depth buffer. After each view section is processed, the buffer is revised for the next section.

(ii) Further disadvantage of the Z-buffer is the difficulty and expense of implementing antialiasing, transparency and translucency effects.

As algorithm writes pixels to the frame buffer in arbitrary order, the necessary information for pre-filtering anti-aliasing techniques is not easily available. For transparency and translucency effects, pixels can be written to the frame buffer in incorrect order, leading to local errors.

9.3.2 A-Buffer Method

To overcome the drawback of Z-buffer that it can only find one visible surface at each pixel position, A-buffer was proposed. It's simply an extension of Z-buffer method. With Z-buffer method, we can only calculate the intensity of opaque objects, whereas, in A-buffer method more than one surface intensity can be taken into consideration at each pixel position.

Each position in the A-buffer has two fields:

(1) Depth field – have a positive or negative real number.

(2) Intensity field stores surface intensity information.

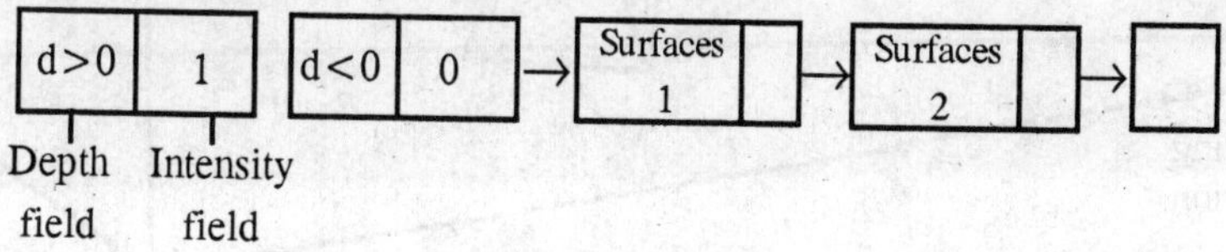

Fig. 9.3 A-Buffer Method

If depth is negative, this indicates visibility of multiple surfaces at a point and intensity field, then stores a pointer to linked list. If depth field is positive, the value stored in depth field is the depth of a single surface.

Surface field contains:

- Surface identifier
- Degree of transparency
- Depth
- RGB intensity components
- Pointer to next surface.

9.3.3 Back Face Removal

A simple object space algorithm is Back Face Removal (or back face cull) where no faces on the back of the object are displayed. Since in general about half of the faces of objects are back faces, this algorithm will remove about half of the total polygons in the image.

9.3.3.1 Algorithm

- Let (x,y,z) be the viewing position.
- Let $Ax + By + Cz + D = 0$ be a polygonal face – A, B, C and D are determined using vertices chosen in a counterclockwise manner.
- If $Ax + By + Cz + D < 0$, then the polygonal face must be a back face and can be eliminated when (x,y,z) is the viewpoint.
- Consider the normal vector to the polygonal face (A,B,C).
  - The viewing direction in left-handed viewing coordinates is along the positive z_v axis.
  - This test alone is sufficient for single convex polyhedron.
  - For more complex scenes, the back-face test eliminates about half the polygonal faces.

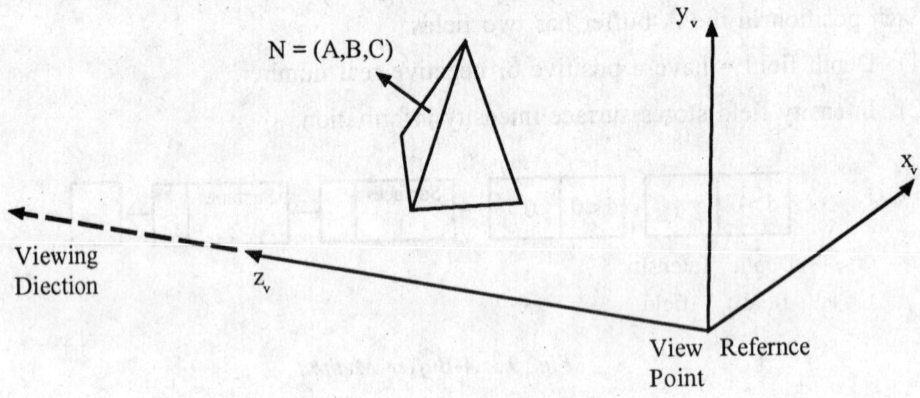

Fig. 9.4 Back Face Removal

- If $c > 0$, the normal points away from the viewing position and the polygonal face must be a back face.
- It is just the opposite condition for a right handed viewing system. Therefore, if $C < 0$ then a back face in a right-handed system.

9.3.3.2 Limitations on Back Face Removal Algorithm

1. It can only be used on solid objects modelled as a polygon mesh.
2. It works fine for convex polyhedron but not necessarily for concave polyhedron.

9.3.4 The Scan Line Method

Scan line algorithms operate at image precision to create an image one scan line at a time.

The basic approach is an extension, of the polygon scan-conversion algorithm and thus uses a variety of forms of coherence, including scan line coherence and edge coherence. The difference is that we deal not with just one polygon but rather with a set of polygons.

Using an active edge table, the scan line algorithm keeps track of the projection beam at a specific time during the scan-line method. When it enters a polygon, a boolean flag goes on, and the scan line switches its intensity from the background intensity to the intensity of the polygon. After the beam leaves the polygon's edge, the intensity again changes back to background intensity. Till this point, no depth information needs to be calculated. However, when the scan-line beam finds itself in more than one polygon, it becomes necessary to use z-buffer algorithm and select the intensity of the highest depth polygon.

The first step is to create an edge table (ET) for all non-horizontal edges of all polygons projected on the projection plane. Horizontal edges are ignored entries in ET are sorted into buckets based on each edges smaller y coordinate and within buckets are ordered by increasing x coordinate of their lower endpoint. Each entry contains:

(i) The x coordinate of the end with the smaller y coordinate.

(ii) The y coordinate of the edge's other end.

(iii) The x increment, Δx, used in stepping from one scan line to the next. (Δx is the inverse slope of the edge.)

(iv) A polygon identification number, indicating the polygon to which the edge belongs.

Also required is a polygon table (PT) that contains at least the following information for each polygon, on addition to its ID:

- the coefficients of the plane equation.
- shading or coloring information for the polygon.
- an in-out boolean flag, initialized to false and used during scan line processing.

The following figure shows the projection of two triangles onto the (x, y) plane:.

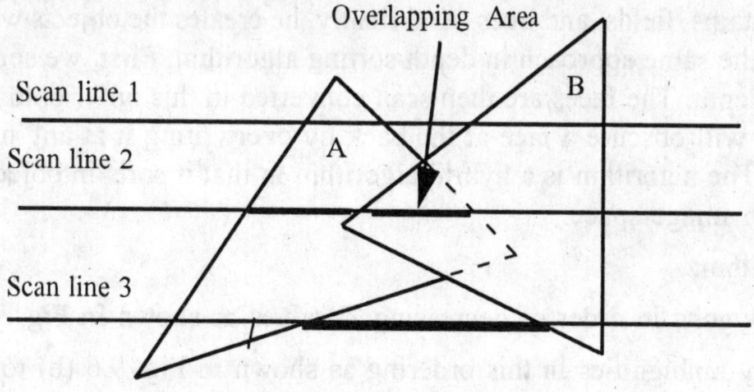

Fig. 9.5 Scan Line Method

The data structure called the 'Active-Edge table (AET)' which keeps tracks of the set of edge it intersects (scan line) and the intersection points are used.

9.3.4.1 Advantages of Scan Line Algorithm

(i) The algorithm concurrently scan converts all polygons in the scene, one scan line at a time.

(ii) Take advantage of coherence between successive scan lines and of span coherence within a scan line.

(iii) Simplifies geometric calculations by reducing a 3-D problem to a 2-D-comparison of segments in the YZ plane.

(iv) It can also be extended to general surfaces apart from polygons. (To accomplish this, ET and AET are replaced by a surface table and active-surface table.)

(v) Simple and high resolution images are readily accommodated

9.3.4.2 Disadvantages of Scan Line Algorithm

(i) Very small or very narrow polygons may fall between the scan line planes.

(ii) A 'hole' may result between adjacent polygons.

(iii) Horizontal edges cannot intersect the scan line and are thus ignored.

The scan line algorithms reduce the visible line/visible surface problem from 3-D to 2-D. A scan plane is defined by the viewpoint at infinity of the positive Z-axis and a scan-line. The intersection of the scan plane and the 3-D scene defines a 1-scan-line high-window. The visible surface problem is solved in this scan-plane window and is reduced to deciding which line segment is visible for each point on the scan line.

9.3.5 Painter's Algorithm

The idea behind the Painter's algorithm is to draw polygons which has the lowest depth (when viewing from positive z coordinate), followed by drawing larger depth polygons. The concept is to map world coordinates to the screen coordinates somewhat like an artist creating an oil painting. An artist first paints the entire canvas with a background color. Next, he adds the more distant objects such as mountains, fields, and trees. And finally, he creates the objects with highest depth. We will also follow the same approach in depth sorting algorithm. First, we sort the polygons in order of decreasing depth. The faces are then scan converted in this order onto the screen. Thus, a face near the front will obscure a face at the back by overwriting it at any points where their projections overlap. The algorithm is a hybrid algorithm in that it sorts in object space and does the final rendering in image space.

The basic algorithm:

1. Sort all polygons in order of decreasing Z-values as shown in Fig. 9.6 (a).
2. Resolve any ambiguities in this ordering as shown in Fig. 9.6 (b) to (e).
3. Scan convert each polygon in the order generated by steps (1) and (2).

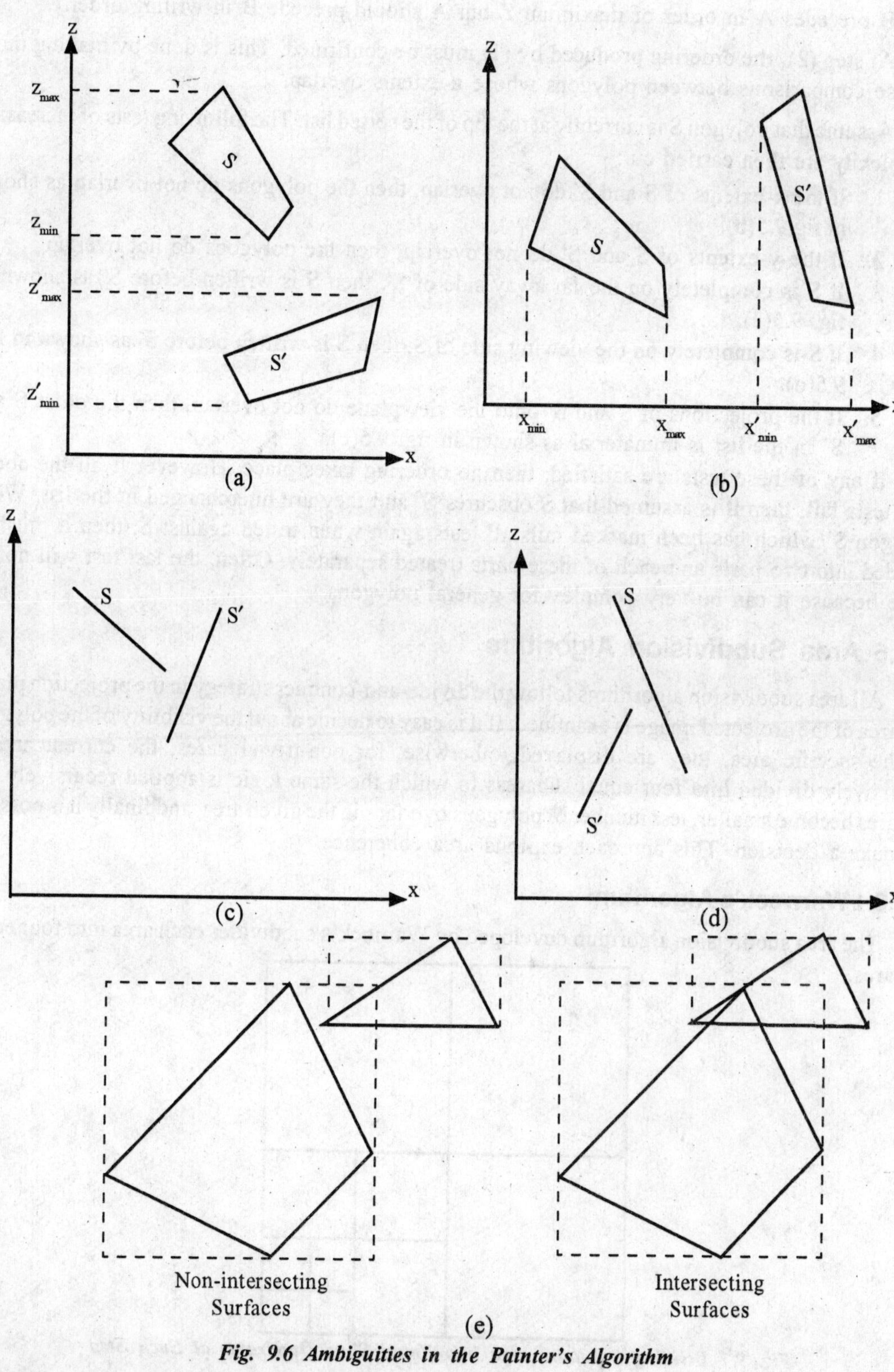

Fig. 9.6 Ambiguities in the Painter's Algorithm

B precedes A in order of maximum Z but A should precede B in writing order.

At step (2), the ordering produced by (1) must be confirmed. This is done by making more precise comparisons between polygons whose z-extents overlap.

Assume that polygon S is currently at the top of the sorted list. The following tests of increasing complexity are then carried out:

1. If the x-extents of S and S′ do not overlap, then the polygons do not overlap as shown in fig.9.5(b).
2. If the y-extents of S and S′ do not overlap, then the polygons do not overlap.
3. If S is completely on the far away side of S′, then S is written before S′ as shown in fig. 9.5(c).
4. If S is completely on the viewing side of S, then S is written before S′ as shown in fig. 9.5(d).
5. If the projections of S and S′ onto the viewplane do not overlap, then the order S and S’ in the list is immaterial as shown in fig. 9.5(e).

If any of these tests are satisfied, then no ordering takes place. However if all the above five tests fail, then it is assumed that S obscures S′ and they are interchanged in the list. When polygon S’ which has been marked fails all tests again when tested against S, then it must be divided into two parts and each of these parts treated separately. Often, the last test will not be done because it can be very complex for general polygons.

9.3.6 Area Subdivision Algorithm

All area subdivision algorithms follow the divide-and-conquer strategy in the projection plane. An area of the projected image is examined. If it is easy to decide about the visibility of the polygons in the specific area, they are displayed; otherwise, for non-trivial cases, the current area is recursively divided into four equal subareas to which the same logic is applied recursively. As the area become smaller, less number of polygons overlaps in the given area, and finally it is possible to make a decision. This approach exploits area coherence.

9.3.6.1 Warnock's Algorithm

The area subdivision algorithm developed by Warnock's subdivides each area into four equal squares.

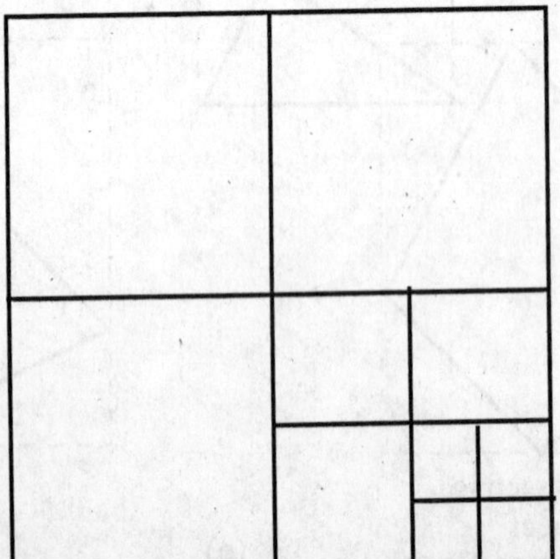

Fig. 9.7 Dividing a Square area into Equal Sized Quadrants at Each Step

At each stage in the recursive subdivision process, the projection of each polygon has one of four relationships to the area of interest.

(i) **SURROUNDING POLYGON** – completely contain the (shaded) area of interest, i.e., one that completely encloses the area.

(ii) **INTERSECTING POLYGON** – intersect the area, also known as overlapping one that is partly inside and partly outside the area.

(iii) **CONTAINED POLYGON** – are completely inside the area, also known as inside polygon.

(iv) **DISJOINT POLYGON** – are completely outside the area, also known as outside polygon.

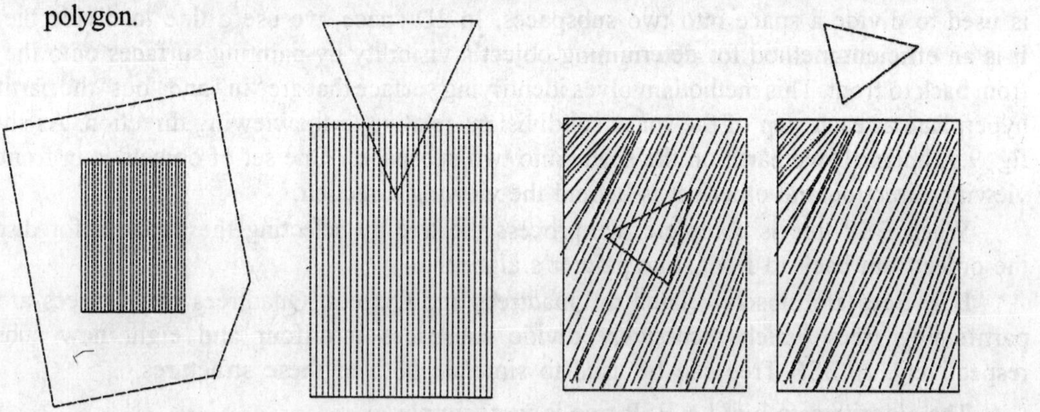

Surounding Polygons | Intersecting Polygon | Contained Polygon (colour of background) | Disjoint Polygon

Fig. 9.8 Area Subdivision Method

Disjoint polygons have no effect on the area of interest, same with the part of an intersecting polygon that is outside the area, whereas, the part of an intersecting polygon that is inside the area of interest is similar to contained polygon.

The tests for finding surface visibility within an area of interest can be written in terms of these four classifications. There is no need to further subdivide the specified area if any of the following conditions is true:

1. For polygons outside from area of interest (Disjoint), set the intensity of the area equal to the background color.
2. There is only one inside or intersecting polygon. Fill the area with the background color, and then render the polygon.
3. There is only one surrounding polygon then fill the area with the polygon's color.
4. If more than one polygon intersects, is inside, or surrounds, then at least one is a surrounding polygon.

Warnock's algorithm has an advantage of elegance and simplicity. The performance of the area subdivision technique can be further improved with other subdivision strategies. Some of these include:

1. Divide the area using an enclosed polygon vertex to set the dividing boundary.
2. Sort polygons by minimum Z and use the front polygon as the window boundary.

9.3.7 BSP Trees

A Binary Space Partitioning (BSP) tree represents a recursive, hierarchical partitioning, or subdivision, of n-dimensional space into subspaces. BSP tree construction is a process which takes a subspace and divides it by any hyperplane that intersects the interior of that subspace. The resultant is two new subspaces of dimension one less than actual one. These two new sub spaces that can be further partitioned by recursive application of the method.

A "hyperplane" is defined as an object of 'n-1' dimension in 'n' dimension plane and which is used to divide a space into two subspaces. In 2D space, we use a line to divide the space. It is an efficient method for determining object's visibility by painting surfaces onto the screen from back to front. This method involves identifying surface that are "in" and "out" the partitioning hyperplane at each step of the space subdivision, relative to the viewing direction. As shown in fig. 9.9, hplane1, we partition the space into two subspaces. One set of objects is in front of the viewing direction and other set is behind the viewing direction.

When BSP tree is complete, we process the tree by selecting the surfaces for display in the order from back to front, like painter's algorithm.

BSP trees are closely related to Quadtrees and Octrees. Quadtrees and Octrees are space partitioning trees which recursively divide subspaces into four and eight new subspaces, respectively. A BSP Tree can be used to simulate both of these structures.

The algorithm to build a BSP tree is very simple:

1. Select a partition plane.
2. Partition the set of polygons with the plane.
3. Recurse with each of the two new sets.

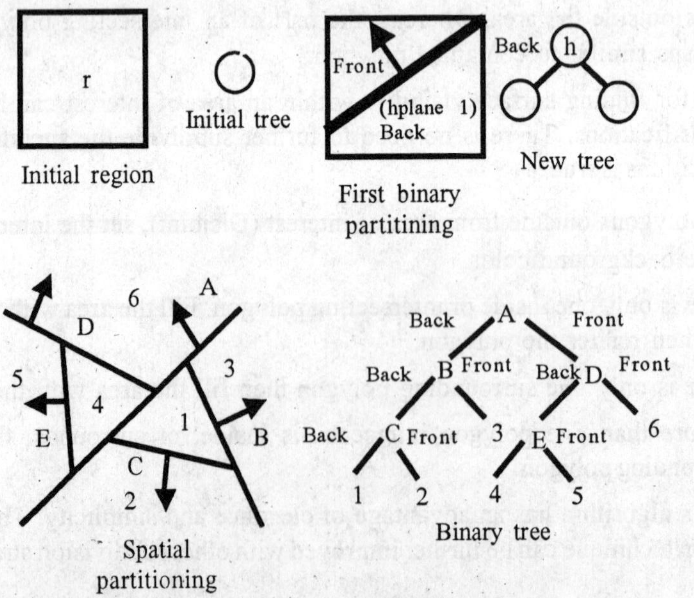

Fig. 9.9 Binary Space Partitioning Tree

9.3.8 Ray Tracing Algorithm

All hidden surface algorithm discussed so far depend upon some coherence characteristic of the scene to efficiently find the visible portions of the scene. In contrast, ray tracing is a brute-force technique.

The basic idea underlying the technique is that an observer views an object by means of light from a source that strikes the object and then somehow reaches the observer. The light may reach the observer by reflection from the surface, or by refraction or transmission through the surface. If light rays from the source are traced, very few reach the viewer. Consequently the process is computationally inefficient. Application originally suggested that rays should be traced in the opposite direction, i.e., from the observer to the object as shown below.

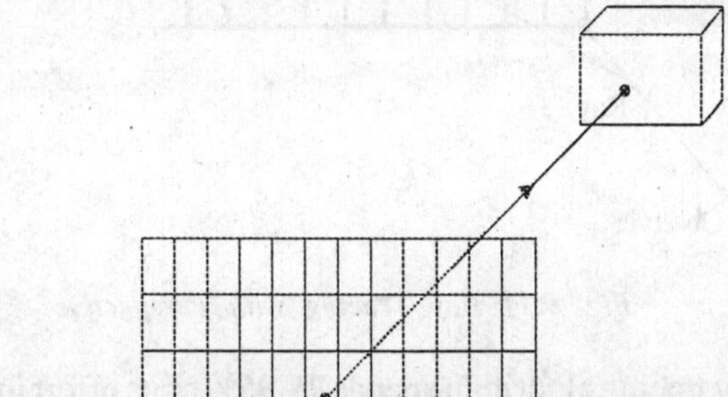

Fig. 9.10 Simple Ray Tracing

The algorithm assumes that the scene is transformed to image space. A perspective transformation is not applied. The viewpoint or observer is assumed to be at infinity, on the positive z-axis, hence all the light rays are parallel to the z-axis. Each ray passes from the observer, through the center of a pixel in the raster, into the scene. The path of each ray is traced to determine which objects in the scene, if any, are intersected by the ray. Every object in the scene must be examined for every ray. If a ray intersects an object, all possible intersections of the ray and object are determined. This process potentially yields multiple intersections for multiple objects. The intersections are sorted in depth. The intersection of the object closest to the observer, i.e., the one with the maximum z value, represents the visible surface for that pixel. The attributes for this object are used to determine the pixel's characteristics.

When the viewpoint is not located at infinity, the algorithm is only slightly more complex. Here, the observer is assumed located on the positive z axis. The image plane, i.e., the raster, is perpendicular to the z-axis as shown below. The effect is to perform a single point perspective projection onto the image plane.

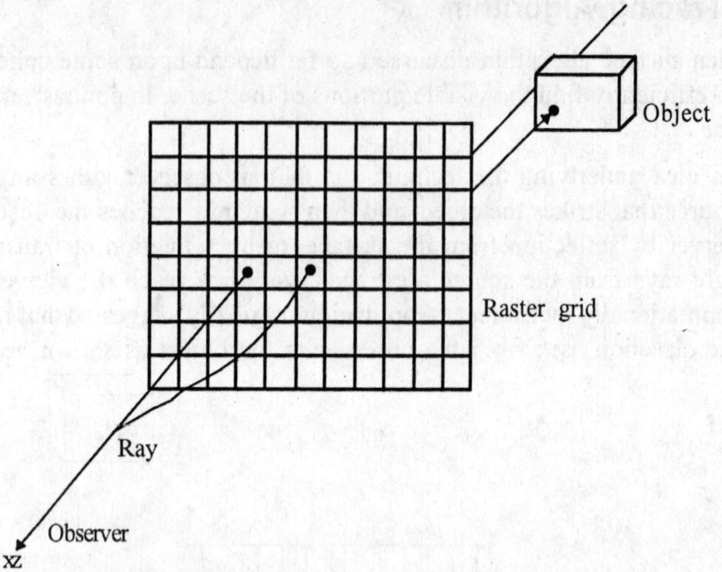

Fig. 9.11 Ray Tracing with Perspective

Since the simple ray tracing algorithm spends 75-95% of its effort in determining intersections, the efficiency of the intersection routine significantly effects the efficiency of the algorithm to eliminate unnecessary intersections, the intersection of a ray with the bounding volume of an object is examined. If the ray fails to intersect the bounding volumes of an object, then the object need not be considered further for the ray.

9.3.9 Bounding Volumes

Although bounding sphere can be inefficient, determining whether a 3-D ray intersects a sphere is simple. In particular, if the distance from the center of the bounding sphere to the ray is more than the radius of the sphere, then the ray does not intersect the bounding sphere. Hence, it cannot intersect the object.

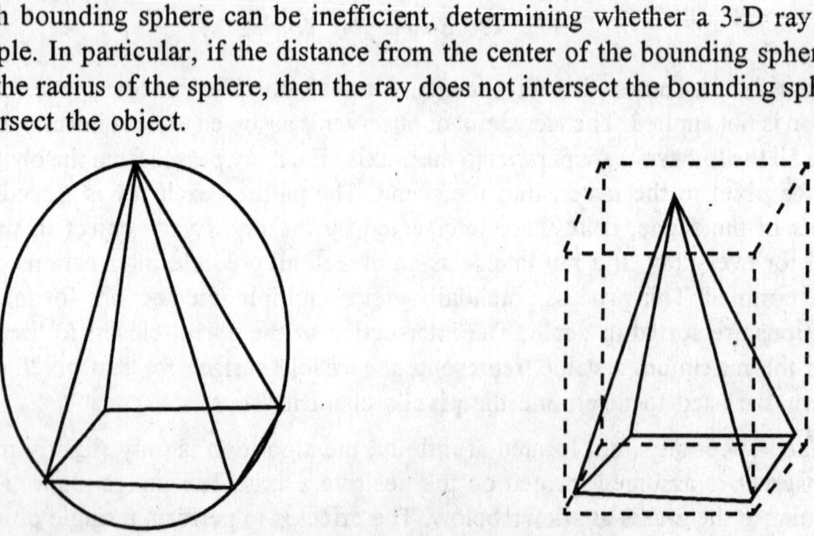

Fig. 9.12 Bounding Volumes

The bounding sphere test thus reduces in determining the distance from a point, i.e., the center of the sphere, to a three-dimensional line, i.e., the ray.

A parametric representation of the line segment, i.e., the ray, between the points $P_1(x_1, y_1, z_1)$ and $P_2(x_2, y_2, z_2)$ is.

$P(t) = P_1 + (P_2 - P_1)t \qquad t \geq 0$

With components

$$x = x_1 + (x_2 - x_1)t = x_1 + at$$

$$y = y_1 + (y_2 - y_1)t = y_1 + bt$$

$$z = z_1 + (z_2 - z_1)t = z_1 + ct$$

Here $(P_2 - P_1)$ and (a, b, c) represent the direction of the ray. The minimum distance, d, from the line to the point P_c (x_c, y_c, z_c), i.e., the center of the sphere, is:

$$d^2 = (x - x_c)^2 + (y - y_c)^2 + (z - z_c)^2$$

Where the parameter, t, specifying the point on P(t) for minimum distance is:

$$t = \frac{-a(x_1 - x_c) + b(y_2 - y_c) + c(z_1 - z_c)}{a^2 + b^2 + c^2}$$

If $d^2 > R^2$, where R is the radius of the bounding sphere, then the ray cannot intersect the object. If t is positive, i.e., $t > 0$, then only we see ray passing through the sphere; if t is imaginary, then may not pass through the sphere and if t is negative, i.e, $t < 0$, then ray is behind eye position.

Ray tracing/Ray casting is a visibility detection tool, based on geometric optics methods, which trace the path of light rays.

Ray tracing is popular for parallel implementation because, in its simplest form, each pixel is computed independently.

9.3.10 Floating Horizon Algorithm

Floating Horizon Algorithm is usually implemented in image space. In image space, aliasing may occur. It is most commonly used for rendering a mathematical defined surface. It can be implemented in object space (with a root finding algorithm, which may be expensive). Floating horizon frequently used to remove hidden lines in 3-D of surfaces represented in the implicit form.

$f(x, y, z) = 0$

The fundamental idea behind the technique is to convert 3-D problem to 2-D problem by intersecting the surface with series of cutting planes at constant values of x, y or z.

Surface is represented by curves drawn on it, say curves of constant height $z = c$ for multiple values of c.

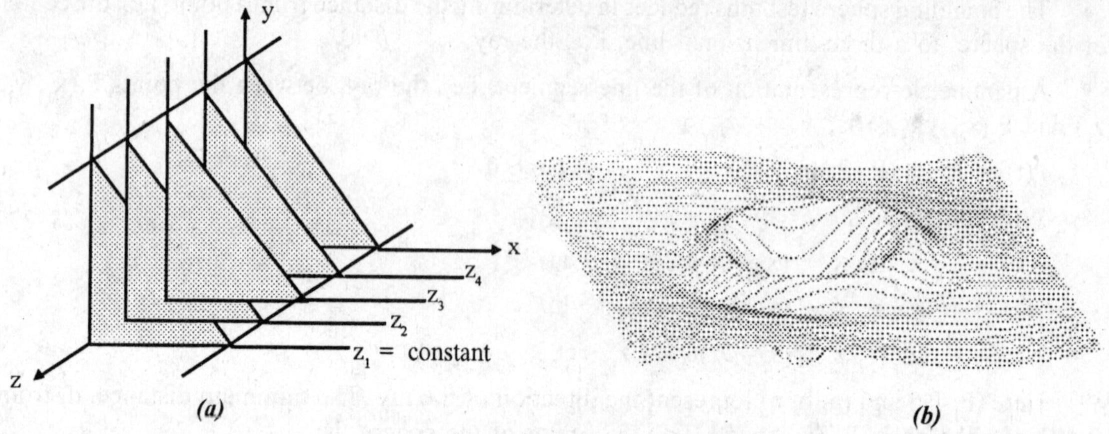

Fig. 9.13 Floating Horizon Method

The function f(x, y, z) = 0 is reduced to a curve in each of these parallel planes,
y = f(x, z) or x = h(y, z)

where z is constant for each of the planes.

The algorithm first sorts the *z* = constant planes by increasing distance from the viewpoints. Beginning with the *z* = constant plane closest to the viewpoint, the curve in each plane is generated, i.e., for each *x* co-ordinate in image space, the appropriate *y* value is determined. The hidden line algorithm is then stated as "If at any given value of *x* and *y* value of the curve in the current plane is larger than the *y* value for any previous curve at that *x* value, then the curve is visible, otherwise it is hidden."

Implementation of algorithm is quite simple. An array of size equal to the resolution of image space in the *x* direction is used to contain the largest value of *y* at each *x* location. The values in this array represent the current "horizon". Thus, the horizon "floats up" as each succeeding curve is drawn. Effectively, this is a one-line hidden line algorithm.

9.4 SUMMARY

When we see an object, only a part of it is visible and rest of the part is not visible from that angle. In computer graphics, to detect which part of an object is visible and which part is not visible, we have a number of algorithms, known as visible surface detection algorithms. These algorithms are classified as image precision and object precision. In this chapter, we have discussed different visible surface detection algorithms.

9.5 GLOSSARY

- One of the most challenging problems in computer graphics is removal of hidden parts from images of solid objects. This is sometimes also referred to as *visible surface detection*.
- The object space algorithm concentrates on the geometrical relationships among the objects in the scene definition in order to determine which parts of which objects are visible.

- Image space algorithm concentrates on the final image and asks what is visible within each raster pixel, i.e., visibility is decided point by point at each pixel position on the projection plane.
- The computation time of an object space algorithm will tend to grow with the number of objects in the scene.
- The image space computation tends to grow with the complexity of the visible parts of the image.
- **Coherence:** It is the degree to which parts of an environment or its projection exhibit local similarities.
- **Scan-line coherence:** It arises because the display of a scan line in a raster image is usually very similar to the display of the preceding scan line.
- **Object coherence:** It is the results from relationships or comparisons between different objects or between separate parts of the same object.
- Number of entries in Z-buffer is equal to the number of entries in frame buffer.

9.6 EXERCISE

Q1. What is visible surface detection?

Q2. What are the types of visible surface detection algorithm?

Q3. Differentiate between image space algorithms and object space algorithm.

Q4. Explain Z-buffer algorithm.

Q5. Explain A-buffer algorithm

Q6. What is coherence? Explain different types of coherence.

Q7. State advantages and disadvantages of Z-buffer algorithm.

Q8. Explain the scan line method of visible surface detection.

Q9. Explain briefly the BSP method.

Q10. Explain Warnock's area subdivision algorithm in detail.

E N D

CHAPTER 10 Drawing Graphics

10.1 INTRODUCTION

Computer Graphics is one of the most powerful and interesting facet of computers. There is a lot that you can do in graphics like animation, video games, films etc. The intension of this chapter is to give you an idea of implementing certain things in C. The main aim is to make you comfortable with the basic concepts of Computer Graphics. Before discussing drawing graphics in C further, a basic understanding of concepts is required.

10.2 BASIC CONCEPTS

10.2.1 Pixel

Pixels (short for picture element) are the basic building blocks of all bitmap images – the individual elements that are grouped to form a picture.

Now a days, the term pixel is used for a number of things like the individual dots on computer screens, dot and laser printer produces and the individual elements of a bitmap graphics. The workings of all these elements are not same, so it can be confusing by calling all of them as pixels. For information, all above elements are defined as:

- Pixels are associated to the individual elements within bitmap graphic files.
- Video pixel is associated to the picture element of computer screen.
- Dots will refer to individual points that are made by laser printers.

10.2.2 Monitor Resolution

Physical Resolution

The physical resolution of your monitor is a measurement of the maximum number of individual dots your computer monitor can produce. This is measured as the number of dots in one horizontal line of dots, and the number of horizontal lines of dots that can be produced vertically.

Display Resolution

The display resolution of your monitor is determined by the device called video card and the software that runs on that device. The display resolution is measured in the number of video pixels displayed on screen. The display resolution is usually written in the form 640 × 480 or 1020 × 768 – referring to the number of pixels being generated horizontally and vertically.

10.2.3 Dot-Pitch

The distance between individual dots (measured in millimetres). It affects how sharp the display of the monitor appear, i.e., the graphics would appear.

10.2.4 Dot Size

Dot size may be defined as the diameter of a single dot on the devices output. Dot size is also called as the Spot size.

10.2.5 Aspect Ratio

Aspect ratio of graphics is referred to ratio of the number of horizontal pixels and number of vertical pixels that go into making up that graphic.

10.2.6 Bit Depth

A bit is the smallest unit of memory used by the computer and can have a value of 0 or 1, i.e., on or off. The color of each pixel is stored by the computer using bits. The more bits the computer uses to store the color, the more colors you get. The number of bits the computer uses for each pixel is the *bit depth.*

Four bits or 'bit depth 4' gives 24 or 16 different colors; 8 bit depth gives 28 or 256 different colors; 24 bit depth gives 2 24 or over 16 million different colors. A 24-bit depth is often called true color since 16 million colors are more than enough to approximate all possible colors the human eye can see.

Relation between Bitmap and File Size

Memory space require to store a bitmap primarily depends upon three factors:

- Dimension of an mage (image aspect ratio).
- Bit depth of pixels.
- File format used to store the image.

10.2.7 Scissoring

In computer graphics, the deleting of any parts of an image which fall outside of a window that has been sized and laid over the original image. Also known as "clipping". Scissoring, solves the problem of separating the visible information from the invisible provided both are kept in high-speed storage. Unfortunately, a memory management problem arises since main memory can overflow in an attempt to accommodate large sheets. The cellular structure, however, solves this problem by pre-scissoring, and the cell becomes the single fundamental unit of display information for transition between visible and invisible and between main memory and disk.

10.2.8 Addressability

In computer graphics, the capability of a display surface or storage device to accommodate a specified number of uniquely identifiable points, or the number of addressable points on a display surface or storage.

10.2.9 Addressable Point

In computer graphics, any point of a device that can be addressed, or a point that can be found, located, or accessed in a predefined coordinate system.

10.2.10 Interdot Distance

Interdot distance is the reciprocal of addressability. If the addressability is large, the interdot distance will be less. The interdot distance should be less to get smooth shapes.

10.2.11 GKS

The Graphical Kernel System (GKS) is a document produced by the International Standards Organization (ISO) which defines a common interface to interactive computer graphics for application programs. GKS has been designed by a group of experts representing the national standards institutions of most major industrialized countries. The full standard provides functional specifications for some 200 subroutines which perform graphics input and output in a device independent way. Application programs can thus move freely between different graphics devices and different host computers. For the first time, graphics programs have become genuinely portable.

10.2.12 GKS Functions

The GKS functions are separated into those which pass values to GKS for control, setting or output, and those which inquire about status information. There are 8 distinct classes:

1. Control Functions
2. Output Attributes
3. Output Primitives
4. Segment Functions
5. Transformations
6. Input Functions

7. Metafile Functions
8. Inquiry Functions

10.2.13 YIQ Color Model

YIQ is the color space used by the NTSC color TV system, employed mainly in North and Central America, and Japan. The Y component represents the luma information, and is the only component used by black-and-white television receivers. I and Q represent the chrominance information. I stands for *in-phase*, while *Q* stands for *quadrature*, referring to the components used in quadrature amplitude modulation. The YIQ system is intended to take advantage of human color-response characteristics. The eye is more sensitive to changes in the orange blue (I) range than in the purple-green range (Q) — therefore less bandwidth is required for Q than for I.

Broadcast NTSC limits I to 1.3 MHz and Q to 0.4 MHz. I and Q are frequency interleaved into the 4 MHz Y signal, which keeps the bandwidth of the overall signal down to 4.2 MHz. In YUV systems, since U and V both contain information in the orange-blue range, both components must be given the same amount of bandwidth as I to achieve similar color fidelity.

10.2.14 Device Drivers

Device drivers are small programs which can communicate directly to the hardware. It is not good to become machine-dependent at any time, so we need these small programs to communicate with the hardware in a standardized manner.

10.3 DRAWING GRAPHICS USING C

Whenever we have to draw any graphics on the screen, it is necessary to include a header file named "Graphics.h" and a library file named "Graphics.lib". In "Graphics.h" we have all the definitions and explanations of all the functions and constants we'll need to draw any graphics; and all the graphics related functions are kept in the graphics library file. TURBO C provides both of these files.

To switch over to the graphics mode that offers the best display resolution, we require to call the function *initgraph()*. It determines the best display resolution and store the number associated to that mode in the variable 'gm'. This number gives the information about the monitor, its resolution, color it supports etc. 'initgraph' initializes the graphics system by loading a graphics driver from disk and putting the system into graphics mode. 'initgraph' also resets all graphics settings (color, palette, current position, viewport, etc.) to their defaults, then resets graph result to 0.

Declaration:

*void far initgraph (int far *graphdriver, int far *graphmode, char far *pathtodriver),* *closegraph()* function switches back the screen from graphics mode to text mode. It clears the screen also. A graphics program should have a *closegraph* function at the end of graphics. Otherwise, DOS screen will not go to text mode after running the program.

graphdriver

Next thing to understand is gdriver (graphic drivers). These are a subset of device drivers and are applicable only in the graphics mode. Integer that specifies the graphics driver to be used. These graphics drivers are the files with a BGI extension. Now corresponding to the value of 'gm' i.e. the graphics adapter is being used, one among these drivers gets selected. To know which driver file is associated to our adapter, i.e., the value assigned to gdriver, we call DETECTO, thereby asking *initgraph()* to determine which BGI is required. This file is then loaded to memory. We can even directly set up 'gdriver' and 'gm' with appropriate values.

graphmode

Next thing that we need to do before glowing any pixel on the screen, is to switch to the right graphics mode (gm). Graphics mode is totally dependent upon the graphics adapter and monitor installed on the system. Mostly, very few graphics modes are available on a system. Each graphics mode is associated with a number. Among all the graphics modes available on our system, our aim is to switch to that one which provides us the best possible display resolution. If *graphdriver = DETECT, initgraph sets *graphmode to the highest resolution available for the detected driver. You can give *graphmode a value using a constant of the graphics_modes enumeration type.

pathtodriver

Specifies the directory path where initgraph looks for graphics drivers (*.BGI) first. If they're not there, initgraph looks in the current directory. If pathtodriver is null, the driver files must be in the current directory.

```
/*My First Computer Graphics Program*/
#include <graphics.h>
#include <conio.h>
void main()
{
int gdriver=DETECT, gm;
initgraph(&gdriver, &gm, "d:\\tc\\");
circle(200,100,150);
getch();
closegraph();
}
```

10.4 BASIC SHAPES

Now let us write a program to draw some basic shapes.

10.4.1 C Program

```
#include <graphics.h>
#include <conio.h>
void main()
{
int gdriver=DETECT, gm;
int poly[12]={350,450,350,410,430,400,350,350,300,430, 350,450};
initgraph(&gdriver, &gm, "d:\\tc\\");
circle(100,100,50);
outtextxy(75,170, "Circle");
rectangle(200,50,350,150);
outtextxy(240, 170, "Rectangle");
ellipse(500, 100,0,360, 100,50);
outtextxy(480, 170, "Ellipse");
line(100,250,540,250);
outtextxy(300,260,"Line");
sector(150, 400, 30, 300, 100,50);
outtextxy(120, 460, "Sector");
drawpoly(6, poly);
outtextxy(340, 460, "Polygon");
getch();
closegraph();
}
```

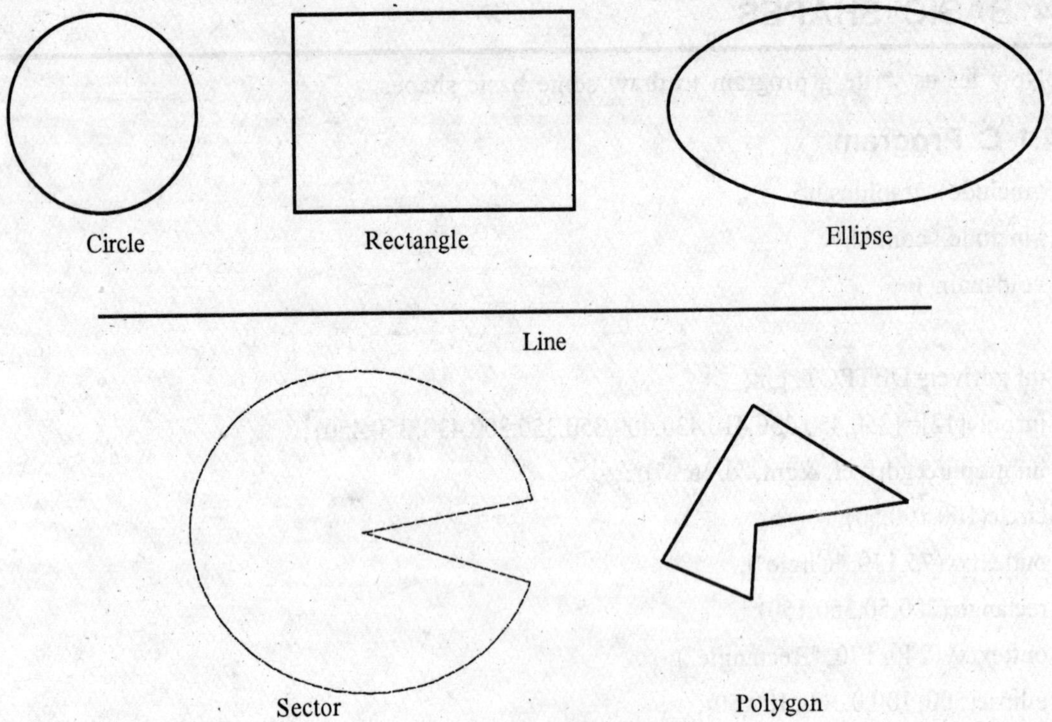

Fig. 10.1 Basic Shapes

Here, *circle()* function takes x, y coordinates of the circle with respect to left top of the screen and radius of the circle in terms of pixels as arguments. Note that, in graphics, almost all the screen parameters are measured in terms of pixels.

Function *outtextxy()* displays a string in graphical mode. You can use different fonts, text sizes, alignments, colors and directions of the text. Parameters passed are x and y coordinates of the position on the screen where text is to be displayed. There is another function *outtext()* that displays a text in the current position. Current position is the place where last drawing is ended. These functions are declared as follows:

```
void far outtextxy(int x, int y, char *text);
void far outtext(char *text);
```

10.5 BASIC COLORS

Here is some idea about colors. There are 16 colors declared in graphics.h as listed below.

BLACK : 0

BLUE : 1

GREEN : 2

CYAN : 3

RED	:	4
MAGENTA	:	5
BROWN	:	6
LIGHTGRAY	:	7
DARKGRAY	:	8
LIGHTBLUE	:	9
LIGHTGREEN	:	10
LIGHTCYAN	:	11
LIGHTRED	:	12
LIGHTMAGENTA	:	13
YELLOW	:	14
WHITE	:	15

To use these colors, use functions setcolor(), setbkcolor() and setfillstyle(). setcolor() function sets the current drawing color. If we use setcolor(RED); and draw any shape, line or text after that, the drawing will be in red color. You can either use color as defined above or number like setcolor(4); setbkcolor() sets background color for drawing. Setfillstyle sets fill pattern and fill colors. After calling setfillstyle, if we use functions like floodfill, fillpoly, bar etc, shpes will be filled with fill color and pattern set using setfillstyle. These function declarations are as follows.

Declaration:

- void far setfillstyle(int pattern, int color);
- void far setcolor(int color);
- void far setbkcolor(int color);

The parameter pattern in setfillstyle is as follows:

Names	**Value**	**Means Fill With...**
EMPTY_FILL	0	Background color
SOLID_FILL	1	Solid fill
LINE_FILL	2	—-
LTSLASH_FILL	3	///
SLASH_FILL	4	///, thick lines
BKSLASH_FILL	5	\\\\\\, thick lines
LTBKSLASH_FILL	6	\\\\\\
HATCH_FILL	7	Light hatch
XHATCH_FILL	8	Heavy crosshatch
INTERLEAVE_FILL	9	Interleaving lines

WIDE_DOT_FILL	10	Widely spaced dots
CLOSE_DOT_FILL	11	Closely spaced dots
USER_FILL	12	User-defined fill pattern

Here is an example program with colors, pixels, bar, cleardevice etc. stdlib.h is used for random number generation. We have a function random(no), it returns a random number between 0 and no. The effect is by drawing random radius, random color circles with same center and random pixels. kbhit() function(defined in conio.h) returns a non-zero value when a key is pressed in the keyboard. So, the loop will continue until a key is pressed.

10.5.1 C Program

```
/* PROGRAM TO DISPLAY SOME GRAPHICS EFFECTS USING RANDOM
NUMBERS.*/
#include <graphics.h>
#include <conio.h>
#include <stdlib.h>
void main()
{
int gdriver=DETECT, gm;
initgraph(&gdriver, &gm, "d:\\tc\\");
setcolor(3);
setfillstyle(SOLID_FILL,RED);
bar(50, 50, 590, 430);
setfillstyle(1, 14);
bar(100, 100, 540, 380);
while(!kbhit())
{
putpixel(random(439)+101, random(279)+101,random(16));
setcolor(random(16));
circle(320,240,random(100));
}
getch();
closegraph();
}
```

10.6 SUMMARY

In this chapter, we have discussed basic definitions in computer graphics and basic shapes and colors. We have also studied how to write graphics programs using C.

10.7 GLOSSARY

- Pixels (short for picture element) are the basic building blocks of all bitmap images – the individual elements that are grouped to form a picture.
- The physical resolution of your monitor is a measurement of the maximum number of individual dots your computer monitor can produce.
- The display resolution of your monitor is determined by the device called video card and the software that runs on that device.
- The distance between individual dots (measured in millimetres). It affects how sharp the display of the monitor appear, i.e., the graphics would appear.
- Aspect ratio of graphics is referred to ratio of the number of horizontal pixels and number of vertical pixels that go into making up that graphic.
- The capability of a display surface or storage device to accommodate a specified number of uniquely identifiable points, or the number of addressable points on a display surface or storage, is known as addressability.
- Device drivers are small programs which can communicate directly to the hardware.

10.8 EXERCISE

Q1. Differentiate between addressability and addressable point?

Q2. Write a program to draw circle, ellipse and line using C.

Q3. What is Aspect Ratio?

Q4. What is a dot size?

Q5. What is interdot distance?

Q6. Explain Dot-pitch.

Q7. Define Pixel in brief.

Q8. Write short notes on:

(i) Physical Resolution

(ii) Display Resolution

(iii) Bit-depth

(iv) Device Drivers

(v) Scissoring

END

Appendix A1 - Short Answer Type Questions

Q1. Can you give some basic features of computer graphics?

Ans. The salient feature of computer graphics is the creation and manipulation of graphics (artificial images) by computer.

Q2. Can you tell which major components (hardware and software) are needed for computer graphics?

Ans. Besides the basic computer, some special devices and software may be required especially for computer graphics. For hardware, a special high-resolution, color monitor is often demanded and some input tools, e.g., mouse and joy-sticker, and hard-copy devices, e.g. high-resolution color printer, may be required. For software, some special purpose utilities (device-dependent and device-independent) are needed for handling processing in computer graphics.

Q3. Can you list at least three important applications of computer graphics?

Ans. There are many interesting applications of computer graphics. Three common applications are graphic user interface (GUI), computer-aided design (CAD), and computer games.

Q4. Define Computer Graphics.

Ans. Computer graphics remains one of the most existing and rapidly growing computer fields. Computer graphics may be defined as a pictorial representation or graphical representation of objects in a computer.

Q5. What is meant by scan code?

Ans. When a key is pressed on the keyboard, the keyboard controller places a code carry to the key pressed into a part of the memory called as the keyboard buffer. This code is called as the scan code.

Q6. What does refreshing of the screen mean?

Ans. Some method is needed for maintaining the picture on the screen. Refreshing of screen is done by keeping the phosphorus glowing to redraw the picture repeatedly, i.e., by quickly directing the electronic beam back to the same points.

Q7. Define Random Scan/Raster Scan displays.

Ans. Random scan is a method in which the display is made by the electronic beam, which is directed, only to the points or part of the screen where the picture is to be drawn.

The Raster scan system is a scanning technique in which the electrons sweep from top to bottom and from left to right. The intensity is turned on or off to light and unlight the pixel.

Q8. Explain the merits and demerits of Penetration techniques.

Ans. The merits and demerits of the Penetration techniques are as follows:

1. It is an inexpensive technique.
2. It has only four colors.
3. The quality of the picture is not good when it is compared to other techniques.
4. It can display color scans in monitors.

Q9. Explain the merits and demerits of DVST.

Ans. The merits and demerits of direct view storage tubes (DVST) are as follows:

1. It has a flat screen.
2. Refreshing of screen is not required.
3. Selective or part erasing of screen is not possible.
4. It has poor contrast.
5. Performance is inferior to the refresh CRT.

Q10. What do you mean by emissive and non-emissive displays?

Ans. Emissive:

The emissive display converts electrical energy into light energy. The plasma panels, thin film electro-luminescent displays are the examples.

Non-emissive:

They are optical effects to convert the sunlight or light from any other source to graphic form. Liquid crystal display is an example.

Q11. Explain the merits and demerits of Plasma panel display.

Ans. Advantages:

1. Refreshing is not required.
2. Produce a very steady image free of Flicker.
3. Less bulky than a CRT.

Disadvantages:

1. Poor resolution of up to 60 d.p.i.
2. It requires complex addressing and wiring.
3. It is costlier than CRT.

Q12. What is persistence?

Ans. The time it takes the emitted light from the screen to decay one tenth of its original intensity is called as persistence.

Q13. What is resolution?

Ans. The maximum number of points that can be displayed without an overlap on a CRT is called as resolution.

Q14. What is Aspect Ratio?

Ans. The ratio of vertical points to the horizontal points necessary to produce length of lines in both directions of the screen is called Aspect Ratio. Usually, the aspect ratio is ¾.

Q15. What is meant by Addressability?

Ans. Addressability is the number of individual dots per inch (d.p.i.) that can be created. If the address of the current dot is (x, y), then the next dot will be (x + y), (x + y + 1) etc.

Q16. What is a dot size?

Ans. Dot size may be defined as the diameter of a single dot on the devices output. Dot size is also called as the Spot size.

Q17. What is interdot distance?

Ans. Interdot distance is the reciprocal of addressability. If the addressability is large, the interdot distance will be less. The interdot distance should be less to get smooth shapes.

Q18. What is the difference between impact and non-impact printers?

Ans. **Impact printers** press formed character faces against an inked ribbon on to the paper. A line printer and dot-matrix printer are examples.

Non-impact printers and plotters use Laser techniques, inkjet sprays, Xerographic process, electrostatic methods and electro thermal methods to get images onto the papers. Examples are: Inkjet/Laser printers.

Q19. What is the features of Inkjet printers?

Ans. Features of inkjet printers:

1. They can print 2 to 4 pages/minutes.
2. Resolution is about 360 d.p.i. Therefore, better print quality is achieved.
3. The operating cost is very low. The only part that requires replacement is ink cartridge.
4. Four colors – cyan, yellow, magenta, black are available.

Q20. What are the advantages of laser printers?

Ans. Advantages of laser printer:

1. High speed, precision and economy.
2. Cheap to maintain.
3. Quality printers.
4. Lasts for longer time.
5. Toner power is very cheap.

Q21. What is the advantages of electrostatic plotters?

Ans. Advantages of electrostatic plotters:

1. They are faster than pen plotters and very high quality printers.
2. Recent electrostatic plotters include a scan conversion capability.
3. Color electrostatic plotters are available. They make multiple passes over the paper to plot color pictures.

Q22. Explain the differences between a general graphics system designed for a programmer and one designed for a specific application, such as architectural design?

Ans. Basically, packages designed for graphics programming contain functions for setting primitives, attributes, and parameters for various graphics operations such as viewing and transformations. Packages designed for applications allow a user to create scenes in terms of the particular application, rather than in terms of graphics functions.

Q23. Consider three different raster systems with resolutions of 640 × 480, 1280 × 1024 and 2560 × 2048.

1. **What size is frame buffer (in bytes) for each of these systems to store 12 bits per pixel?**
2. **How much storage (in bytes) is required for each system if 24 bits per pixel are to be stored?**

Ans. 1. Because eight bits constitute a byte, frame buffer sizes of the systems are as follows:

640 × 480 × 12 bits π 8 = 450KB

1280 × 1024 × 12 bits π 8 = 1920KB

2560 × 2048 × 12 bits π 8 = 7680KB

2. Similarly, each of the above results is just doubled for 24 (12 × 2) bits of storage perpixel.

Q24. Consider two raster systems with the resolutions of 640 × 480 and 1280 × 1024.

1. **How many pixels could be accessed per second in each of these systems by a display controller that refreshes the screen at a rate of 60 frames per second?**
2. **What is the access time per pixel in each system?**

Ans. 1. Since 60 frames are refreshed per second and each frame consists of 640 × 480 pixels, the access rate of such a system is:

(640 × 480) × 60 = 1.8432 × 107 pixels/second.

Likewise, for the 1280 × 1024 system, the access rate is:

(1280 × 1024) × 60 = 7.86432 × 107 pixels/second.

2. According to the definition of access rate, we know that the access time per pixel should be 1/(access rate). Therefore, the access time is around 54 nanoseconds/pixel for the 640 × 480 system, and the access time is around 12.7 nanoseconds/pixel for the 1280 × 1024 system.

Q25. Consider a raster system with the resolution of 1024 × 768 pixels and the color palette calls for 65,536 colors. What is the minimum amount of video RAM that the computer must have to support the above-mentioned resolution and number of colors?

Ans. Recall that the color of each pixel on a display is represented with some number of bits. Hence, a display capable of showing up to 256 colors is using 8 bits per pixels. Notice, first that the color palette calls for 65,536 colors. This number is but 216, which implies that 16 bits are being used to represent the color of each pixel on the display. The display's resolution is 1024 by 768 pixels, which implies that there is a total of 786,432 (1024 × 768) pixels on the display. Hence, the total number of bits required to display any of 65,536 colors on each of the screen's 786,432 pixels is 12,582,912 (786,432 × 16). Dividing this value by 8 yields an answer of 1,572,864 bytes. Dividing that value by 1,024 yields an answer of 1,536 KB. Dividing that value by 1,024 yields an answer of 1.5 MB.

Q26. What is a Display file?

Ans. The display file is a set of ***graphic orders*** that are commands to the display unit to generate an image. The display file for a sheet thus contains a large number (perhaps thousands) of commands taken from a small set of graphic orders **(DESIGNPAD** uses only eight with any frequency). If this file is presented to the display unit, the sheet will be displayed. Unfortunately, this makes no sense in **DESIGNPAD** since the sheet is very large compared to the screen size. Most display units will display unintelligible information when presented with a display file that requests offscreen images. To overcome this problem, two solutions – scaling and windowing'-were considered. Scaling reduces an image to fit into a given area, whereas windowing (or scissoring) "cuts out" and displays a portion of the image. To provide the user with flexibility, either technique must be done dynamically so that the windowing or scaling can be quickly changed under user control.

Q27. What is a thermal printer? Explain the mechanism of the thermal printer.

Ans. ***Thermal Printers***

A thermal printer produces a printed image by selectively heating coated thermochromic paper, or thermal paper as it is commonly known, when the paper passes over the thermal print head. The coating turns black in the areas where it is heated, producing an image. Two color direct thermal printers are capable of printing both black and an additional color (often red), by applying heat at two different temperatures. Thermal transfer printing is a related method that uses a heat-sensitive ribbon instead of heat-sensitive paper.

Efficient Mechanism

A thermal printer comprises these key components:

1. Thermal head — generates heat; prints on paper
2. Platen — a rubber roller that feeds paper
3. Spring — applies pressure to the thermal head, causing it to contact the thermo-sensitive paper
4. Controller boards — for controlling the mechanism

In order to print, one inserts thermo-sensitive paper between the thermal head and the platen. The printer sends an electrical current to the heating resistor of the thermal head, which in turn generates heat in a prescribed pattern. The heat activates the thermo-sensitive coloring layer of the thermo-sensitive paper, which manifests a pattern of color change in response. Such a printing mechanism is known as a thermal system or direct system. Thermal printers print faster and more quietly than dot-matrix printers. They are also more economical.

Q29. Write a short history of graphics?

Ans. – 1950: MIT Whirlwind (CRT)

– 1955: Sage, Radar with CRT and light pen

– 1958: Willy Higinbotham "Tennis"

– 1960: MIT "Spacewar" on DEC PDP-1

– 1963: Ivan Sutherland's "Sketchpad" (CAD)

– 1969: ACM Siggraph founded

– 1968: Tektronix storage tube ($5-10.000)

– 1968: Evans and Sutherland (flight simulators) founded

– 1968: Douglas Engelbart: computer mouse

– 1970: Xerox: GUI

– 1971: Gourand shading

– 1974: Z-buffer

– 1975: Phong model

– 1979: Eurographics founded

– 1980: Whitted: Ray tracing

– 1981: Apollo Workstation, IBM PC

– 1982: Silicon Graphics (SGI) founded

– 1984: X Window System

– 1984: First Silicon Graphics Workstations (IRIS GL)

– Until mid/end of 1990s: Dominance of SGI in the high end

- HW: RealityEngine, InfiniteReality, RealityMonster, ...
- SW: OpenGL, OpenInventor, Performer, Digital Media Libs, ...

– End of 1990s: Low- to mid range taken over by "PCs" (Nvidia, ATI, ...)

- HW: Fast development cycles, Graphics-on-a-chip, ...
- SW: Direct 3D and OpenGL, computer games

– Today

- Programmable graphics hardware, Cg

Appendix A2 - Question Papers

GURU GOBIND SINGH INDRAPRASTHA UNIVERSITY
END TERM EXAMINATION (REAPPEAR)
SECOND SEMESTER (MCA), MAY – 2011

Paper Code: MCA108 **Subject: Computer Graphics**

Time: 3 Hours **Maximum Marks: 75**

Note: Section A is Compulsory. Attempt any three questions from Section B.

SECTION – A

Q.1. Write short notes on any FOUR of the following:

(a) Principle Vanishing Points

(b) 3-D Transformation matrices of Scaling, Rotation and Shear

(c) Octrees

(d) Illumination model for diffused reflection

(e) Testing for first and second order continuities

(f) DVST (Direct View Storage Tube)

Q.2. (i) Explain Scan Line algorithm for Hidden Surface Removal (4)

(ii) Why Mid point sub division algorithm is preferred over Cohen-Sutherland algorithm for line clipping.? (3)

(iii) Write Mid point algorithm for drawing a circle (3)

SECTION – B

Q.3. (a) Describe the advantages of using homogeneous coordinates (4)

(b) Consider the square (0,0), (0,2), (2,0). Perform a composite transformation of the square using the following steps. Give the coordinates of the square at each intermediate step.

(i) Scale by using $S_x = 2$ and $S_y = 3$

(ii) Rotate by 45° in the anti-clockwise direction

(iii) Translate by using $T_x = 3$ and $T_y = 5$ (6)

Q.4. (a) Write the empirical model for calculating specular reflection range given in the Phong Model (5)

(b) Determine the blending functions of uniform, periodic B-spline curves for 4 control points and degrees of polynomial equal to 2 (5)

Q.5. (a) Discuss RGB color model in brief (3)

(b) What is meant by gamma correction? (3)

(c) Derive window to viewport transformations (4)

Q.6. (a) Describe sweep representations for solid modeling (3)

(b) Write and discuss the depth buffer algorithm to display the visible surfaces in a scene containing any number of polyhedrons (7)

Q.7. (a) Explain briefly Transparency, Shadows and Object reflection (2)

(b) Find a transformation that aligns the vector: (2)

V = 2I – J – K with z-axis.

(c) Explain Fractal dimensions with examples.

(d) What is meant by CSG? Explain. (2)

(e) Explain image processing in brief.

GURU GOBIND SINGH INDRAPRASTHA UNIVERSITY
END TERM EXAMINATION
SECOND SEMESTER (MCA), MAY – 2010

Paper Code: MCA108 **Subject: Computer Graphics**

Time: 3 Hours **Maximum Marks: 75**

Note: Question 1 is Compulsory. Attempt any one question from each unit.

Q.1. Answer following questions: (2 × 10 = 20)

(a) List and explain the applications of computer graphics.

(b) Consider the raster system with resolution of 1280 by 1024. What size frame buffer (in bytes) is needed for the system to store if 24 bits pixels are to be stored?

(c) Define clipping. What is polygon clipping?

(d) Explain Octrees.

(e) Why are hidden surface algorithms needed?

(f) Explain Bezier Surface.

(g) What is scan conversion?

(h) What do you mean by Lllumination Model?

(i) Explain the purpose of BSP Tree.

(j) What do you mean by Constructive Solid Geometry?

UNIT – I

Q.2. (a) Explain Bresenham's line drawing algorithm. Give the advantages of this algorithm over DDA algorithm. (5)

(b) Compute the intermediate points on the line drawn from (0,0) to (5,10) using Bresenham's algorithm. (5)

Q.3. (a) Define window to viewport transformation. (5)

(b) Compute 2-D transformation matrix for rotating a point (12,6) about the point (3,2) by an angle 30^0 in clockwise direction. (5)

UNIT – II

Q.4. (a) Give the properties and limitations of a Bezier curve. (5)

(b) Construct equations for a Bezier curve with two, three and four control points using casteljau's algorithm. (5)

Q.5. (a) Prove that the open uniform B-spline curve for n = 3, k = 4 is the cubic Bezier curve. (5)

(b) Four control points P0(a,b), P1(2,5), P2(4,4) and P3(7,c) are on a uniform quadratic B-spline. Determine the values of a, b and c if the curve starts from the points (1,4) and terminates with the slope (-0.5). (5)

UNIT – III

Q.6. (a) Give the properties of a good representation of solids. (4)

(b) Describe spatial occupancy enumeration method for spatial partitioning representation of solids. What are the advantages of octrees? (6)

Q.7. (a) What do you mean by parallel projection and perspective projection? (4)

(b) Drive a matrix for projection of a point P(x,y,z) onto a projection plane at a distance Z_p from the origin and perpendicular to z-axis. (6)

UNIT – IV

Q.8. (a) Describe Gouraud shading. What are mach bands? (4)

(b) What are the two main approaches used for hidden surface removal? Explain briefly the methods used in each approach. (6)

Q.9. (a) Describe how the z-buffer hidden surface removal algorithm works. (4)

(b) Write the empirical model for calculating specular reflection range given in the Phong Model. (6)

WEST BENGAL UNIVERSITY OF TECHNOLOGY
MCA EXAMINATIONS, JUNE -2009
GRAPHICS & MULTIMEDIA
SEMESTER – 4

Time: 3 Hours **[Full Marks: 70]**

GROUP – A

(Multiple Choice Type Questions)

1. Choose the correct alternatives for the following: (10 × 1 = 10)

(i) Raster scan display means that the screen is scanned

(a) Top to bottom and right to left

(b) Left to right and top to bottom

(c) Bottom to top and left to right

(d) Bottom to top and right to left

(ii) The correct statement for Bezier curve is

(a) Best curve is drawn when stating and end slope of a curve are same

(b) A curve is proper only if cubic polynomials for *X* & *Y* identical

(c) The control points may lie anywhere on screen

(d) The control points should be so placed that the values of X coordinate are in increasing order.

(iii) When transforming a random Axis-Aligned Bounding Box defined by the points (near x, near y, near z) and (far x, far y, far z) to the standard orthographic viewing box, which affine transforms are used?

(a) Shear and translation (b) Rotation and scale

(c) Scale and shear (d) Translation and scale

(iv) Dragging in computer graphics can be achieved through which of the following transformations?

(a) Translation (b) Rotation

(c) Scaling (d) Mirror Reflection

(v) The format of storing digital audio in multimedia application is

(a) JPEG (b) TIFF

(c) WAV (d) BMP

(vi) Fill in the following matrix. This is to be the general reflection matrix for Y = -X

|0 ?|

|-1 0|

(a) -1 (b) 1

(c) 0 (d) ½ (e) 1-/2

(vii) If P0, P1, P2 be the control points(in sequential ordering), then the Bezier curve must pass through

(a) P0 and P1 (b) P1 and P2

(c) P2 and P0 (d) points close to P0, P1 and P2

(viii) The total no. of pixels put 'ON' for the line starting at (1,1) and ending at (12,7) would be

(a) 7 (b) 11

(c) 12 (d) more than 12

(ix) In 2-D graphics, if S1and S2 are scaling matrices and T1 and T2 are two translation matrices then

(a) S1 S2 = S2 S1 (b) S1 T1 = S2 T2

(b) T2 S2 = T1 S1 (d) S1 T2 = T2 S1

(x) GIF supports

(a) 256 colors (b) 512 colors

(c) 1024 colors (d) 16 million colors

GROUP – B
(Short Answer Type Questions)

Answer any three of the following. (3 ×5=15)

2. What is the aspect ratio? Consider three different raster systems with resolutions of 640 by 480, 1280 by 1024 and 2560 by 2048. What size of frame buffers is needed for each of these systems to store 12 bits per pixel? How much storage is required for each system if 24 bits per pixel are to be stored? (1 + 4)

3. Explain the term "scan conversion". Find out all intermediate pixel values between (10, 11 and 20, 19) through Bresenham's line drawing algorithm. (1 + 4)

4. What do you mean by morphing? Write dwon the advantages and disadvantages of using MIDI over digital audio. Why is text encryption needed? (1 + 2 + 2)

5. What is affine transformation? Show that the composition of two rotations is additive. (5)

6. Give the best steps/algorithm of JPEG compression. (5)

7. Derive the conditions for smooth joining of two Bezier curve segment of degree three. (5)

GROUP – C
(Long Answer Type Questions)

Answer any three of the following. (3 × 15 = 45)

8. What do you mean by "window" and "viewport"? Describe the relationship for window to viewpoint mapping. A clipping window ABCD is specified as A(0, 0), B (40,0), C(40, 40), D(0, 40). We want to clip two lines P(-20, 70), Q(20, 30) and R(50, 10) S(70, 70) against the window. Use endpoints code of the lines to find out if the lines are totally invisible or partially visible. Use a standard clipping algorithm to find out visible portion of a line. (3 + 4 + 8)

9. Discuss the digitization principle of audio. What are the different components of multimedia system? Compare hypertext and hypermedia with suitable example. What are the different animation principles? (3 + 3 + 4 + 5)

10. (a) Describe the Z-buffer algorithm.

    (b) "Moving the control points only affects the shape of a section of the given B-spline curve". Justify the statement.

    (c) What is the difference between the raster graphics and vector graphics?

    (d) What is image resolution? (4 + 6 + 3+ 2)

11. (a) What are the conditions for point clipping?

    (b) Describe the midpoint subdivision algorithm for line clipping. Compare efficiency of clipping obtained using midpoint subdivision technique and Cohen-Sutherland method.

    (c) Derive a composite matrix to scale a unit square placed at the origin along its diagonal (0, 0) – (1, 1) by a scale factor 2. Find the vertices of the transformed figure. (2 + 8 + 5)

12. (a) What are the hypertext and hypermedia? What is the relation between multimedia, hypertext and hypermedia?

    (b) What do you mean by I-frame B-frame and P-frame in the context of video compression?

    (c) Which tag is used for hyperlinking? Explain the use of this tag with example.

    (d) Write down two attributes of <BODY> tag. Explain their utility with suitable example. (4 + 3 + 5 + 3)

WEST BENGAL UNIVERSITY OF TECHNOLOGY
MCA EXAMINATION 2009
COMPUTER GRAPHICS AND MULTIMEDIA
SEMESTER - 4

Time: 3 Hours **Full Marks: 70**

GROUP-A
(Multiple Choice Questions)

1. Choose the correct answer from the given alternatives:

(i) Transpose of a matrix A = [a1 b1 c1]

[a2 b2 c2] is:

(a) [a1 a2]
[b1 b2]
[c1 c2]

(b) [a1 b1]
[a2 b2]
[c1 c2]

(c) [a1 c1]
[a2 c2]
[b1 b2]

(d) [a1 a2]
[c1 c2]
[b1 b2]

(ii) Lambert's cosine law is defined by

(a) L_{bett} = I1 Kd cosθ
(b) I_{diff} = I1 Kd cosθ
(c) I_{bett} = I1 Kd sinθ
(d) I_{diff} = I1 Kd sinθ

(iii) Convex polygon mean

(a) Opposite of concave polygon
(b) same as concave polygon
(c) All a and b
(d) none

(iv) The parametric equation of a line within P1 and P2 is

(a) P = P2 + (P1-P2)t
(b) P = P2 + (P2-P1)t
(c) P = P1 + (P2-P1)t
(d) NONE

(v) The value of t varies between

(a) $t \leq 0$
(b) $0 \leq t \leq 1$
(c) $t \leq 0$
(d) none

(vi) Boundary condition matrix is represented as:

(a) [B] = [P1]
[P2]

(b) [B] = [P0]
[P1]

[P1′]	[P2]
[P′2]	[P3]
(c) [B] = [P1]	(d) [B] = [P0]
[P2]	[P1]
[P3]	[P1′]
[P4]	[P2]

(vii) Hermite blending function is

(a) F1(t), F2(t), F3(t), F4(t) (b) P1(t), P2(t), P3(t), P4(t)

(c) all the above (d) none of the above

(viii) A triangle is defined by [2 4 4]

[2 2 4]

Find the transformed coordinate after the following transformation – Reflection about line y = -x.

(a) [-2 -4 -4]	(b) [2 -4 -4]
[2 2 -4]	[-2 2 -4]
[1 1 1]	[1 -1 -1]
(c) [-2 4 -4]	(d) none
[2 -2 -4]	
[1 1 1]	

(ix) Aspect ratio means

(a) Ratio of Y pixel to the X pixel (b) Ratio of X pixel to the Y pixel

(c) both of them (d) none

(x) In CRT, cathode is

(a) Positively charged (b) negatively charged

(c) all of the above (d) none

GROUP-B
(Short Answer Type Questions)

Answer any three of these question: (3 × 5 = 15)

2 (a) Define FLOODFILL.

(b) What do you mean by Phosphorescence? (3 + 2 = 5)

3 (a) Describe JPEG compression scheme. (5)

4 (a) What do you mean by MIDI?

(b) What is Hermite Blending Function? (2 + 3 = 5)

5. In case of Bresenham line drawing algorithm, find out the value of Pk and intermediate values when starting point is (0,2) and ending point is (4,5). (5)

6. Describe the steps of Cohen-Sutherland line clipping algorithm. (5)

GROUP-C
(Long Answer Type Questions)

Answer any three of these questions: (3 × 15 = 45)

7 (a) Describe the working principal of Cathode Ray Tube (CRT) with diagram.

(b) Describe the Bresenham Circle Drawing Algorithm. (8 + 7 = 15)

8 (a) Describe Polygon fill algorithm.

(b) A unit square is transformed by a 2*2 transformation matrix. The resulting position vectors are:

[0 2 8 6]

[0 3 4 1]

What is the transformation matrix?

(c) Describe scaling with respect to any arbitrary point (6 + 5 + 4 = 15)

9. (a) Q′, Q(3,11), P(3,5) Consider the scaling transformation of PQ to PQ′. Let the scale factor is (s=2). Find out the value of Q′.

(b) Describe cubic Bezier curve

(c) Describe Z-buffer algorithm. (5 + 5 + 5 = 15)

10. Write short notes on the following (any three): (3 × 5 = 15)

(a) Describe diffused light model in Illumination model.

(b) Describe about HTML.

(c) Phong shading.

(d) Boundary fill algorithm.

WEST BENGAL UNIVERSITY OF TECHNOLOGY
B.TECH (CSE) EXAMINATION 2010
COMPUTER GRAPHICS AND MULTIMEDIA
SEMESTER - 6

Time Allowed: 3 Hours **Full Marks: 70**

The figures in the margin indicate full marks. Candidates are required to give their answers in their own words as far as practicable.

GROUP – A

(Multiple Choice Type Questions)

1. Choose the correct alternative for any ten of the following: (10 × 1 = 10)

(i) If blue is represented as 001 the yellow is represented as

(a) 001 (b) 010 (c) 101 (d) 110

(ii) A 24-bit plane colour frame buffer with three 10-bit wide color look up tables can have .... number of colours.

(a) 2^{24} (b) 2^{8} (c) 2^{48} (d) 2^{30}

(iii) DAC means

(a) direct access coding (b) digitally activated compression

(c) direct area clipping (d) digital to analog converter

(iv) .... acts as anode in CRT.

(a) The phosphorous coating (b) The glass panel

(c) The deflectors (d) None of these

(v) Slope of the line joining the points (1, 2) and (3, 4) is

(a) 0 (b) 1 (c) 2 (d) 3

(vi) In Bresenham's circle generating algorithms, if (x, y) is the current pixel position then the x-value of the next pixel position is

(a) x (b) x-1 (c) x + 1 (d) x + 2

(vii) Run length coding is used for

(a) image smoothening (b) image compression

(b) image colouring (d) image dithering

(viii) If X_L, X_R, Y_B, Y_T represent the four parameter of x-left, x-right, y-bottom and y-top of the clipping window and (x, y) is a point inside the window then

(a) $X_L \le x \le X_R$ and $Y_B \le y \le Y_T$ (b) $X_L \le x \le X_R$ and $Y_B \ge y \ge Y_T$

(c) $X_L \ge x \ge X_R$ and $Y_B \le y \le Y_T$ (d) $X_L \ge x \ge X_R$ and $Y_B \ge y \ge Y_T$

(ix) A line with end point codes as 0000 and 0000 is

(a) partially invisible (b) completely visible

(c) trivially visible (d) completely invisible

(x) Which device is used to grasp a 'virtual object'?

(a) Space ball (b) Data glove (c) Digitizer (d) Touch panels

(xi) How many channels are specified by MIDI standard?

(a) 16 (b) 24 (c) 32 (d) None of these

(xii) Lossy image simplification is based on .... operation.

(a) DCT (b) CCIT (c) ISO (d) DMS

GROUP – B
(Short Answer Type Questions)

Answer any three of the following. (3 × 5 = 15)

2. Write the properties of B-spline. In what respect it differs from Bezier's curve? (3 + 2)

3. Write boundary-fill algorithm for region filling. Compare and contrast the boundary-fill algorithm and flood fill algorithm. (3 + 2)

4. Explain Liang-Barsky algorithm for line clipping. (2 + 3)

5. What do you mean by MIDI? Write down the components of MIDI. (2 + 3)

6. Define projection and mention its importance. Derive the transformation matrix for a perspective projection. (3 + 2)

GROUP – C
(Long Answer Type Questions)

Answer any three of the following. (3 × 15 = 45)

7. (a) Derive Midpoint circle drawing algorithm.

(b) Using Midpoint drawing algorithm draw a circle with radius 10 unit.

(c) Define random and raster scanning. (7 + 5 + 3)

8. (a) Derive the transformation matrix for rotation about any axis.

(b) Explain the reflection of a 2-D figure on y = mx + c. Derive its component matrix.

(c) What is homogeneous co-ordinate? Why is a homogeneous co-ordinate system needed in transformation matrix. (5 + 7 + 3)

9. (a) Derive the transformation matrix for perspective projection.

(b) Suppose window has its lowest left line corner t (-3, -2) and its upper right corner at (4, 2). Find the visible portion of the line joining points (-4, 2) and (3, 5) using Cohen-Sutherland line clipping algorithm.

(c) Write and explain Sutherland-Hodgeman algorithm to clip a polygon. (5 + 6 + 4)

10. (a) Define morphing and masking.

(b) Write down the basic step of JPEG.

(c) What do you mean by key frame and tweening?

(d) Write few audio file formats. Explain the advantages and disadvantages of MIDI over digital audio. (2 + 2 + 5 + 2 + 1 + 3)

11. Write short notes on any three of the following: (3 × 5)

(a) MPEG

(b) Shading Model

(c) Virtual reality

(d) Cohen Sutherland line clipping algorithm

(e) CRT

WEST BENGAL UNIVERSITY OF TECHNOLOGY
B.TECH (CSE) EXAMINATION 2009
COMPUTER GRAPHICS AND MULTIMEDIA
SEMESTER - 6

Time Allowed: 3 Hours **Full Marks: 70**

GROUP – A
(Multiple Choice Type Questions)

1. Choose the correct alternative for any ten of the following: (10 × 1 = 10)

(i) The best hidden surface removal method(s) used for complex scenes with more than a few thousand surface is/are

(a) Depth sorting method (b) Scan line algorithm

(c) Depth buffer algorithm (d) Octree method

(ii) When the angle between the projectors and the plane of projection is not equal to 90°, the projection is

(a) Orthographic (b) Isometric (c) Perspective (d) Oblique

(iii) Under the parallel projection, the point (2,3,-1) has been viewed at (3,3,0), then the direction of the vector should be

(a) (1,1,0) (b) (1,0, -1) (c) (0,1,1,) (d) (0,-1,1)

(iv) The reflection matrix of a point P(x, y) about the straight y = -x is

(a) $\begin{matrix}-1 & 0\\ 0 & -1\end{matrix}$ (b) $\begin{matrix}0 & -1\\ -1 & 0\end{matrix}$ (c) $\begin{matrix}-1 & 0\\ -1 & 0\end{matrix}$ (d) $\begin{matrix}-1 & 0\\ 0 & -1\end{matrix}$

(v) The DDA algorithm is a faster method for calculating pixel positions than direct use of line equation using y = mx +c, because

(a) It eliminates floating point addition
(b) It eliminates floating point multiplication
(c) It eliminates rounding operation that drift away from true line path
(d) none of these

(vi) In Bresenham's circle generating algorithms, if points are generated from 90° to 45° and (x, y) are the coordinate of last scan converted pixel then the next pixel coordinate is

(a) (x + 1, y + 1) or (x – 1, y – 1) (b) (x + 1, y) or (x, y + 1)

(c) (x, y + 1) or (x + 1, y – 1) (d) (x + 1, y) or (x + 1, y – 1)

(vii) Aliasing means

(a) Rendering effect (b) Shading effect

(b) Staircase effect (d) Cueng effect

(viii) Sutherland-Hodgman algorithm is used for

(a) line clipping (b) point clipping

(c) polygon clipping (d) hybrid clipping

(ix) The technique of using a minimum number of intensity levels to obtain increased visual resolution is

(a) Dithering (b) Half toning

(c) Depth-Cueing (d) Rendering

(x) Z-buffer algorithm is used for

(a) frame buffer removal (b) hidden line removal (c) rendering (d) animation

(xi) The format for storing digital audio in multimedia application is

(a) JPEG (b) TIFF (c)WAV (d) BMP

(xii) The people of the planet Mars designed a scale for measuring the temperature in which water freezes at 100 units and boils at 250 units. The people of Jupiter designed a scale in which water freezes at 75 units and boils at 300 units. A temperature of 200 units in Mars will measure .... units in Jupiter.

(a) 300 (b) 225 (c) 250 (d) 175

(xiii) The Model Human Processor is comprised of three components, which are

(a) Cognitive system, perceptual system, and affective system

(b) Cognitive system, propriceptive system and affective system

(c) Perceptual system model system and cognitive system

(d) Perceptual system, locomotion system and cognitive system

(xiv) A raster colour display processor supports a resolution of 1024 × 800 with up to 16 million colours simultaneously displayed. What will be the approximate size (in bytes) of the frame buffer used in the display processor?

(a) 1.2×10^6 (b) 2.4×10^6 (c) 16×10^6 (d) 10^5

(xv) A Bezier cubic curve with control points P_0, P_1, P_2 and P_3 is defined by the equation

(a) $(1-u)^3$ (b) u^3 (c) $3u(1-u)^2$ (d) $3u^2(1-u)$

GROUP – B
(Short Answer Type Question)

Answer any three of the following. (3 × 5 = 15)

2. Explain ant-ialiasing. A cubic Bezier Curve Segment is described by the control points P1(20, 20), P2(40, 80), P3(80, 80), P4(90, 50). Another curve segment is described by Q1(a, b), Q2(c, 20), Q3(150, 20), Q4(180, 20). Determine the values a, b, c so that the two curve segments join smoothly. (2 + 3)

3. Perform a 300 rotation of a triangle A(2, 2), B(3, 3), C(6, 5) about

   (a) the origin

   (b) a point P(-8, -5) (2 + 3)

4. Define projection and mention its importance. Derive the transformation matrix for a perspective projection.

5. Write the steps of the Z-buffer algorithm. Discuss its advantages and disadvantages.

6. What do you mean by staircase effect? How does this staircase effect affect the generation of graphic primitives? What was the proposed solution to this effect?

7. Distinguish between window and viewport. Describe how window to viewport mapping is done.

GROUP – C
(Long Answer Type Questions)

Answer any three of the following. (3 × 15 = 45)

8. (a) Why are homogeneous coordinates used for transformation computations in Computer Graphics?

   (b) Show how reflections in the line y = x and in the line y = -x can be performed by a scaling operation followed by a rotation.

   (c) Describe how a 3-D object is presented on the screen using perspective projection. Take a simple object for illustration.

   (d) An object "ABCD rectangle" is defined with respect to a coordinate system whose units are measured in inches. If a local coordinate system which uses mm as the basic unit is used to describe the object details "abcd rectangle" as shown in the figure below, then indicate the necessary transformation matrix for describing the object in the local coordinate system:

9. (a) Differentiate between Flood Fill and Boundary Fill algorithms.

   (b) A Bezier curve is to be drawn by the given control points as P1(40, 40), P2(10, 40), P3(60, 60) and P4(60, 0). Calculate the coordinates of the points on the curve corresponding to the parameter t = 0.2, 0.4, 0.6. Show the rough sketch of the curve with the coordinates of various points on it.

   c) Using midpoint circle drawing algorithm, draw a circle with radius of 8 units. 4 + 5 + 6

10. (a) What are meant by key framing and Tweening?
    (b) What are Hypertext and Hypermedia?
    (c) What is the difference between the following?
        (i) Video and Motion picture
        (ii) Video and animation
    (d) What are meant by luminance and chrominance? Discuss about their quantitative expressions.
    3 + 2 + 5 + 5
11. (a) Write the midpoint ellipse drawing algorithm (only the algorithm).
    (b) Derive the midpoint circle drawing algorithm.
    (c) Using midpoint circle drawing algorithm, draw a circle with radius 10 units. (6 + 6 + 3)
12. (a) What do you mean by B-Spline curve? Discuss the properties of B-Spline curves.
    (b) Write down the basic steps of MPEG video compression..
    (c) What are the major components of a multimedia document? How can they be compiled together?
    (2 + 4) + 6 + 3
13. Write short notes on any three of the following: (3 × 5)
    (a) Virtual Reality
    (b) Sampling and Quantization
    (c) MPEG and JPEG
    (d) Sutherland-Hodgeman Polygon clipping algorithm
    (e) Phong's Shading Model
    (f) Cubic B-Spline.

UTTAR PRADESH TECHNICAL UNIVERSITY
B.Tech.
(Sem. VI) Examination, 2007
COMPUTER GRAPHICS

Time: 3 Hours **Total Marks: 100**

1. Attempt any two: (2 × 5 = 10)

   (a) Distinguish between Rastar and Vector graphics methods. When do we prefer? What?

   (b) Describe briefly Bresenham's circle drawing algorithm. Why do we prefer incremental algorithm over DDA?

   (c) How do we represent polygon using polygon table and vertex table explain with example?

2. Attempt any two: (2 × 5 = 10)

   (a) Distinguish between window port and viewport. In 2-D clipping, how are lines grouped into visible, invisible and partially visible categories?

   (b) Give a 3 × 3 homogenous matrix to rotate the image clockwise by 90°. Then shift the image to the right by 10 units. Finally scale the image by twice as large. All these transformations are to be done one after another in sequence.

   (c) What is a segment table. How do we create it? Why do we need segments? Explain in detail.

3. Attempt any two: (2 × 5 = 10)

   (a) A cube is placed at the origin of 3-D system. Such that all its vertices have positive coordinate values and sides are parallel to the three principal axes. Indicate a convenient position of a viewer at which he can see a 2-point perspective projection. Verify that such a view is generated.

   (b) Define vanishing points. Is the location of vanishing point directly related to the viewing point? Explain how?

   (c) What are the various logical graphic input primitives? What are the various input modes in which they work?

4. Attempt any two: (2 × 5 = 10)

   (a) What is ray tracing algorithm for hidden surface removal? Explain mathematically how do we find which planes are visible using ray tracing algorithm.

   (b) What are the two spaces in which hidden surface algorithms work? How does sorting and coherence speed up calculation in such algorithms?

   (c) Given control points (10,100), (50,100), (70,120) and (100,150). Calculate coordinates of any four points lying on the corresponding Bezier curve.

5. Attempt any two: (2 × 5 = 10)

   (a) Derive simple illumination model. Include the contribution of diffuse, ambient and specular reflection.

   (b) How are periodic B-spline curves different from non-periodic B-spline curves?

   (c) Which clipping algorithm is best suited for hardware implementation? Give how this algorithm works.

PUNJAB TECHNICAL UNIVERSITY
SIXTH SEMESTER B.E. DEGREE EXAMINATION, JULY 2007
COMPUTER SCIENCE AND ENGINEERING
COMPUTER GRAPHICS

Time: 3 Hours **Max. Marks:100**

Note: Answer any five full questions.

1. (a) What is aliasing? Explain the properties of a good line generation algorithm. (10 Marks)

   (b) Write an algorithm to generate a complete circle using midpoint technique, using eight-way symmetry function. (10 Marks)

2. (a) Explain the edge coherence and the scan line algorithm using appropriate data structure. (10 Marks)

   (b) Describe random and raster display systems with the help of neat sketches. (10 Marks)

3. a) Derive the mathematical formulation required to scale for rotate an object with respect to arbitrary axis in a 3-D space. (10 Marks)

   (b) Perform a 45° rotation of triangle A(0,0), B(1,1) and C(5,2) about the origin and the point (-1,-1). (10 Marks)

4. (a) Explain the following with the help of neat sketches:

   (i) Two-point perspective projection of a cube.

   (ii) Cabinet and cavalier projections. (10 Marks)

   (b) Obtain the front one-point perspective view of the house shown below, the overall set of viewing parameters is as follows:

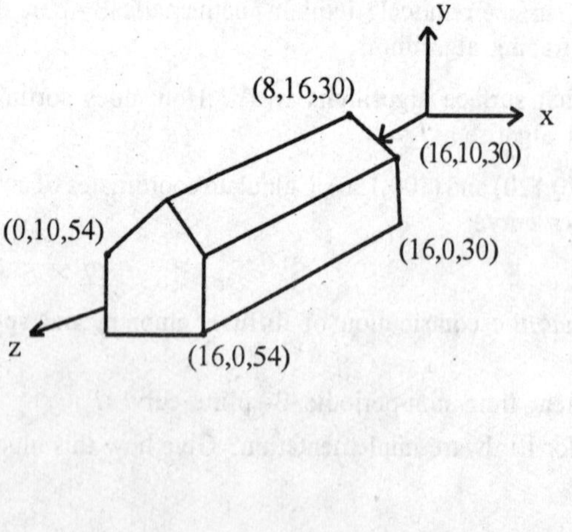

VRP (WC) 0,0,0

VPN (WC) 0,0,1

VUP (WC) 0,1,0

PRP (VRC) 8,6,84

WINDOW (VRC) (-50,50,-50,50)

(i) Sketch the output view for the above case.

(ii) To produce more centered projection of the house, which extends 0 to 16 in both x and y (a window extending from -1 to 17 in x and y direction) write the corresponding set of viewing parameters. (10 Marks)

5. (a) Explain the concept of data Glove as a 3-D interactive device, with the help sketches. (10 Marks)

   (b) Explain the three common styles for user computer interfaces. (10 Marks)

6. (a) Write the pseudocode for the Z-buffer algorithm and explain its working principle to sort the objects/planes in Z-direction using plane equation. (10 Marks)

   (b) Explain the following concepts in hidden surface elimination process:

   (i) Area subdivision algorithm

   (ii) BSP Trees (10 Marks)

7. Explain the following with the help of neat sketches:

   (a) Mathematical formulation for cubic Bezier curves and sketch the blending functions (for n = 3) (10 Marks)

   (b) List the properties of B-spline curve and derive the B-spline basis matrix. (10 Marks)

8. Write short notes for the following:

   (a) Light pen

   (b) Character generation in graphics mode

   (c) Window to viewport transformation

   (d) Geometric construction of deterministic self similar fractals. (10 Marks)

GURU GOBIND SINGH INDRAPRASTHA UNIVERSITY
END TERM EXAMINATION
SECOND SEMESTER (MCA), MAY – 2009

Paper Code: MCA108 **Subject: Computer Graphics**

Time: 3 Hours **Maximum Marks: 75**

Note: Question 1 is Compulsory. Attempt four questions from the rest.

Q. 1. Answer any ten from the following questions: (2 × 10 = 20)

(a) Explain Octrees.

(b) Why are hidden surface algorithms needed?

(c) Explain Bezier Surface.

(d) What is scan conversion?

(e) In Back face detection method, derive the condition to detect if a polygon is back face. (viewing direction along –ve z-axis)

(f) What is scan conversion?

(g) What is meant by addressability?

(h) What is interdot distance?

(i) What is the difference between impact and non-impact printers?

(j) What is resolution?

(k) Explain the relevance of the following diagram to 2-D clipping.

1001	1000	1010
0001	0000	0010
0101	0100	0110

(l) What is dot-size?

Q.2. (a) What is solid modeling? Explain it with one of its techniques. (5)

(b) Derive matrix representation for perspective projection and with the help of this expression. Find the perspective view of cube for centre of projection at (0, 0,-5) with image plane to be XY plane. (5)

Q.3. (a) Draw a Bezier curve with respect to control points p(1,3), q(2,4), r(5,5), s(7,3) and draw its convex hull. (4)

(b) Answer the following w.r.t. Cohen-Sutherland line clipping algorithm. (6)

(i) Describe when the clipping of a line segment is considered to be a trivial case.

(ii) How are bit codes assigned to the regions?

(iii) Find the Region Codes for a given line segment PQ with the end points given as P(-1, 5) and Q(3,8) and then clip the line with respect to a Rectangular window with lower left corner at (-3, 1) and upper right corner at (2,6).

Q.4. (a) What is the use of approximated curve in Computer graphics? What is the advantage of parametric form of curves with respect to the explicit form of curve in Computer Graphics? (5)

(b) In the Bresenham Line drawing algorithm, calculate p_{k+1} in terms of p_k, ^x and ^y. (5)

Q.5. (a) Explain Bezier Surface. (5)

(b) Find out the projected value for a plane z + d = 0 and centre of projection is at (0, 0, -d). (5)

Q.6. (a) Describe the steps of Depth-sort algorithm. (5)

(b) Explain different techniques to generate solid models in Computer Graphics. (5)

Q.7. (a) Prove that the blending function of Open uniform B-Spline is equal to that of Bezier curve for d = n + 1 (where number control point = n + 1 and degree = d - 1). (5)

(b) Find out the effect of multiple control points in B-spline using exmple. (5)

Q.8. (a) In back face detection method, derive the condition to detect if a polygon is a back face (viewing direction along –ve z-axis.). (5)

(b) Write briefly about different projections and explain the concept vanishing point. (5)

GURU GOBIND SINGH INDRAPRASTHA UNIVERSITY
END TERM EXAMINATION
SECOND SEMESTER (BCA), MAY – 2011

Paper Code: BCA **Subject: Computer Graphics and Multimedia Applications**
Paper ID: 306
Time: 3 Hours **Maximum Marks: 75**

Note: Question 1 is compulsory and attempt one question from each unit.

Q.1. Attempt any ten parts. Each part carries 2.5 marks. (10 × 2.5)

(a) When and why we use homogeneous coordinate system?

(b) What is clipping?

(c) Describe aliasing.

(d) Polygon meshes.

(e) What do you understand by the term multimedia? List a few applications of multimedia.

(f) Differentiate interactive and non-interactive graphic.

(g) How millions of colours are created in graphics with only 3 basic colours?

(h) Resolution of monitors.

(i) Refreshing.

(j) Representation through parametric geometry.

(k) B-splines.

(l) 3-D transformation requires information of projection.

UNIT – I

Q.2. (a) List various methods learnt by you to draw a line. Discuss the method you think is the best and why. (6.5)

(b) Scan convert the straight line with endpoints (5, 10) and (15, 35) using the algorithm discussed by you earlier the part (a). (6)

OR

Q.3. (a) Describe Cyrus-Back clipping techniques. What are its merits/demerits compared to other techniques of clipping. (6.5)

(b) Briefly describe evolution of input/output graphic tools. (6)

UNIT – II

Q.4. (a) Consider a square with coordinates (2,2), (6,2), (2,6), (6,6).

(b) Rotate the square with 90 degree, anticlockwise with respect to (2,2).

(c) Now scale it to twice its size.

(d) Describe all operation through composite matrix.

(e) Also guess the shape of the final figure. (5 × 2.5)

OR

Q.5. (a) What is the difference between window and viewport? What happens, to the scene if viewport is displaced? (6.5)

(b) Describe Cohen-Sutherland algorithm of clipping. (6)

UNIT – III

Q.6. (a) What is a B-spline curve? How are they generated? Describe the algorithm to generate a B-spline.

(b) Describe Constructive Solid Geometry for solid modelling. (8 + 4.5)

OR

Q.7. (a) Describe sweep representation for solid modelling.

(b) Explain how Bezier curves are represented parametrically. Consider a Bezier curve having control points P1(20, 0), P2(0, 20), P3(80, 40) and P4(40,0). Compute the coordinates of points on the curve for I = 0, 0.2, 0.6, 1.0. Draw a rough sketch of the curve.

UNIT – IV

Q.8. (a) Describe evolution of skills in multimedia. Today, the multimedia techniques are replacing old concepts of advertisements. Discuss, also bring out power of multimedia with examples.

(b) Describe authoring tools. (8 + 4.5)

OR

Q.9. (a) How important is the software and software skills for the development of multimedia application? (4)

(b) Describe any software of multimedia you have studied. (4)

(c) Describe interactive multimedia. (4.5)

Index

D

E

F

G

H

I

J

P

Q

R